"If your payroll carries the permanent
every position, here's an alternative w
Adopt this cunningly simple idea, and y
should become more diverse, more agi

Rich ... .ytner, Blue Hat Man,
Adjunct Professor of Marketing, London Business School
and Author, *Consiglieri: Leading from the Shadows*

"As someone who has worked as a fractional CFO for a number of
years, I can attest to the C-suite burnout which Sara so eloquently
describes, and how this new way of working is definitely the way
forward for C-suite individuals."

Dax Mehta, Part-time CFO and former CFO,
Sony Pictures Distribution

"Forget what you think you know about the 'gig economy.' Sara
Daw's *Strategy and Leadership as Service: How the Access Economy Meets
the C-Suite* is a fascinating read packed with key insights! The access
economy is more than just a transient trend – in the global race
for talent, traditional talent acquisition models are becoming outdated. Fueled by technology, changing attitudes, demographics and
economic conditions, the future belongs to those with agile talent
supply chain strategies. Sara cuts to the core of the Strategy and
Leadership as Service model with real-world examples, making this
a practical, useful, helpful, fun, and above all, indispensable book for
businesses and the C-suite alike!"

Kirthi Mani, Managing Principal of New York, CLA
(CliftonLarsonAllen LLP)

"Leaders face many challenges in today's turbulent environment.
Workforce planning and providing meaningful work that will attract
and retain talent is high on that list of challenges. This well written,
empirically rich book provides many insights into a different way of
getting work done. The access economy is explained and evidenced
as an exciting and effective sustainable alternative to the traditional
full-time work model. A must read."

Professor Sue Dopson, Deputy Dean, Saïd Business School,
University of Oxford

"Great eye opener, also a pragmatic and well thought out framework for how to evolve current CXO models and benefit from the rapidly emerging access economy. I would have loved to utilize this approach in my previous executive roles and now as a portfolio CFO I see that it really works."

Uwe Stelter, Portfolio CFO and former Group
Chief Financial Officer, Atos SE

"Converging workforce trends are fuelling the most squeezed labour markets since WWII. Organisational staffing needs an urgent reboot for optimal resilience and prosperity. Sara Daw presents a proven method of accessing 'on-demand' leadership expertise that no CEO can afford to overlook."

Cat Barnard, Director, Working the Future

"Sara's book is an important addition to the thinking on the C-suite. It puts forward what the future C-suite could look like and is a must read for anyone who influences the C-suite or who aspires to be in it."

John Jeffcock, CEO, Winmark and Author, *The Suite Spot*

"Within professional services, as Sara highlights, we are increasingly experiencing the continued rise of the access economy as organisations, small and large, supplement their teams with required expertise and capacity, and professionals choose a flexible career and make lifestyle choices. This excellent book challenges us as leaders to think about the organisation of the future."

Mark Britton, Chief Operating Officer of Global Consulting, JMJ

"Fractional execs are a secret superpower that most CEOs and boards haven't discovered yet, but for those that are considering embarking on this journey, this book provides both a map and a compass."

David Jack, Serial CTO, Board Member, and PE Advisor

"I've no doubt that using a Strategy and Leadership as Service model was a key factor in being able to obtain a good exit for our shareholders in a four-year timeframe. We needed expertise in finance and marketing that we could not afford on a full-time basis, but that wasn't well-matched to short, intense contract roles. Engaging professionals who had been through a rigorous vetting process, who had big and small company expertise (including helping other businesses on their growth journeys) and who were interested in being mentors to and part of the management team was transformational. Having trusted team members also deeply involved in other (non-competing) businesses also gave us access to best practice ideas and networking opportunities that would have been time-consuming for me to have developed on my own."

Jo Kettner, Co-Founder Vantage Ventures and
former CEO, Company Watch

"Strategy and Leadership as Service describes a smart new way for business leaders to build their top team of talent with the flexibility, agility, and capability to not only keep pace with change but also stay ahead of the competition."

Nancy MacKay, PhD, Founder and CEO, MacKay CEO Forums

"While all of us are talking about the future of work, some leaders are already bringing pockets of the future into the present. In this timely book, Sara Daw shows us what is possible – helping us not only to imagine, but to create new ways of adding value to the C-suite. Her research, grounded in her real-world experience at The Liberti Group and drawing from ideas about the sharing economy, reveals how psychological ownership can bridge the gap between insiders and outsiders in the C-suite. For those of us who are looking for ways to contribute our C-level expertise to organisations without being limited by traditional corporate models, Sara Daw makes an inspiring case for how the model pioneered at The Liberti Group can be a win-win for individual leaders and the innovative organisations that need them."

Tara Montgomery, Founder and Principal,
Civic Health Partners, NY

"Sara Daw's book develops the idea of the access economy to include how organisations source external talent to support strategic objectives when resources are limited. It provides a well thought through framework for leaders to consider when sourcing such talent and gives valuable cases on how the approach works in practice. It shines a light on an area which has so far been neglected and will be a foundational contribution."

Dr Marc Thompson, Senior Fellow in Strategy and
Organisation, Saïd Business School, University of Oxford

"Having worked with The CFO Centre over the years, their ingeniously simple model was ahead of its time in a hybrid and portfolio world. Fabulous for financials, delivering customer delight, and critically creating the opportunity for meaning and purpose to those working in the model. This is evidence, not just from theory but from having done it in the real world!"

Mark Robb, Consultant and Speaker

"During my own career at The CFO Centre, I've been fortunate enough to work with many outstanding portfolio C-suite leaders. Sara's narrative comprehensively informs the reasons why portfolio working for C-suite executives offers a transformative approach to leadership amplifying productivity and versatility. Sara leverages her deep understanding of the C-suite dynamics to highlight the benefits of diversity and the unique perspectives that portfolio professionals bring to senior leadership positions. This is a great read for anyone considering a portfolio career."

Patrick Murray, Portfolio CFO with The CFO Centre

"Accessing talent and creating an environment where it can thrive is a business differentiator. This book is an inspiring and practical guide for both individuals wanting to further maximise their potential and businesses who desire high performance."

Chris Starkey, former Accenture Managing Director and current Managing Director, The Marketing Centre

"Sara introduces the concept of the access economy as a means of challenging and refreshing the traditional approach to strategy and leadership through a closed C-suite model and brings the concept to life with her description of psychological ownership."

Paul Dodd, Experienced CFO, Business Builder, and Group Risk Advisor to The CFO Centre

"I encountered Sara as a smart, curious, empathetic, and inspiring entrepreneur. In her book, she offers a fresh perspective to navigate and thrive in the ongoing acceleration and pixelization of our world."

Claude Rumpler, Chief People Experience Officer, L'Oréal

"Becoming a portfolio People Director has transformed my life. Firstly, it's enabled me to be the father I want to be and secondly, I've helped CEOs and MDs grow their businesses through Strategy and Leadership as Service, driving value beyond my functional People/HR expertise."

Shaun O'Hara, Portfolio People Director, People Puzzles and former Director of Talent, Britvic Soft Drinks PLC

"Today's working environment (also!) in the C-suite is characterised by increasing demands on the company's side, which is countered on the demand side by a strongly decreasing willingness to work a 24/7 job and a growing interest in networking and sharing knowledge. Sara Daw wisely and understandably shows how these developments can be countered by transferring the principles of the access economy. A must read for members of the C-suite or those who want to be!"

Professor Doctor Norbert Neu, Partner at dhpg, Bonn, Germany

"Strategy and Leadership as Service presents a noteworthy alternative to the traditional employment model – a win for both individuals and organizations. The model offers freedom from corporate constraints for C-suite professionals and a breadth and depth of skills otherwise unobtainable to organizations."

Catherine Jessup, former CFO, Diageo North America

"Portfolio working as described in *Strategy and Leadership as Service* has transformed my professional and personal life. I love working with a diverse client base and adding true value through our collective knowledge and expertise. There's also an amazing sense of belonging within the team of brilliant People Directors."

Debra Lee, Regional Director, People Puzzles and former Senior Director of Diversity and Inclusion, ASDA

"As a CFO I've been bringing C-suite experience to SME clients for 11 years now. This book brilliantly captures the benefits both to the 30+ clients I've worked with and to me. Truly an insight into the future of business management."

Michael Reeder, Portfolio CFO

"Based on a combination of over 20 years of experience and solid academic research, Sara Daw paints a compelling picture of a new business model for the deployment of C-suite executives. A must read both for people engaging C-suite executives and for C-suite executives that want to gain a new perspective on their career and their life!"

Wim Van der Smissen, Portfolio CFO

Strategy and Leadership as Service

Strategy and Leadership as Service isn't just a nice idea; it is a practical, alternative vision of the future of work for senior executives that is starting to gain significant interest and is being adopted by businesses globally. Disrupting and challenging the traditional full-time employment model, the Strategy and Leadership as Service framework provides businesses with access to the complete range of functional, emotional, and collective intelligence at the C-suite level by moving their positions from the "payroll" to an "access-role."

Many entrepreneurial and growing businesses don't need, don't want, and can't afford full-time C-suite executives. For larger organisations, it is becoming harder to find the skills and knowledge required to fulfil all the obligations of a functional C-suite with a fixed group of individuals. By moving to the Strategy and Leadership as Service framework, the outcomes are better for all stakeholders: more engagement, access to the right skillsets and mindsets at the right time and in the right quantity to match the changing business agenda, more flexibility for senior leaders, and strengthened risk management. Through presenting a working business model, and real-world case studies throughout, this book provides executives and leaders with a complete understanding of this groundbreaking approach and its key benefits, the theory upon which it is based, its essential ingredients, the mindset change required and, most importantly, how to apply it in practice.

The book provides business leaders, C-suite portfolio executives, human resource professionals, strategy consultants, leadership coaches, organisational development consultants, recruiters, professional service firms, academics, and forward-thinking business students with a radical new view of how the access economy can be applied to business strategy and leadership for more sustainable futures.

Sara Daw is Co-Founder and Group CEO of The CFO Centre Group and The Liberti Group, the global number one provider of C-suite portfolio professionals to entrepreneurial, owner managed, mid-tier businesses, and larger organisations.

Strategy and Leadership as Service

How the Access Economy Meets the C-Suite

SARA DAW

Routledge
Taylor & Francis Group

LONDON AND NEW YORK

Cover design: © Julie Lodge

First published 2024
by Routledge
4 Park Square, Milton Park, Abingdon, Oxon OX14 4RN

and by Routledge
605 Third Avenue, New York, NY 10158

Routledge is an imprint of the Taylor & Francis Group, an informa business

© 2024 Sara Daw

British Library Cataloguing-in-Publication Data
A catalogue record for this book is available from the British Library

Library of Congress Cataloging-in-Publication Data
Names: Daw, Sara, author.
Title: Strategy and leadership as service: how the access economy meets the c-suite / Sara Daw.
Description: New York: Routledge, 2024. | Includes bibliographical references and index.
Identifiers: LCCN 2023047863 (print) | LCCN 2023047864 (ebook) | ISBN 9781032390529 (hardback) | ISBN 9781032436111 (paperback) | ISBN 9781003368090 (ebook)
Subjects: LCSH: Leadership. | Executives.
Classification: LCC HD57.7 .D398 2024 (print) | LCC HD57.7 (ebook) | DDC 658.4/092--dc23/eng/20231019
LC record available at https://lccn.loc.gov/2023047863
LC ebook record available at https://lccn.loc.gov/2023047864

ISBN: 978-1-032-39052-9 (hbk)
ISBN: 978-1-032-43611-1 (pbk)
ISBN: 978-1-003-36809-0 (ebk)

DOI: 10.4324/9781003368090

Typeset in Avenir and Dante
by SPi Technologies India Pvt Ltd (Straive)

This book is dedicated to business leaders and C-suite professionals who want to change their lives by adopting this new way of working – Strategy and Leadership as Service.

Contents

Illustrations

Figures

Tables

About the Author

Sara Daw is passionate about designing the future of work for C-suite professionals and the organisations they serve. She has helped thousands worldwide build successful team-based portfolio careers in the access economy. The Strategy and Leadership as Service framework changes the lives of business leaders and C-suite professionals forever.

She is Co-Founder and Group CEO of The CFO Centre Group and The Liberti Group, the global number one provider of C-suite portfolio professionals to entrepreneurial, owner-managed, mid-tier businesses, and larger organisations.

Sara is a graduate in Chemistry from Oxford University, a Chartered Accountant, holds an MBA from The London Business School, and a Mastère Spécialisé® in Consulting and Coaching for Change from HEC, Paris.

Preface

This book is long overdue.

We've accepted traditional ways of working for the C-suite, which don't fully meet their needs nor those of the businesses they serve, for too long. The C-suite construct hasn't been revisited since its introduction in the 1980s, and the needs of our top talent and their organisations are changing rapidly to cope with the ever-complex demands of the global megatrends.

I've written this book because C-level talent and business leaders deserve better.

Strategy and Leadership as Service is a practical, alternative vision of the future of work. It challenges the traditional full-time employment model to deliver functional, emotional, and collective intelligence to organisations on-demand and adopts a flexible, agile, team-based approach to accessing C-level talent rather than employing it.

I want to share this new approach widely for more of us to evaluate and make informed choices for our futures.

Why now, though, you might ask?

I have been helping thousands of business leaders and top talent adopt this model for many years. It is a simple idea that has been successfully used by enlightened top calibre executives and forward-thinking business leaders of small and large organisations to achieve their company goals and life ambitions. At Liberti, we have studied the business model tirelessly to understand how it works, but until recently, we didn't know why. There's still more to do here, but undertaking the research for my Mastère Spécialisé® in Consulting and Coaching for Change at HEC, Paris, gave me the space and time to explore some of the reasons why it is fit-for-purpose and what it needs to thrive.

It is now time to share this best-kept secret along with what it takes to gain full value from its implementation. This book shares the perspectives of the C-suite professionals, their clients, and a new breed of organisation, the firms of C-suite providers required to support and provide a home for these top-flight executives looking for a new way to combine life and work.

The access economy is in its infancy and not yet fully understood as a concept, nor is it widely adopted. Yet as more participate, as both suppliers and customers, through necessity or choice, society could change substantially to one where we increasingly access goods and services as a substitute for ownership.

The advance of mobile technology as an enabler, connecting us all, and the younger generations' focus on social capital mean ownership can be substituted for on-demand access to goods and services that are affordable, convenient, and fulfil needs. Up to now, some of us are economically forced into the access economy as suppliers and customers due to hardship, possibly due to the global financial crisis and, more recently, the Covid-19 pandemic. Others choose to participate to make better use of idle assets and promote sustainability, reduce over-consumption, and decrease the rate of climate change. Yet, to triumph, we still need to psychologically feel ownership of our goods and services without legal ownership. We need them to feel part of our extended selves.

The presence of psychological ownership within the access economy could be the game-changer for its adoption and proliferation. Studies show psychological ownership exists in the access economy for material goods and digital services.

This book describes the first known qualitative study demonstrating that psychological ownership can exist within the access economy for sharing professional C-suite services, enabling us to move our C-suite from the "pay-roll" to an "access role" and giving us options other than traditional employment.

I put forward in this book that psychological ownership is a crucial lever for change in promoting the adoption and longevity of these service relationships for clients and C-suite talent. Developing the skills to create psychological ownership by the C-suite is a significant determinant of success. It can contribute to a departure from the traditional approach of working through ownership by employment to a future of work of providing skills as a service in the access economy.

This is a pathway for organisations to consistently have access to the dynamic and flexible leadership capabilities they need for growth, fuelled by a C-suite who love what they do, working with the people they like, earning the money they need.

Acknowledgements

First, I would like to acknowledge all the remarkable business leaders, C-suite professionals, and my colleagues at Liberti (past and present) who have taken the leap to engage with Strategy and Leadership as Service. You are the pioneers, and your forward thinking has helped promote this way of living and working and prove that it is a credible alternative to traditional employment and the C-suite construct.

I want to thank Colin and Julie Mills for starting The FD Centre and giving me the opportunity to help shape the idea and take it forward with them to create Liberti.

The journey to writing this book started in 2019 as I embarked on my Masters in Consulting and Coaching for Change (CCC), run jointly by HEC, Paris, and Saïd Business School, Oxford University. I owe special thanks to Steve Gilroy and Lucy Hogarth for supporting my initial desire to study again and to all my CCC professors and colleagues, particularly my tutor group – Tara Montgomery, Pete Naschak, and Patrick Zola. Your passion for learning and ability to ask awkward and challenging questions, along with your positivity, have pushed me to offer my very best in terms of this book.

I owe a great deal to Professor Sue Dopson, whose constant wise and expert mentorship and encouragement throughout my CCC Masters, particularly during the depths of Covid, kept me going to build the foundations of research to support Strategy and Leadership as Service. Following my graduation, she inspired me to take my work even further and helped me find the confidence to write this book and bring this concept to the awareness of more who can benefit from it.

Thank you to Rebecca Marsh, Lauren Whelan, and the Routledge and Taylor & Francis team for backing me to write about this ground-breaking approach and for their excellent support and guidance.

I am incredibly grateful to all the business leaders and C-suite professionals who gave up their time to be interviewed in depth for my research and to have the privilege to write case studies about Anthony Clacher, Neil Crofts, Scott Smyth and Kirk Zavieh. Living examples, anecdotes, advice, and introductions – thank you to Kate Longworth, Lucy Czakan, Rowan De Klerk, Richard Gant, Alex Kinchin-Smith, Nathan King, Richard McCandless, Andrew Milbourn, Sarah Rozenthuler, Steve Settle, Zara Skinmore, Helen Stenhouse, Richard Walker, and Raymond Yager.

My thanks go to everyone who has taken the time to read my drafts and provide endorsements. I am incredibly grateful for your support and humbled by your comments.

I am extremely lucky to have worked with Julie Lodge, who designed the cover and internal artwork to convey the spirit of the idea. Her never-ending patience, creativity, and responsiveness to my thoughts are second to none.

I wrote this book as we hosted Lesya, Masha, and Valeriia from Ukraine. Despite the content being unrelated to the conflict with Russia, for me, it will always be inextricably linked and remind me of the difficulties facing our guests and their unbelievable resilience and kindness, which shine through.

Finally, I cannot thank my family enough for their constant support. They contributed in countless ways and are probably relieved that the book has now made it onto the shelves … until the next one!

Abbreviations

24/7	Twenty-four hours per day, seven days per week
ABC	Access-Based Consumption
ABS	Access-Based Services
AI	Artificial Intelligence
APAC	Asia Pacific
AR	Augmented Reality
B2B	Business to Business
B2C	Business to Consumer
Baby boomers	Individuals born between 1946 and 1964
BBC	British Broadcasting Corporation
Big Four	The four largest global accounting and professional service firms: Deloitte, EY, KPMG, and PwC.
Board	Board of Directors
BRP	Business Rescue Practitioner
CCC	Consulting and Coaching for Change
CCO	Chief Communications Officer
CD	Compact Disc
CEO	Chief Executive Officer
CFO	Chief Finance Officer
CFOC	The CFO Centre
CFRO	Chief Financial and Reporting Officer
CHRO	Chief Human Resources Officer
CIO	Chief Information Officer
C-Level	C-suite level
CLO	Chief Legal Officer

CMDO	Chief Multi-Disciplinary Officer
CMO	Chief Marketing Officer
COO	Chief Operating Officer
CSR	Corporate Social Responsibility
CTO	Chief Technology Officer
CV	Curriculum Vitae
DE&I	Diversity, Equity, and Inclusion
DVD	Digital Versatile Disc
ESG	Environmental, Social, and Governance
FD	Finance Director
FDC	The FD Centre
FMCG	Fast-Moving Consumer Goods
FTSE 100	Financial Times Stock Exchange Top 100 public companies
Generation X	Individuals born between 1965 and 1979
Generation Y	Individuals born between 1980 and the late 1990s
Generation Z	Individuals born from the late 1990s
HBR	Harvard Business Review
HMRC	His Majesty's Revenue and Customs
HR	Human Resources
IR35	Inland Revenue (now HMRC) 35
IT	Information Technology
KPI	Key Performance Indicator
MBA	Master of Business Administration
Millennials	Individuals born between 1980 and the late 1990s
PLC	Public Limited Company
PO	Psychological Ownership
RD	Regional Director
S&P 50	Standard & Poor's Top 50 of the largest companies in the Top 500
SME	Small Medium Enterprise
TMT	Top Management Team
TV	Television
UK	United Kingdom
US	United States
VUCA	Volatile, Uncertain, Complex, Ambiguous
ZAR	South African Rand

Introduction: The Access Economy Meets the C-Suite

Real problems to solve

Jacinta's ambition

Jacinta is the founder and owner of a fast-growing e-commerce business. It has been a roller coaster ride building it up to a team of 75 employees after starting five years ago from her kitchen table, yet momentum is building.

She has always dealt with the finances and just about managed them. They occupy a lot of her time because she isn't qualified, and she finds it an energy drain. In contrast, she has plenty of exciting ideas in other areas of the business she wants to pursue. Jacinta is keen to expand internationally but has yet to learn how to build a solid strategic financial plan for growth. She needs a Chief Finance Officer (CFO) and dreams of working alongside one, but she thinks this is a long way away. She knows that would be a six-figure sum investment, which is out of the question. While her business means everything to her and keeps her fully occupied, she realises these high-flying professionals might want to work with a more sophisticated organisation than hers.

Will's dilemma

Will is a seasoned Chief Executive Officer (CEO) of a sizeable private distribution business. Its former CFO had to retire due to ill health, and

DOI: 10.4324/9781003368090-1

Will needs to find a replacement. After reviewing his organisation's requirements, he realises that what he thought was just one role had many aspects.

He needs someone centrally to steer the ship, liaise with the board, lead the financial planning, and sort out the funding. Then there is a stand-alone division located remotely with a different set of financial needs, not to mention the corporate finance skillset required to go on the acquisition trail that Will has been planning. He has been talking to various recruitment agencies. They have yet to come up with any credible candidates with all the skills he wants and who want to work in the part of the country where his firm is based.

Nadim's regret

Nadim is a very knowledgeable CFO. He's in his mid-fifties, and retirement has popped its head over the horizon, yet he knows he's not ready for that. His current role in a large corporation is ending after ten years due to a recent takeover. He dreads the thought of doing the rounds with the recruitment agencies again. He knows he could do one more big CFO job before winding down and concentrating on his golf handicap, yet this prospect doesn't excite him.

He has had a respected career, working with the best in the hospitality sector. He has travelled the world extensively, been exposed to, and conquered virtually all CFO challenges he could wish for, and his employers have treated him well.

However, if he is honest with himself, he knows the role has also taken its toll. He has missed seeing his children grow up, leaving for work on Sunday evenings and returning tired and irritable on Fridays, most weeks, most years. His relationship with his wife needs attention too. He has loyally carried out the corporate agenda without fail, always putting his employer before his family and himself. He has filled his life rushing from meeting to meeting and from task to task. That has been his total focus.

He is now asking himself the question, "For what purpose? Is life passing me by?" His overwhelming emotion is one of regret. He has missed out on many family things. He knows now is the time to make amends, and now is the time to focus on himself too.

Nadim wants to make an impact and "give back." He wants to have the opportunity to use all his experience and help other businesses grow, applying the best of his skills and knowledge. He has learnt so much over the years. Surely other organisations will value this? However, it must be on his terms now. He wants control over his agenda and with whom he works. He yearns for freedom of choice and the flexibility to progress in the areas of his life he has neglected. Nadim knows what he wants but needs to see if it exists.

Tara's purpose

Tara is in her late 30s. From her relatively short career to date, she has already decided she does not want a traditional corporate life. She has worked hard to gain experience and landed the top job as Chief Marketing Officer (CMO) in a software business. Tara likes the role and the people but feels restrained by the bureaucracy and organisational expectations. She feels she is missing something.

She finds that the relentlessness of the corporate agenda lacks meaning and authenticity. Conforming to the status quo and the expected career progression of her predecessors needs to be more compelling. She thinks, "There must be more to work than this."

Tara knows she wants more excitement and stimulation from her career. She wants to learn and progress her skillsets. She wants to develop herself continually, grow professionally and personally, and balance that with time to be with her family and friends.

Looking around at other roles on offer, she keeps seeing more of the same.

A new vision for the C-suite

There are thousands, if not millions, of business owners and CEOs like Jacinta and Will and C- suite executives like Nadim and Tara worldwide. Many are grappling with the same or similar issues. They don't know it, but they can solve their problems with a new business model: Strategy and Leadership as Service.

This book paints the picture of this new way of working for C-suite executives within organisations. Not only that, but it also brings this approach alive with real-world examples from an established global operating business model. It provides a perspective which disrupts and challenges today's traditional full-time employment model, which, I contend, is outdated and unfit for purpose. We need a rethink.

Let me explain.

Entrepreneurial and growing businesses, like Jacinta's, don't want, don't need, and can't afford a full-time C-suite professional. It is just not an option for a small-medium enterprise (SME). Besides, the high-level C-suite professionals they want to attract are not interested or fulfilled in working in these smaller organisations full-time.

At the other end of the spectrum in larger organisations, the complexity, uncertainty, and increased pace of today's business environment mean it is becoming harder to find all the skills and knowledge required to fulfil a functional C-suite position wrapped up in a single individual. Most organisations (like Will's) are looking for a superhuman; they don't exist. This forces larger firms to buy additional skills to complement and support the board, which increasingly doesn't know what it doesn't know.

In tandem with this, C-suite professionals like Nadim and Tara are searching for more purpose and meaning in and at work, with freedom, flexibility, variety, and control being top of their agendas. They feel overworked and disillusioned with the unrealistic demands of their corporate roles. This was the case before Covid, yet the pandemic has turbo-charged these feelings, resulting in them considering leaving these roles and looking for alternatives.

A new way of working is called for.

Organisations must discard their prejudices and preferences to put these individuals on the payroll and embrace an access economy, team-based approach utilising deeply knowledgeable, committed, and connected portfolio C-suite executives (those working at the more privileged end of the gig economy).

This is Strategy and Leadership as Service.

This ground-breaking approach is already gaining significant traction with SMEs who need access to C-suite skills but not full-time. It's a carefully designed solution for them and the C-suite individuals who want to break free from corporate life, become self-employed, and build a portfolio of clients, each of whom they service on a part-time or fractional basis. Part-time and fractional are terms used to describe this approach, and I use them interchangeably throughout this book.

The temptation is for organisations to see this new approach as only appropriate for SMEs, who use it to scale and then hop back onto the traditional model of employing the C-suite when they are more mature.

However, the landscape for mid-to-large corporates is also changing. If they only want to engage their C-suite through employment, they could find that their available talent pool has diminished. Relying on a single individual to lead a C-suite function in these complex times heightens risk.

The usual answer to shoring up capacity and skillset gaps through a mix of external consultants is sub-optimal.

This is their chance to think differently about how they resource up, with whom, and why.

If we can see past the myth that employing our C-suite is the only way to do things, Strategy and Leadership as Service is a way forward. It provides the roadmap to accessing C-suite skills for both SMEs and mid-to-large corporates. An access economy team approach from a new breed of professional services organisation, "the firm of C-suite providers," can deliver much-needed support for employed C-suite talent struggling to cover all the bases, and go beyond, to provide an alternative solution to full-time employment.

The purpose of this book

This book showcases Strategy and Leadership as Service from the perspectives of the pioneering C-suite executives who want to work differently and the organisations who need access to the complete range of functional, emotional, and collective intelligence at the C-suite level.

Its purpose is two-fold:

- To provide executives and business leaders with a complete understanding of this innovative approach and its key benefits. Most importantly, through illustration with real-life case studies, it will focus on how to put this business model into practice; and
- To understand the concepts behind Strategy and Leadership as Service, why it works, its essential ingredients, and the mindset shift required.

As CEO and co-founder of Liberti, a community of businesses operating a global working business model and successfully delivering Strategy and Leadership as Service, I am passionate about improving the lives of C-suite level executives and business leaders through its adoption.

Liberti has worked this way for over 20 years, proving the model in hundreds of locations worldwide across five continents. The business leaders and C-suite executives in all these geographies grapple with the same issues this new approach solves. Nevertheless, while Liberti has been clear on how to implement this way of working through extensive development of intellectual property and best practice from experimentation over the years, it has yet to explore why the model works.

First known study of the access economy for sharing professional services

In 2019, I embarked on a specialised master's degree from HEC, Paris, run jointly by HEC and Saïd Business School, Oxford University, called Consulting and Coaching for Change. I was interested in the factors influencing change and was keen to see how the offerings of current and future competitors compared with the Liberti business model.

Platform businesses (Acquier et al., 2017) in other sectors (e.g., Spotify and Netflix) were gaining traction. Through research into how these manifested, I realised that Liberti's business model had similarities. I started to research the sharing economy and learned about the access economy. There are many definitions of the access economy. For this book, I have chosen "The access economy covers a set of initiatives *sharing underutilized assets (material resources or skills) to optimize their use*" (Acquier et al., 2017, p. 4).

From my research, it became clear that the Liberti business model forms part of the sharing economy. It operates specifically in the access economy by giving businesses access to part-time or fractional C-suite services. The under-utilised asset (the C-suite executive) is shared, typically by a portfolio of between three and ten SME clients. This makes it affordable for the clients as they only require the services part-time, and the professionals can work as much as they want. For larger firms, a full-time solution can be delivered through a joined-up team of fractional C-suite members, ensuring the company always gets the right skills for the role as and when required.

Up to this point, I had yet to consider the Liberti business model to be part of the sharing economy since it was founded in 2001, long before accessing services started to emerge. However, the more I researched the sharing and access economy, the more I was convinced that it could provide some answers to why the business model worked and consequently improve how to deliver it. Liberti had areas that needed a boost, notably:

- The length of client relationships varied from a few months to over ten years. What was driving this variation? and
- Widespread service adoption in new geographical markets can take up to five years. How could this time be reduced?

Simultaneously, I became aware that while there was increasing research into the access economy for goods and digital services, there was limited information regarding sharing professional services, i.e., Strategy and Leadership as Service. This became my thesis topic for my master's degree and is now the subject of this book.

A sea change for the C-suite

For Strategy and Leadership as Service to gain further adoption, it requires three industry players: the firms of C-suite providers, their clients, and the C-suite professionals.

While globally, there are a growing number of independent C-suite executives and firms of C-suite providers, throughout this book and for illustration purposes only, I found it helpful to use the Liberti business model to showcase Strategy and Leadership as Service. I believe this is the beginning of a movement focused on a different way of living and working, providing a credible alternative to traditional employment.

The firms of C-suite providers

These firms enable their clients to gain access to the critical C-suite skills they need to grow and develop. The firms typically specialise in a particular function. They provide a community for like-minded C-suite professionals within that function and support them in building their portfolios of clients.

The Liberti business model takes this concept a step further. It is a community of independently owned and run C-suite level firms sharing the same business model, ethos, and approach, with each firm focusing on a specific domain within the C-suite. The business model facilitates collaboration within the community for the benefit of each firm's clients and team members.

The clients

Clients benefitting from Strategy and Leadership as Service take one of two forms:

Entrepreneurial businesses
These are generally owner-managed, growing SMEs like Jacinta's. Typically, they have revenues between £2 million and £100 million and don't need,

don't want, and can't afford full-time C-suite level professionals but recognise they need their skillsets on an ongoing basis or as the need arises.

Each C-level executive will have a portfolio of SME businesses (usually between three and ten companies), each of which they serve permanently and on a part-time basis. A typical client will work with their C-suite executive for a day a week, yet the range of time commitments can be from half a day per month up to three or four days per week. The number of clients in a professional's portfolio will vary depending on each company's time and skillset demands.

The goal is for each executive to have a stable client portfolio and build long-term, productive, and value-adding relationships, delivering the relevant C-suite services needed. Due to the clients' entrepreneurial nature and growing size, most will have had limited prior engagement with a skillset akin to those offered by this business model. However, a full-time resource would have been too expensive and unnecessary, and a fractional service like this has only recently existed.

These growing clients will be serviced predominantly by one individual, who becomes their C-suite professional in the relevant discipline, e.g., CFO, CIO (Chief Information Officer), and CMO. This individual will build a deep relationship with the business owner and leadership team.

These businesses sometimes require a specialist skillset for critical objectives within a discipline; here, a broader team approach comes in. C-suite executives from the wider team within a C-suite firm with relevant expert skillsets can deliver these projects. For example, a business may need specialist CFO skills to acquire another company. A team member with this expertise can work alongside the incumbent part-time CFO to deliver this project.

In addition, the added benefit to a client of engaging with a C-suite firm which is part of a wider community is that it can gain access to the skills of C-suite professionals from additional functional disciplines. This breadth and depth of skillset and capacity, combined with a joined-up, coordinated, and flexible approach, mean clients are fully supported in their ambitions.

Larger organisations

Like Will's business, these are more established, often with revenues over £100 million. They suit a team approach of part-time C-suite professionals to meet their diverse needs rather than a single individual working full-time.

One option is for the C-suite team to assist the incumbent full-time C-level employee by providing joined-up and coordinated support to fill their capacity and skillset gaps with specialist C-suite expertise as needed.

Alternatively, the C-suite team can offer a complete alternative to full-time employment. This approach comprises a Lead C-suite team member, working part-time, who holds the primary relationship with the client. They are supported by other C-suite professionals from the wider team brought in as required to service the diverse and varying needs of the business – all with the most relevant skillset and aptitude for the roles required. Some of these roles will be full-time interim, and project-based interventions, while others will be ongoing part-time.

The C-suite professionals

Critically, unlike traditional professional services businesses, the C-suite professionals are not employed by their firm of C-suite providers. They are self-employed. This is a crucial ingredient of the business model. It enables the C-suite level executives to feel more in control over their working lives. They have freedom of choice. They can choose with whom they want to work and which clients are a match for them, ensuring the amount of work they take on can fit with their lives. This mindset shift away from employment requires a move from job security to income security – more on that later.

What is the access economy?

The access economy enables sharing of assets to optimise their use. Outcomes involve broader and cheaper access without ownership, more intensive adoption, and an attractive, sustainable offering.

Spotify and Netflix are just two examples of an increasing number of digital services that have grown exponentially. Consumers realise that they no longer need to own and store vinyl records or DVDs to enjoy the benefits of listening to music and watching films and TV whenever they want.

An example of an access economy business model for more traditional goods would be Zipcar, which enables non-car owners to access a pool of cars when needed. The user pays for the vehicle when it is required but doesn't have the responsibility and expense of owning it full-time.

On learning more about the access economy, I realised that clients benefitting from Strategy and Leadership as Service were, in the broadest sense, "sharing" the services of their C-suite professional and that the model is one of access within the sharing economy. I furthered my research into the concepts underpinning this approach. I found that it is possible for users to feel they are "renting" the asset. Without legal ownership and something I later discovered called psychological ownership (PO), the relationship can be temporary, even uncaring, with a lack of self-identification with the asset. In the example of Zipcar, while the access economy business model enables convenient usage, it does not promote ownership (Bardhi & Eckhardt, 2012).

I started to explore the role of PO in these relationships, specifically how feelings of PO without legal ownership could enhance an access economy business. This led me to consider whether PO would also impact relationships between clients and C-suite executives within the access economy for professional services.

Psychological ownership fills the gap

The Liberti business model underpins thousands of client relationships globally, some are very long-term, yet others are much shorter. The Liberti community has studied part-time executives' behaviours in detail over the years. It has built ideal profiles, value sets, mindsets, and required behaviours for attracting team members, best practice development, coaching, and training, often tailored to each discipline. Nevertheless, there is still an opportunity to marry these data up with the clients and investigate their feelings towards the firms delivering the services, the offerings, and the C-suite professionals.

The clients using the model gain access to C-suite professionals rather than owning the services through legal employment. This mindset has always been vital for clients to adopt. Getting over that hurdle of traditional employment and ownership versus access has been critical in new client acquisition and enhancing engagement longevity.

On digging deeper, I realised that the lack of PO could explain why some relationships are brief, with clients demonstrating low levels of care for the C-suite executives (and vice versa). Some clients still want to migrate to legal employment as soon as it is affordable, even though the business case does not support it. In these situations, the ingrained mindset of ownership prevails.

Attracting more professionals to the fractional portfolio industry and developing their skills to have long-term, productive, rewarding, and value-adding client relationships are issues that keep me awake at night. I am passionate about building this industry globally so that as many business leaders and C-suite professionals as possible can benefit from working together.

I had discovered existing research on access-based consumption (Bardhi & Eckhardt, 2012) and PO (Pierce et al., 2001) where the assets or targets of ownership were products or digital services. Nothing similar existed for PO's role in the access economy for professional services, and my interest in this gap encouraged me to write this book. This is a game-changer for the industry and extends the current body of knowledge in PO in the access economy to a new context: professional services.

Overview of my study

From this accumulated knowledge of the access economy and the critical role of PO, I embarked on a research project. I wanted to test whether the known factors which underpin PO in other contexts were present and influential within the relationships using the Liberti business model.

I conducted a qualitative study on the largest C-suite provider in the Liberti community, The CFO Centre (CFOC), which provides part-time CFO services to owner-managed entrepreneurial enterprises globally. I chose their most established market to study, the UK.

This research focuses on the three-way relationships illustrated in Figure 0.1.

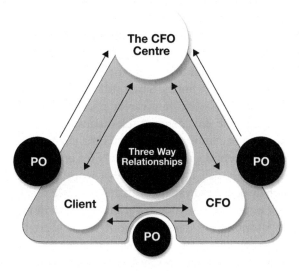

Figure 0.1 The Strategy and Leadership as Service relationships for The CFO Centre

Specifically, I focused on feelings of PO as follows:

- Both ways between the client (primary contacts, most often CEO, Managing Director, or entrepreneur) and the CFO;
- From the CFO towards CFOC; and
- From the client towards CFOC.

It is important to note that from PO theory, it is possible to consider other people as "extensions of self" (Belk, 1988, p. 156). This is not a reference to slavery but "Rather ... the symbolic extension of self that James (1890, pp. 291–292) saw in 'his wife and children, his ancestors and friends'" (Belk, 1988, p. 156).

Lastly, the study was one of business-to-business (B2B) rather than business-to-consumer (B2C). Many former studies have focused on B2C provisions of goods and services. To my knowledge, this was the first study of PO in the access economy for sharing B2B professional services.

The future of work

A critical success factor for Strategy and Leadership as Service is that the C-suite professionals are all self-employed. Their motivation to leave significant corporate roles and become independent is to break free from corporate life. They want to gain control over their lives. They seek work-life balance and flexibility, a variety of clients to work with, and want to "give back" and "make a difference" using their considerable skills and experience. They often wish to supplement working with other commitments like caregiving for children or elderly parents, becoming a micro-entrepreneur, or pursuing a hobby. Some still want to work full-time yet relish the opportunity to become a career portfolio executive, thriving working with many different clients simultaneously.

This transition to becoming self-employed is a change in their state of mind and a very different approach to working for one employer at a time and being employed. It is an alternative way of working that can bring fulfilment through diversity and variety, with income rather than job security.

The increase in portfolio working will be a significant change in society. This shift contributes to a new future of work where the traditional ownership and employment model is no longer the only route forward.

Strategy and Leadership as Service has its foundations in the "'portfolio' approach to life" (Handy, [1994]2002, p. 71). In *The empty raincoat*

Charles Handy described organisations of the future as "organisers not employers" (ibid., p. 171). He suggested that "The age of the organisation may be coming to an end in one sense, when to be a full-time employee is a minority occupation" (ibid., p. 39). He was referring to how organisations and workers would adapt to the future chaos and confusion of the paradoxes of our times. He introduced the concept of the Doughnut Principle to work and live successfully with these paradoxes. It involves organisations with a small core of essential employed professional staff with a surrounding ring of space filled with flexible portfolio workers. Equally, individuals will build their Personal Doughnuts. Handy described his doughnut as:

> A collection of different groups and activities, of bits and pieces of work, like a share portfolio, I could get different things from different bits. A part of that portfolio would be 'core', providing the essential wherewithal for life, but it would be balanced by work done purely for interest or for a cause, or because it would stretch me personally, or simply because it was fascinating or fun.
>
> (Handy, [1994]2002, p. 71)

In *The age of unreason*, Handy ([1989]1995) had described the organisation of the future as "The Shamrock Organization" (Handy, [1989]1995, p. 70). It has three parts represented by the three leaves of a shamrock. The first leaf is the core of professionals who lead the organisation. They are well-rewarded but pay the price as the organisation demands their complete attention. There is little room for anything else in their lives. The second leaf comprises non-essential work contracted out to individuals or firms, paying for results, not time. The third leaf is the flexible labour force delivering just-in-time solutions, which the organisation can flex up and down depending on demand.

Thirty years on, we are seeing Handy's insights becoming a reality. The third leaf of the flexible labour force is being serviced by the lower end of the gig economy, with workers on zero-hours contracts, which suit some but not all. There is tension in the labour market regarding ensuring they receive decent pay and conditions. In the second leaf, individuals with non-essential skills set themselves up as self-employed or small firms to service organisations.

Finally, we see the C-suite, who would form part of what Handy might have been tempted to call his four-leaf clover, becoming fed up with corporate demands and moving to portfolio work.

The impact of Covid-19

In 2020, the Covid-19 virus appeared in China and began worldwide transmission within the community resulting in millions of deaths. The global deployment of effective vaccines, social distancing, economic lockdowns, increased hygiene, and wearing protective clothing contained its spread and death toll. Society and human behaviours have changed considerably, and look set to continue for the medium term with vast implications.

Many individuals suffered significantly, losing loved ones, experiencing economic hardship, job losses, redundancies, and lower mental health and well-being levels.

During lockdowns, there was an enormous shift to remote working, conducting business, and communicating using technology platforms such as Zoom and Teams to enable social distancing and prevent the spread of the virus. As we have gained control over the transmission and impact of the virus and started to socialise more, we have moved back to working together in offices. Many businesses have adopted a hybrid policy of mixing working from home and the office.

Many entrepreneurial businesses engaged with Strategy and Leadership as Service throughout the pandemic. The C-suite firms shifted their offerings online and continued to deliver them successfully. They experienced increased demand among new and existing clients because their services were affordable, flexible, and essential for survival and growth.

The remote working style became normalised, and the C-suite professionals were no longer "the odd ones out" as many employees also worked remotely from home.

The lockdowns have allowed C-suite executives in traditional employment to reflect on their lives and purposes. Many see that their ties to a particular company or sector bring risk and realise that security from employment is just an illusion. Others who have lost their positions are rethinking their next move, with building a portfolio career being a significant contender. Hence, more and more C-suite professionals are considering working this way.

The new normal

Given the Covid-19 pandemic and the enormous society-wide changes it is causing, there is a widespread belief that life will never be the same again. Over time, we will transition to a new, undefined normal.

In *The paradox of success*, O'Neil (1995) describes how leaders can move forward in life and let go of their past. The general idea is what has served us in the past to get us here isn't going to keep us here or move us forward. Charles Handy (2015) introduces the concept of the second curve as a pathway to move through change. By carefully timing changes in thinking, strategies, and teams, we can find a new and different way forward for continued success.

Our old system and way of working could be the traditional employment model, and the emerging system or second curve could be part-time portfolio working. Effectively a transition from ownership to access. This transition had already begun slowly and has accelerated through Covid.

Extensive research by MIT Sloan Management Review and Deloitte throughout 2021 and 2022 based on interviews with thousands of global leaders and managers found that a third of respondents expected to increase their dependence on external workers in the next two years (Altman et al., 2021). A minority of progressive organisations already recognise that they need to design and lead workforce ecosystems and cultures made up of temporary workers, gig workers, consultants, contractors, job-sharers, and full and part-time employees (Altman et al., 2022). Organisations are finally realising that an employee-only workforce is limiting, and external workers are here to stay and do important work, not just more work (Altman et al., 2021).

Introducing the Strategy and Leadership as Service framework – the Four Rs

Here is an overview of the Strategy and Leadership as Service framework, see Figure 0.2, which I have built from my research and provides a preview of the rest of the book.

I developed The Strategy and Leadership as Service framework from the Four Rs:

- The roots;
- The routes;
- The relationships; and
- The roadmap to access.

The roots and routes are terminologies adopted from the research in the seminal papers "Toward a theory of psychological ownership in

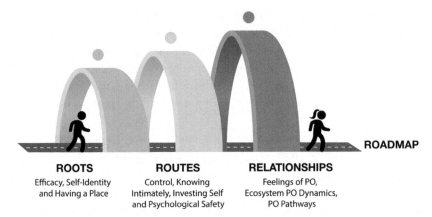

ROOTS	ROUTES	RELATIONSHIPS
Efficacy, Self-Identity and Having a Place	Control, Knowing Intimately, Investing Self and Psychological Safety	Feelings of PO, Ecosystem PO Dynamics, PO Pathways

Figure 0.2 The Strategy and Leadership as Service framework – The Four Rs

organizations" (Pierce et al., 2001) and "The state of psychological owner-ship: Integrating and extending a century of research" (Pierce et al., 2003) and are described in detail in Chapter 4. The study explained in this book focuses on testing the presence of these roots and routes within the pro-fessional services context of the Liberti business model.

The roots – WHY PO exists in relationships

As explained by the work of Pierce et al. (2001), there needs to be three roots or motives of PO which underpin why the state exists: efficacy, self-identity, and having a place, explained as follows:

- *Efficacy*: for PO to emerge, clients and C-suite executives have to understand each other's needs, feel knowledgeable about the range of services offered, and be confident that the service and relationship are working to meet desired goals;
- *Self-identity*: possessions contribute to our sense of identity and self-definition. People use ownership to define themselves, express self-identity to others, and ensure the continuity of the self across time. In this context, C-suite executives and clients work together with shared identities and use them to establish and contribute to their own iden-tities, fostering feelings of PO; and
- *Having a place*: individuals desire to have a particular territory or place, for belonging, and to call home and dwell (Ardrey, 1966). Working

together enables C-suite executives and clients to be part of a group of like-minded people, contributing to their feelings of PO towards each other.

The routes of PO – HOW to create PO in relationships

There are three major routes to develop PO which are interrelated (Pierce et al., 2001):

- *Controlling the target*: the extent to which clients and C-suite executives can control and access each other impacts feelings of ownership. This includes how accessible, approachable, and available they find each other;
- *Intimately knowing the target*: the more information and intimate knowledge the client and C-suite executive have about each other, the deeper the relationship between them and the stronger the feelings of PO;
- *Investing self into the target*: individuals own the objects they have created in much the same way as they own themselves (Durkheim, 1957). Investment can take many forms: time, skills, ideas, physical and psychological, and intellectual energies. The more the investment, the more the individual feels connected to the target. An example here would be that the more the client and C-suite executive work together to co-create outputs, the stronger the feelings of PO; and
- *Psychological Safety – an additional route to PO*: a meta-analysis found through a review of 141 studies published over 20 years that psychological safety (defined as "feeling able to show and employ one's self without fear of negative consequences to self-image, status, or career" (Kahn, 1990, p. 708), is an emerging antecedent leading to PO (Zhang et al., 2021). Both client members and C-suite executives need to feel psychologically safe in their group settings to build feelings of PO.

The relationships required for Strategy and Leadership as Service

Once the roots and routes are in place in an access economy model for delivering C-suite services, PO can develop. Relationships flourish through the interaction and combination of roots and routes. The following factors determine how these relationships extend across the system and sustain in balance for the longer term:

- *Feelings of PO*: aspects such as matching the client and the C-suite executive, organisational norms, C-suite skills, and personal context all influence the establishment of PO;
- *PO Pathways*: given the number of roots and routes of PO, I found that there were many different pathways to creating PO through various combinations of roots and routes, ultimately giving more flexibility in generating effective relationships held together with PO; and
- *Ecosystem PO Dynamics*: I identified some key influencers contributing to enabling or disabling dynamics within the system, for example, balancing PO across the three relationships between the client, C-suite executive, and C-suite firm.

The roadmap to access professional services

Finally, I share how to use the Strategy and Leadership as Service framework to design a roadmap for delivering professional C-suite services in the access economy at an individual and team level for SMEs and larger organisations.

Overview of the book

Following this introduction are thirteen chapters and a conclusion in six sections, as follows:

Part I The Forces Shaping Change in the C-Suite

This section analyses the history of the Board of Directors and the C-suite's emergence and adoption in managing and leading organisations. The global perspective highlights the benefits and limitations of the current C-suite construct. I then share a detailed review of the megatrends shaping how C-suite executives are beginning to want to work now and how this will change further, alongside the challenges facing organisations to remain relevant and maintain growth throughout constant turbulence.

These forces and the impact and repercussions of the Covid-19 pandemic demand a different way of engaging with C-suite executives in the future, which embraces collective intelligence, flexible working, a sense of belonging, and harnessing the power of many. We need a shift towards accessing C-suite skills rather than legally employing them.

Part II Access to the C-Suite through Psychological Ownership

This focuses on the rise of the access economy as an alternative method of engaging C-suite professional services skillsets. The access economy is still a relatively new phenomenon, so this part introduces the various definitions of the access economy and distinguishes between ownership, access, and sharing. It then reviews the emerging access economy's growth, barriers, drivers, and how it changes user behaviour, particularly for goods, digital, and B2B services.

I then introduce and define the concept of PO, suggesting it bridges the gap between access and legal employment.

Part III The C-Suite Industry Players

The access economy for the C-suite requires three industry players, the C-suite professionals themselves, their clients, and the firms of C-suite providers. This part shares the characteristics, attitudes, needs, and wants of all three players and highlights how they fit together for mutual benefit. I share case studies of C-suite executives and firms already putting this business model into action in individual and team-based contexts. I highlight the differences with traditional employment and the role of PO in building relationships for the long term.

Part IV Evidence for C-Suite Access

In this part, I present and discuss how I tested the concepts underpinning PO using The CFO Centre UK as the case study. I share the essential findings and interpret what this means in practice for C-suite industry players to build long-term and productive relationships using PO.

Part V Strategy and Leadership as Service Framework: The Four Rs

Here I examine the framework in detail. I describe each of the Four Rs: the roots (why PO exists), the routes (how they manifest), the relationships (how they develop and interact across the system), and the industry roadmap to building an access economy business model for delivering professional C-suite services at scale.

I discuss how to upskill C-suite executives and the businesses they serve and why and how to develop their skills in establishing PO across the whole ecosystem.

The roadmap demonstrates how to use the framework. It highlights that organisations can engage at an individual or team business model level. The more complex and ambitious the business agenda, the more likely a team approach would be a better solution.

Part VI The Changing Face of the C-Suite

The book will close by addressing its central purpose: to provide a more substantial evidence base for changing the nature of the C-suite to align with the developing needs of C-suite professionals and the external challenges facing organisations.

In this chapter I start by highlighting the advantages of the access economy C-suite alongside the downsides and barriers to adoption. I then distinguish Strategy and Leadership as Service from consulting business models and share implications for Human Resource (HR) practices, such as managing accountability of the C-suite executives within their clients. I discuss how the business model impacts other factors, such as understanding business risk and maintaining corporate governance.

Finally, I share the study's limitations and consider future directions for further research. I conclude by reviewing the significance to practice, theory, and the future of work, as offerings like Strategy and Leadership as Service develop to disrupt and challenge the traditional employment model.

Who is this book for?

This book is for a range of people interested in the latest thought leadership, which challenges the current orthodoxy of employment and how C-level professionals live and work. This includes:

- CEOs, board members, and business leaders in owner-managed, growing, entrepreneurial organisations who don't want, don't need, or can't afford a full-time C-suite executive but recognise they need the skillset on an ongoing basis or as needed;
- The owners and leaders of larger organisations who recognise that the fast pace of business and breadth of knowledge expected of C-suite functions could be better filled through a team-based approach;
- Budding and existing portfolio C-suite executives who want to live and work differently, with more freedom of choice, purpose, flexibility, variety, and control;
- Leaders of professional services firms who would like to venture away from the traditional business model of employment to create a more progressive workplace;
- HR professionals of organisations concerned with attracting, selecting, energising, and developing high-calibre C-suite executives;
- Leadership coaches, strategy, and organisational development consultants, and recruiters; and
- Academics and forward-thinking business students who want to learn about cutting-edge working business models that challenge the status quo and want to be in touch with the latest thinking.

In summary, Strategy and Leadership as Service is reinventing the professional services business model and the traditional way of working. Teams of self-employed C-suite executives have a different perspective: one of greater agency in designing their careers, work, and home lives. They are just as committed to their clients and roles, perhaps even more so than when they were employed. They belong to a global team of like-minded individuals who are serial masters in their disciplines and fully supported by each other. At the same time, the organisations they service gain access to a diverse team and set of skills, which is what they need when they need it, subscribing to the philosophy "You are what you can Access" (Belk, 2014, p. 1595).

References

Acquier, A., Daudigeos, T., & Pinkse, J. (2017). Promises and paradoxes of the sharing economy: An organizing framework. *Technological Forecasting and Social Change*, *125*, 1–10. https://doi.org/10.1016/j.techfore.2017.07.006

Altman, E. J., Schwartz, J., Kiron, D., Jones, R., & Kearns-Manolatos, D. (2021). Workforce ecosystems: A new strategic approach to the future of work. *MIT Sloan Management Review and Deloitte*.

Altman, E. J., Kiron, D., Jones, R., & Schwartz, J. (2022). Orchestrating workforce ecosystems: Strategically managing work across and beyond organizational boundaries. *MIT Sloan Management Review and Deloitte.*

Ardrey, R. (1966). *The territorial imperative: A personal inquiry into the animal origins of property and nations.* Atheneum Books.

Bardhi, F., & Eckhardt, G. M. (2012). Access-based consumption: The case of car sharing. *Journal of Consumer Research, 39*(4), 881–898. https://doi.org/10.1086/666376

Belk, R. (1988). Possessions and the extended self. *Journal of Consumer Research, 15*(2), 139–168. https://doi.org/10.1086/209154

Belk, R. (2014). You are what you can access: Sharing and collaborative consumption online. *Journal of Business Research, 67*(8), 1595–1600. https://doi.org/10.1016/j.jbusres.2013.10.001

Durkheim, É. (1957). *Professional ethics and civil morals.* Routledge & Kegan Paul, Ltd.

Handy, C. ([1989]1995). *The age of unreason* (2nd ed). Arrow Books Limited.

Handy, C. ([1994]2002). *The empty raincoat: New thinking for a new world.* Arrow.

Handy, C. (2015). *The second curve: Thoughts on reinventing society.* Random House Books.

James, W. (1890). *The principles of psychology.* Holt.

Kahn, W. A. (1990). Psychological conditions of personal engagement and disengagement at work. *Academy of Management Journal, 33*(4), 692–724.

O'Neil, J. R. (1995). *The paradox of success: When winning at work means losing at life: a book of renewal for leaders.* McGraw-Hill Publishing Co.

Pierce, J. L., Kostova, T., & Dirks, K. T. (2001). Toward a theory of psychological ownership in organizations. *Academy of Management Review, 26*(2), 298–310. https://doi.org/10.5465/amr.2001.4378028

Pierce, J. L., Kostova, T., & Dirks, K. T. (2003). The state of psychological ownership: integrating and extending a century of research. *Review of General Psychology, 7*(1), 84–107. https://doi.org/10.1037/1089-2680.7.1.84

Zhang, Y., Liu, G., Zhang, L., Xu, S., & Cheung, M. W. (2021). Psychological ownership: A meta-analysis and comparison of multiple forms of attachment in the workplace. *Journal of Management, 47*(3), 745–770. https://doi.org/10.1177/0149206320917195

Part I

The Forces Shaping Change in the C-Suite

Time for a New Version of the C-Suite? $\quad$ **1**

In 2014, Deloitte coined the term CFO to mean Chief Frontier Officer (Comeau et al., 2014). They refer to Troy Alstead, Chief Finance Officer of Starbucks, whose role shifted to a global focus with responsibility for worldwide initiatives. He was not only CFO but also titled group president of global business services because Starbucks recognised his role's increasing complexity and responsibility in overseeing their global financial, technological, and supply chain operations. Deloitte quotes the growth of Starbucks from 170 shops in 1992, when Alstead joined, to 19,000 globally in 2013 as evidence for the sheer scale of the role. Alstead became Starbucks's COO (Chief Operating Officer) in 2014 with an even broader remit to address the expanding requirements of going global with pace and scale.

Similarly, as far back as 2009, the role of the CMO was enlarging, from being in charge of advertising, brand management, and market research to a much broader and public role, leading change efforts, shaping public profiles, managing complexity and building new capabilities (Court, 2007). It is beyond doubt that this evolution of the role of the CMO has occurred. As an illustration, in 2022, Forbes announced the world's most influential CMOs (Matlins, 2022) in conjunction with their research partner Sprinklr and data and analysis from LinkedIn. They measured the influence of the brands and businesses of these CMOs, i.e., their ability to change human attitudes and behaviours.

It is the same for CIOs. They started as functional heads and became strategic partners responsible for aligning technology with the business. The next step was to get involved in driving business strategy, and eventually, they became part of the C-suite (Ross & Feeny, 1999). Today they

DOI: 10.4324/9781003368090-3

spearhead many organisations' digital transformation efforts, with 80 per cent interviewed by Genpact saying they drive business transformation or partner for it (Srivastava et al., 2021). However, it is more than that. Along with their fellow C-suite colleagues, they have become co-creators of new business models, and almost all expect their roles to expand going forwards.

Chief Human Resources Officers (CHROs) are also experiencing further demands from their organisations and roles. The role is expanding. It already includes responsibility for the strategic direction of resource forecasting, talent management, compensation programmes, succession planning, training, and learning and development within digital transformation. It must also be on top of corporate responses to emerging future work trends. These include creating agile organisational structures which embrace new workforce models such as contracting, freelancers, temporary, and consultant contributors, and understanding changing behavioural wants and needs of the workforce. Employees want more flexibility and work-life balance in an inclusive, diverse workforce with inspiring leadership (Link, 2019).

As far back as 2001, Peter Drucker, in his article "Will the corporation survive?" for *The Economist* noted the increased failure rate of CEOs in large American companies within a year or so of being appointed. He referred to the advanced pace of change and complexity facing companies at the turn of the century. With organisations still structured to meet the business demands of the 1950s, he described the roles of CEOs and their executive teams as undoable and that a new organising concept was needed for very senior management in large organisations (Drucker, 2001).

The book *Reinventing the C-suite* (White, 2020) refers to the world evolving and responding to a series of revolutions over time. Firstly, agricultural, some 10,000 years ago, then industrial, which started in about 1760, and now the digital revolution is upon us. The digital age enables our organisations to build scale without mass. Data can be digitised and more easily stored and communicated. The process of getting these data into a digital state is digitisation, and it is this process that is changing our behaviours. We are developing new ways to consume goods and services, enjoy experiences, share information, and digest media. Digitalisation permeates everyday life, requiring organisations to internally change their behaviours and processes to produce these goods and services to remain competitive.

How organisations digitalise is just one of the complex megatrends they face today. They are encountering many wicked problems, defined as novel, recalcitrant, and complex, with no definition of success, only trade-offs and better or worse outcomes (Brookes & Grint, 2010). What is more, solutions tend to be partial with unintended consequences. Wicked problems (e.g., how to prevent climate change, provide clean water for all, optimise the use of artificial intelligence, deal with ageing populations, world conflict, and societal changes) live in complex emerging systems. They fall within the realm of the modern leader and the C-suite.

However, most organisational change efforts fail (Kotter, 1995). A significant contributing factor could be that there is no single, shared vision of reality. We operate in many interactive, complex emerging systems that we will only partially understand. A future stable state is just an illusion (Morgan, 1997).

Paradoxically, understanding the environment of an organisation is considered by leaders to be vital. The political, economic, social, technological, and environmental contexts (Boulton et al., 2015), which are different in each location where global corporations operate, all play a part. Leaders strive to control organisations, and there is much research into why this is so difficult. There are many discontinuities to deal with. Leaders must reconsider their role and face the challenge of simultaneously positioning their organisations for the present and future.

Time for a new version of the C-suite?

The demands and expectations for the C-suite roles of the future mean more and more organisations are piling the pressure onto their top teams and widening their remits to deliver organisational change to address emerging trends and to stay competitive. With the current C-suite concept, they have little choice but to ask and expect more of their leaders, with transformational skills paramount.

Nevertheless, are all C-suite members equipped to handle these vast and complex agendas for transformation?

This leads to the follow-on question: is it even time to rethink our model for the C-suite?

Writing for Deloitte Insights, Eamonn Kelly asks if it is "Time for version 3.0" of the C-suite (Kelly, 2014)? He refers to a group of general managers making up the Board of Directors being version 1.0, originating in the 1920s. Then in the 1980s and 1990s, functional C-suite leaders were introduced, version 2.0, which is the structure we still use today.

However, is this enough to deliver the constant transformation required of organisations to remain on top?

The signs are that this model is now at its limits. A C-suite composed of a core of individual functional heads made sense; organisations certainly do not want to throw this out. They want to have it all. They still search out the best leaders with functional intelligence, who know that discipline inside out and are adept at leading and developing that functional capability within enterprises.

However, they also want these individuals to have more advanced skillsets above and beyond their specific discipline's rational and logical technical expertise. They need emotional intelligence, i.e., people skills, communication capabilities, and social abilities. These enable them to influence and mobilise large workforce groups internally; to work as one and deliver on corporate strategies and externally; to represent the public face of the brand and business to the broader world. The book, *Frames of mind* (Gardner, 1983) presents eight intelligence types. These include interpersonal intelligence, which involves understanding and interacting with others and being skilled in assessing their emotions, desires, and intentions, along with intrapersonal intelligence (understanding oneself). Both are essential skills for leaders to inspire others and navigate their way successfully through organisations.

Social skills are critical C-suite leader traits described in the *Harvard Business Review* (HBR) article "The C-suite skills that matter most" (Sadun et al., 2022). They refer to specific capabilities such as high levels of self-awareness, excellent listening and communication skills, the ability to work well with a variety of people and groups, and what psychologists refer to as "theory of mind" – the ability to infer what others are thinking and feeling – are just a few examples (Sadun et al., 2022). Furthermore, Alvarez and Svejenova (2022) highlight the importance for C-suite executives to develop and understand the different styles of executive power open to them in their roles.

Leaders must be good networkers and master boundary spanning which is the collection of interactions between individuals within and between organisations to coordinate and communicate across various institutional, cultural, and organisational contexts (Schotter et al., 2017). Internally leaders must build alliances across and within departments and business lines, externally with other stakeholder groups, and within organisations in their extended ecosystem.

Outstanding social skills and networking will also help leaders navigate the generational challenges they face in the workforce and their customer base. There are currently three generations in the workforce: Baby Boomers (born between 1946 and 1964), Generation X (born between 1965 and 1979), and Generation Y or Millennials (born between 1980 and the late 1990s), with Generation Z (born from the late 1990s) only just starting to work (O'Boyle, 2021). Research shows that while categorising people like this can lead to generalisations, there is broad agreement that each generation exhibits specific traits and characteristics that result in differing workplace needs, lifestyles, and buying habits. The *Global leadership forecast* (Development Dimensions International Inc. et al., 2018) reported that of 25,812 leaders and 2,547 HR professionals studied, 18 per cent were Baby Boomers, 62 per cent were Generation X, and 20 per cent were Millennials. The current C-suite is, therefore, primarily Generation X leaders with their attitudes, working styles, beliefs, and ways of building relationships. However, they must communicate meaningfully with Baby Boomers, who will likely still hold investment and decision-making power in their organisations. Additionally, they will need to inspire the Millennials, who will make up most of the workforce.

On top of that, to cope with the complexity of issues facing large companies and the relentless pace of change, C-suite leaders must elevate their mindset and thinking. They will be required to think systemically and holistically rather than linearly. They must be forever curious to seek out new and different perspectives from others. Roger Martin, a Professor Emeritus at the Rotman School of Management at University of Toronto and former dean, believes this type of thinking is the competency most needed by the individuals at the C-suite. He describes it as integrative thinking, which is a way of holding several opposing points of view at once and, rather than being overcome by the discomfort and ambiguity that results, utilising it to come up with fresh and better solutions (Martin, 2009).

Dr. George Land described developing creative, multiple solutions, and visualising many possibilities for problems as a skillset called divergent thinking (Ainsworth-Land & Jarman, 1992). He believed many of us need to learn outside of traditional schooling systems, where they focus on convergent thinking, which is critical, judgemental, and deciding. Both, of course, are needed.

Leaders who are integrative thinkers will see the value of diversity in thinking. They will design and build their teams and organisations with a culture which deliberately encourages multiple perspectives for discussion and debate. These leaders will value collective intelligence and harness it for growth and business transformation.

There is an extensive shopping list of new and enhanced skills that future C-suite leaders need to master. Is it just a case of upskilling these individuals? Or, in addition, can the current functional C-suite construct be organised differently to use the collective?

Since the middle of the 1990s, the strategic leadership perspective has dominated the study of senior leadership teams' structures and neglected structure and dynamics (Beckman & Burton, 2011).

Less is known about the organisation and division of responsibilities among the different positions reporting to the CEO and how these have evolved over time (Guadalupe et al., 2014). In addition, it is surprising that the majority of scholarship on the top management team (TMT) treats it as a stable entity, especially given different C-suite members come and go, as if playing a game of musical chairs fuelled by frequent changes in organisational structure (Beckman & Burton, 2011).

Asking how we can reimagine the C-suite for the future is the core question that this book explores by introducing a revolutionary access economy business model as an alternative to the traditional employment model. This new way of working may have some of the answers.

It offers a solution for entrepreneurial and growing businesses by providing a model to bring C-suite skills into their organisations early in their lifecycle. This solution has previously been widely unavailable and unaffordable.

For mid-market corporates and substantial global organisations, it provides some answers by giving them access to the functional, emotional, and collective intelligence they need for transformation through dynamically accessing teams of C-suite portfolio professionals.

In all contexts and stages of development of an organisation, the C-suite individuals will need to upskill beyond the technical and functional to develop emotional intelligence and elevated thinking. However, this is a big ask.

Development of this breadth of skills to a high level requires deliberate and concentrated personal and professional development over a committed period. The HBR article "Seven transformations of leadership" (Rooke & Torbert, 2005) shares that only 15 per cent of managers sampled were at the Individualist level and above and capable of thinking systemically. The population of C-suite professionals who have already mastered all the functional and emotional skills required and developed an elevated mindset is likely insufficient to meet the demands of the business world going forwards. Even if this hypothesis for the C-suite is accepted and promoted, it will take time for organisations to transition their leadership and development programmes to support it and then shift their top teams to the next stage of mindset development.

Therefore, a different way of organising the C-suite could be a partial solution. An access economy business model using multiple skillsets, engaged dynamically and flexibly over time, could provide an alternative and additional way to have the organisational capability needed for the future and sooner.

Most importantly, this new way of working through the access economy addresses a crucial part of the equation that needs to be added to the emerging theory and practice underpinning the current direction of travel for C-suite development. It meets the changing needs of individual C-suite professionals, which must be addressed in any future version of the C-suite as described in depth in Chapter 2.

In this chapter, I share an understanding of the Board of Directors' role and the adoption of the C-suite. The global perspective reviews the benefits and limitations of the current C-suite construct. It then highlights the emerging trends we see developing within the C-suite to make it fit for the future.

Throughout this chapter and the next, I share the access economy business model and how it builds on and addresses the current trends experienced in the C-suite. It is an innovative and alternative way for organisations to engage and structure their C-suites in the future to benefit from collective intelligence, broader and deeper skillsets, and more robust risk management. Most importantly, I will explain how this novel approach aligns with emerging global trends and the needs of C-suite executives of the future.

The Board of Directors – version 1.0

The term Board of Directors originated in the 16th century. The "board" was where people came together for significant meetings. The word's meaning changed from the furniture piece to the individuals seated around it (Nordqvist, 2019). The term "Board of Directors" (board) was first recorded in 1712 (Morrish, 2020).

Public companies must have a board, and some private companies and non-profit organisations will also have one. The board is the governing body of a company, elected by shareholders in the case of public companies to set strategy and oversee management (Chen, 2022).

It is usual for large organisations with a board to select a leadership team, often called the C-suite executive team, to lead and be responsible for the company's strategy and performance. The board, presided over by a chairperson, is responsible for the organisation's governance and represents the shareholders' and sometimes other stakeholders' interests.

Corporate governance flows from the organisation's owners through the board to the C-suite and into the organisation. The value created by the organisation passes the opposite way through the leadership team and board back to the owners and shareholders, usually in the form of equity rewards and dividends.

Smaller organisations and certainly many entrepreneurial SMEs looking to engage with part-time C-suite professionals often have shareholders, board members, and C-suite executive team members who are the same people. For example, a growing company's 100 per cent owner and shareholder founder is also likely to be the CEO who leads the business daily, sits on the board, and may even be the board chair.

The same individuals holding different roles at this level of the organisation can bring some ethical considerations regarding conflict of interest. The founder, owner, chairperson, and CEO are required to have different responsibilities in each of these positions. This conflict is often one of the reasons that these smaller organisations want to bring in portfolio professionals with expertise across the C-suite. It introduces professional rigour into the leadership team in the required corporate disciplines, divorcing ownership from leadership and management and bringing more objectivity to the business.

In contrast, some vast and undoubtedly phenomenally successful global organisations like Amazon and Meta Platforms (formerly Facebook, Inc.) had the same individuals as their CEO, part of the shareholder group, and chairperson throughout their development. Jeff Bezos is currently the founder, executive chair, and former president and CEO of Amazon, stepping down as CEO in July 2021. He is also still a shareholder. Mark Zuckerberg is a shareholder, co-founder, executive chair, and CEO of Meta Platforms.

There is overlap between board members and the C-suite in all sizes of organisations. Nevertheless, as businesses develop and progress, they tend to expand their C-suite to bring in leaders to focus on the execution of strategy.

Profit or purpose and the multi-stakeholder board

Over the last 50 years, there has been a shift from seeing organisations as profit-making machines existing to serve their shareholders (Friedman,

2007) to ones which serve a more comprehensive set of stakeholders (Freeman, 2010) and purpose-related goals. As a result, they are considering a wider set of stakeholders beyond shareholders, including staff, customers, suppliers, the community, and the environment.

Despite the stock markets still being a key barometer of organisational success with financial metrics at their heart, the external context for what makes a successful organisation is changing. Increasingly stakeholders, including employees and customers, are searching for companies that also "do good" and have a higher purpose, which these individuals can make sense of and attach meaning to, other than making money. An excellent example of this would be Patagonia, whose purpose talks straight to the sustainability movement to "Protect our home planet" (Patagonia, 2023, para. 3).

Two organisations which are very successful under financial metrics but have a focus which goes beyond producing good commercial outcomes are Handelsbanken (customer focus) and the Tata Group (community focus). They both have a higher purpose that unites their employees, customers, and other stakeholders, providing meaning and engagement within the organisation. These businesses align both purpose and profits. However, which comes first?

Purpose and meaning lead naturally to profits, as illustrated by the work in "Combining purpose with profits" (Birkinshaw et al., 2014). In their study, goal-framing theory explains how organisations can manage two goals simultaneously (not linearly). The theory shows how goals make a difference when they work on the employees' beliefs, with the most valuable goals being the pro-social goals supporting collaborative work. These goals compete for mindshare with other financial gain and hedonic goals. They need to be emphasised by the leaders for constant prominence and reinforcement within the business, with systems and internal structures developed to ensure they show up and are meaningful in day-to-day operations. Of particular interest is that pro-social goals highlight the need for obliquity (Kay, 2011) i.e., the other goals are not removed by pro-social goals but are realised more effectively.

Research shared in "The purpose of profit" (Edmans, 2019) supports this theory. Serving the community should be central to how a business runs, and not just a department of corporate social responsibility (CSR) (Edmans, 2019). Edmans' approach is that by investing in stakeholders companies create profits for investors and value to society. Profits can be a by-product of serving a purpose, with purpose-led businesses typically being more profitable in the long term anyway (Sisodia et al., 2014). This shifts our thinking regarding investors, who are often considered "the enemy" looking for short-term financial gains at all costs. Instead,

Edmans believes the other stakeholders have agency in their roles as employees and customers and the capacity to act independently and influence their environment. With all stakeholders working together and focusing on a common purpose for the long term, we shift our thinking from business "or" society to business "and" society (Edmans, 2019).

Organisations focusing on purpose alongside profits are changing their structures and increasing the representation on their boards from all stakeholders, not just shareholders. Representation of employees, customers, society, the environment, and investors is occurring and will likely increase as organisations expand their focus beyond the financials. Regulation will also play its part in moving this stakeholder model forward, for example, by insisting on reporting on ESG goals (Environmental, Social, and Governance) along with Diversity, Equity, and Inclusion (DE&I) reporting of individual board members, amongst others.

We are therefore seeing the board developing in some organisations to a broader stakeholder composition, focusing on return to stakeholders, financial and otherwise, and corporate governance.

Expansion of the C-suite – version 2.0

Regardless of its composition and inclusion of board members, shareholders, and founders holding these positions, the C-suite executive team has a separate role from the board. Led by the CEO, it executes strategy and performance to deliver a return to stakeholders. The separation of powers between the board and C-suite allows more transparent lines of responsibility and accountability.

The C-suite comprises a varying number of CXOs (Jeffcock, 2022), defined as follows:

1. C represents the Chief, head of the function, business unit, or department and either a C-suite executive team member or the level below. It illustrates the hierarchy in the organisation;
2. X represents the Expert. Individuals will have deep expertise and specialism in the functional discipline they head up, gained through experience or characterised by a technical or professional qualification or accreditation in the field; and
3. O represents Officer, which denotes the seriousness of the role and requires the individual to represent and generate value for the whole company, not just their function

The exact make-up of the C-suite team varies from organisation to organisation depending on their size and stage of the lifecycle, the sectors they serve, and the challenges and opportunities they face.

A study of the FTSE 100 C-suite roles by Jeffcock (2022) showed that, on average, the executive team comprised nine people. This team included the CEO, with five staff C-suite executives in order of frequency of CFO (in 100 per cent of companies), CLO (Chief Legal Officer), CHRO (Chief Human Resources Officer), CIO (Chief Information Officer), CTO (Chief Technology Officer), or COO (Chief Operations Officer), and CMO (Chief Marketing Officer) or CCO (Chief Communications Officer) plus three line C-suite executives responsible for the critical product, geography, or service lines.

Jeffcock (2022) found that the American-based digital giants such as Apple, Amazon, and Alphabet also had nine in the C-suite executive. They had two line C-suite members responsible for technology or product-focused lines and six staff C-suite executives. Of the six staff members, the CFO and CLO were both in place in 100 per cent of cases, followed by, in order of frequency, the CMO, CHRO, CTO, and then the COO.

In addition, this study of the FTSE 100 referred to approximately 45 other C-suite roles, and the average staff C-suite member was responsible for eight other C-level roles. A trend is therefore developing in C-suite families with hierarchies. For example, the CHRO who would be a member of the C-suite executive team could have several C-level roles reporting to them, i.e., their C-suite family comprising Chief Talent Officer, Chief Leadership Officer, and Chief Learning Officer. Wikipedia corroborates this increase in C-level positions by listing 56 C-level titles, including less well-known ones such as Chief Gaming Officer, Chief Visionary Officer, and Chief Cloud Officer ("List of corporate titles," 2023).

These findings align with the C-suite having doubled between the 1980s and mid-2000s "from 5 to 10, with approximately three-quarters of the increase attributed to functional managers rather than general managers" (Guadalupe et al., 2014, p. 825). The current trend of CXO proliferation or inflation in job titles is also described by the article "Too many chiefs" (Schumpeter, 2010).

An analysis of the S&P50 companies, 2015, in *The changing C-suite* shows the expansion of CXO roles reporting directly to the CEO and reporting to the CEO's direct reports (Alvarez & Svejenova, 2022).

The executive search industry is also highlighting this trend of enlargement of C-suite roles in the top team, such as the introduction of the Chief Digital Officer, Chief Happiness Officer, and Chief Automation

Officer to address the future of work challenges such as cultural and digital transformations (Half, 2022).

The C-suite is evolving through growing its C-level roles to cover more and more specialisms required to address transformation. Digital adoption is just one of the enormous challenges facing organisations, and the C-suite needs to be able to run their companies to meet the requirements of how customers want to interact with them digitally. Technology will drive competitiveness and create new and improved products and services. Automation will change the way humans work. The resulting cultural shift for organisations and their people is immense. This is in addition to how businesses meet other global challenges, such as the energy crisis, demographic changes, and sustainability and decarbonisation, to name a few. It is hardly surprising that the C-suite is expanding. Nevertheless, with so many at the C-suite level, the titles become meaningless, and outsiders have no proper concept of seniority, decision-making authority, and responsibilities of any given CXO.

The future C-suite – version 3.0

These trends of expansion of C-level roles and titles, the need to develop an elevated mindset and deepen capabilities in social skills and emotional intelligence prompt the question, "What is the best way to structure the C-suite going forwards?"

There is an opportunity to study TMTs in more depth, given the assumption in scholarship that senior leadership teams are a stable entity (Beckman & Burton, 2011). I now share four recommendations and insights from my research into how the structure of the C-suite might develop and change going forward.

The Multi-Disciplinary approach with variable chairs

In his extensive work, Jeffcock (2022) acknowledges that there is no clear-cut answer to what the future C-suite will look like. He puts forward a structure which builds on the current formation. He proposes that the modern C-suite includes nine roles, including the CEO, three fixed seats for divisional product CEOs, and five variable seats for the advisory and multi-disciplinary functional leaders.

The critical development Jeffcock promotes is that the Chief Multi-Disciplinary Officers (CMDOs) will have more breadth in their strategic areas and be more generalist and relational in their skillsets. For example, the Chief Financial and Reporting Officers (CFROs) will have many CXOs responsible for specialisms reporting to them. The disciplines included within these functions can also change over time to suit the organisational needs and make the roles more interesting. In addition, these variable and rotating seats will make the C-suite more fluid, bringing in new and temporary expert advisors and more merged roles over time. The emphasis for the top C-suite members is to work collaboratively as a team, aligned with a common purpose and values.

This view of the future C-suite acknowledges its need to be dynamic and flexible with breadth and depth through the CMDO and advisor roles.

Self-managed teams and self-organising systems

In contrast, Terry White (2020) proposes a radical, new approach to C-suite evolution: self-managed teams within self-organising systems. He refers to the book *Reinventing organizations*, which studies organisational development and shares the emergence of self-managed entities (called Teal organisations). These operate under the principles of self-managed teams, wholeness (i.e., treating people as humans and removing the corporate mask), and an evolutionary purpose (Laloux, 2014).

Working to a set of objectives agreed upon through consultation across the whole organisation towards a common goal, self-managed teams take collective responsibility for meeting targets. The whole organisation will work within an overarching framework vision or evolutionary purpose. Within teams, the individuals with the most expertise and knowledge on a particular issue will lead that objective. This way, leadership is fluid and dynamic, changing as the priorities and challenges vary and ensuring the most appropriate leader is always in place.

In this context, business systems are considered complex adaptive systems managed by distributed rather than central control, which means the top-down approach of command and control will not work. Instead, a driving sense of purpose governs these systems. There are three or four rules units must obey to act within the purpose, along with constantly scanning the system's environment.

A small yet emerging number of global organisations are successfully adopting this approach, including Buurtzorg in the Netherlands. However, it cuts to the heart of most traditional leadership models, which operate through hierarchical titles, roles, and power structures.

Transitioning to this way of working will represent a massive leap into the unknown for most businesses and their leadership. It will "question their authority, control, role, power, self-image, ego, and even their livelihood. It will take a strong and secure executive to undo their legacy and implement this very different way of running their organization" (White, 2020, p. 109).

For these reasons, early-stage organisations and those run by the younger generations might adopt this approach as they can set up this way from the start.

The executive constellation

"A radically new C-suite model has yet to emerge" (Alvarez & Svejenova, 2022, p. 165). Alvarez & Svejenova (2022) agree with the requirement for a cohesive top team aligned on shared values and outcomes and focused on the CEO's need to be surrounded by a supportive and collaborative team. They concur with the consensus in the field of research that just expanding the C-suite to include more specialist CXO roles is an inadequate response to the complexity of the future facing organisations. They refer to a C-suite comprising multiple stakeholders and a CEO role, which is rotated (De Yonge, 2019). This would involve a move away from the traditional "hub-and-spoke model, with the CEO as the hub, to a much more dynamic executive constellation" (Alvarez & Svejenova, 2022, p. 166).

The doughnut organisation

Lastly, "Organisations will organise, but to do so they will no longer need to employ" (Handy, [1994]2002, p. 39). Organisations would no longer be full of "jobs;" instead, we would work for ourselves and offer our services to organisations. Firms would be doughnut-shaped, with a small core of key people and a collection of portfolio workers around the core. Handy was conscious that individuals must find a balance between what we can and should do to serve society and exercise our individual freedom (Handy, [1994]2002).

He considered the organisation as a whole rather than the senior leadership team. Nevertheless, it is possible to see the similarities between Handy's insights and Strategy and Leadership as Service.

Conclusion

The themes I have identified from the thinking described in this chapter are that future top team structures need to be dynamic and flexible as the organisation changes, which may require some roles to be temporary. We need both breadth and depth in skillsets, i.e., generalists and specialists, and encouraging collaboration through collective knowledge is paramount.

Much more research and experimentation are needed to find the optimal principles that promote an agile and fit-for-purpose C-suite, specific to industry, organisational size, and geography. The existing research moves our thinking forward by spotlighting the need for change, the issues we must address, and the challenges to getting there. However, much of this research is from the organisation's perspective and what it might need to be sustainable.

One essential aspect of the future of the C-suite is the changing needs of the individuals within it now and going forwards. Of the future models described Handy's Doughnut Organisation considers the needs and wants of the C-suite individuals. These professionals and their work requirements will be a further factor to consider when deciding on a new version's business model and structure.

In the next chapter, I share the megatrends influencing the attitudes and views of top executives regarding the working environment and, specifically, what it needs to look like to become compelling for them. This careful matching of needs, both now and anticipated in the future, between organisations and C-level executives is core to developing an access economy business model for C-suite professionals.

The innovative business model of Strategy and Leadership as Service contributes to the debate regarding the future structure and form of the C-suite. It offers organisations an alternative approach to embrace functional, emotional, and collective intelligence at the top level while meeting the needs of the team within it.

References

Ainsworth-Land, G. T., & Jarman, B. (1992). *Breakpoint and beyond: Mastering the future today*. Harpercollins.

Alvarez, J. L., & Svejenova, S. (2022). *The changing C-suite: Executive power in transformation*. Oxford University Press. https://doi.org/10.1093/oso/9780198728429.001.0001

Beckman, C. M., & Burton, M. D. (2011). Bringing organizational demography back in: Time, change, and structure in top management team research. *The Handbook of Research on Top Management Teams*, 49–70. https://doi.org/10.4337/9780857933201.00009

Birkinshaw, J., Foss, N. J., & Lindenberg, S. (2014). Combining purpose with profits. *MIT Sloan Management Review*, *55*(3), 49–56.

Boulton, J. G., Allen, P. M., & Bowman, C. (2015). *Embracing complexity: Strategic perspectives for an age of turbulence*. Oxford University Press.

Brookes, S., & Grint, K. (2010). Wicked problems and clumsy solutions: The role of leadership. In *The new public leadership challenge* (pp. 169–186). Palgrave Macmillan.

Chen, J. (2022, April 14). *Board of directors: What it is, what its role is*. Investopedia.com. Retrieved March 26, 2023, from www.investopedia.com/terms/b/boardofdirectors.asp

Comeau, B., Rorem, R., Silvers, S., & Ehernhalt, S. (2014, April 1). *CFO as chief frontier officer*. Deloitte Insights. Retrieved March 26, 2023, from www2.deloitte.com/xe/en/insights/focus/business-trends/2014/cfo-as-chief-frontier-officer.html

Court, D. (2007, August 1). *The evolving role of the CMO*. McKinsey & Company. Retrieved March 26, 2023, from www.mckinsey.com/capabilities/growth-marketing-and-sales/our-insights/the-evolving-role-of-the-cmo#/

De Yonge, J. M. (2019, September 24). *Has your C-suite changed to reflect the changing times?* EY.com. Retrieved August 14, 2023, from www.ey.com/en_uk/growth/has-your-c-suite-changed-to-reflect-the-changing-times

Development Dimensions International Inc., The Conference Board Inc., & EYGM Limited. (2018). *Global leadership forecast 2018: 25 Research insights to fuel your people strategy*. DDI. Retrieved March 26, 2023, from www.ddiworld.com/research/global-leadership-forecast-2018

Drucker, P. F. (2001, November 1). Will the corporation survive?: Yes, but not as we know it. *The Economist*. Retrieved March 26, 2023, from www.economist.com/special-report/2001/11/03/will-the-corporation-survive

Edmans, A. (2019). The purpose of profit. *Think, London Business School Review*, *30*(2–3), 18–21. https://doi.org/10.1111/2057-1615.12304

Freeman, R. E. (2010). *Strategic management: A stakeholder approach*. Cambridge University Press. https://doi.org/10.1017/cbo9781139192675

Friedman, M. (2007). The social responsibility of business is to increase its profits. In *Corporate ethics and corporate governance*. (pp. 173–178). Springer Ebooks. https://doi.org/10.1007/978-3-540-70818-6_14

Gardner, H. (1983). *Frames of mind*. Basic Books.

Guadalupe, M., Li, H., & Wulf, J. (2014). Who lives in the C-suite? Organizational structure and the division of labor in top management. *Management Science*, *60*(4), 824–844. https://doi.org/10.1287/mnsc.2013.1795

Half, R. (2022, October 14). *C-suite explained: Your guide to current and future exec level roles*. Retrieved March 26, 2023, from www.roberthalf.co.uk/advice/c-suite/c-suite-explained-your-guide-current-and-future-exec-level-roles

Handy, C. ([1994]2002). *The empty raincoat: New thinking for a new world*. Arrow.

Jeffcock, J. (2022). *The suite spot: Reaching, leading and delivering the C-suite.* Bloomsbury Publishing.

Kay, J. (2011). *Obliquity: Why our goals are best achieved indirectly.* Profile Books.

Kelly, E. (2014, April 1). *The C-suite: Time for version 3.0?* Deloitte Insights. Retrieved March 26, 2023, from www2.deloitte.com/us/en/insights/focus/business-trends/2014/c-suite-3-0.html

Kotter, J. P. (1995). Leading change: Why transformation efforts fail. *Harvard Business Review.* Retrieved March 26, 2023, from https://hbr.org/1995/05/leading-change-why-transformation-efforts-fail-2

Laloux, F. (2014). *Reinventing organizations: A guide to creating organizations inspired by the next stage of human consciousness.* Nelson Parker.

Link, J. (2019, January 8). *The CHRO's role as the organization's "future of work expert".* Forbes. Retrieved March 26, 2023, from www.forbes.com/sites/forbeshumanresourcescouncil/2019/01/08/the-chros-role-as-the-organizations-future-of-work-expert/?sh=2e689add7427

List of corporate titles. (2023). In *Wikipedia.* Retrieved March 26, 2023, from https://en.wikipedia.org/wiki/List_of_corporate_titles

Martin, R. L. (2009). *The opposable mind: How successful leaders win through integrative thinking.* Harvard Business Press.

Matlins, S. (2022, June 23). *The Forbes world's most influential CMOs list: 2022.* Forbes. Retrieved March 26, 2023, from www.forbes.com/sites/sethmatlins/2022/06/23/the-forbes-worlds-most-influential-cmos-list-2022/?sh=e4c1cb21b8ab

Morgan, G. (1997). *Images of organization.* Sage Publications.

Morrish, J. (2020, August 30). *Where does the word board (of directors) come from?* Retrieved March 26, 2023, from www.managementtoday.co.uk/does-word-board-of-directors-from/article/1340275

Nordqvist, C. (2019, July 19). *Board of directors – definition and meaning.* Market Business News. Retrieved March 26, 2023, from https://marketbusinessnews.com/financial-glossary/board-of-directors/

O'Boyle, E. (2021, March 30). *4 things Gen X and Millennials expect from their workplace.* Gallup.com. Retrieved April 16, 2023, from www.gallup.com/workplace/336275/things-gen-millennials-expect-workplace.aspx

Patagonia. (2023). *Our core values.* Patagonia, Inc. Retrieved March 26, 2023, from https://eu.patagonia.com/gb/en/core-values/

Rooke, D., & Torbert, W. R. (2005). Seven transformations of leadership. *Harvard Business Review, 83*(4), 66–76. https://hbr.org/2005/04/seven-transformations-of-leadership

Ross, J. W., & Feeny, D. (1999). The evolving role of the CIO. *RePEc: Research Papers in Economics.* https://dspace.mit.edu/bitstream/handle/1721.1/2758/SWP-4089-43797710-CISR-308.pdf

Sadun, R., Fuller, J., Hansen, S., & Neal, P. (2022, September 26). The C-suite skills that matter most. *Harvard Business Review.* Retrieved March 26, 2023, from https://hbr.org/2022/07/the-c-suite-skills-that-matter-most

Schotter, A., Mudambi, R., Doz, Y. L., & Gaur, A. S. (2017). Boundary spanning in global organizations. *Journal of Management Studies, 54*(4), 403–421. https://doi.org/10.1111/joms.12256

Schumpeter (2010, June 24). Too many chiefs: Inflation in job titles is approaching Weimar levels. *The Economist*. Retrieved March 26, 2023, from www.economist. com/business/2010/06/24/too-many-chiefs

Sisodia, R., Sheth, J. N., & Wolfe, D. B. (2014). *Firms of endearment: How world-class companies profit from passion and purpose*. Pearson Education.

Srivastava, S., Davenport, T., & Mahidhar, V. (2021, March). Pilots, co-pilots, and engineers: Digital transformation insights from CIOs for CIOs. *Genpact*. Retrieved March 26, 2023, from www.genpact.com/insight/digital-transformation-cio-research

White, T. (2020). *Reinventing the C-suite: Evolving your executive team to meet today's challenges*. Routledge.

Future of Work Megatrends

2

Change is constant, and its pace is increasing.

That is the consensus developed by theorists, academics, and the business world. We haven't got the luxury anymore of business imperatives slowing down so we can all catch our breath, take stock, and build a new five-year plan to deal with each discrete change thoroughly and sequentially. Instead, top teams and organisations must develop agile and collaborative cultures designed to live with the unknown and progress through the complexity.

One thing is sure, and that is uncertainty lies ahead.

The future way of working for C-suite executives is changing rapidly due to unprecedented global forces. As discussed in Chapter 1, top teams are expected to keep abreast of global and technological change in real-time, stretching their human capabilities to the limit and potentially exposing their organisations to increased risk. At the same time, individuals seek more meaning and purpose in and at work. They search for freedom, flexibility, and control over their lives and some turn to the gig economy for answers. They need to upgrade their skillsets and retrain as they face the prospect of multiple careers throughout their lengthening working lives.

These forces and the impact and repercussions of the Covid-19 pandemic demand a different way of engaging with C-suite executives in the future: one which embraces collective intelligence, flexible working, a sense of belonging, and engaging with the power of many. This suggests a two-step shift: first, towards accessing skills and second, a move away from the more traditional employment model.

DOI: 10.4324/9781003368090-4

The future of work is impacted by the pace of change, which has accelerated and continues to do so. Inter-connectedness means that information and viruses spread almost instantly, and shocks to the system have global effects ("who appreciated that Ukraine was such a big grain producer?"). It's a VUCA (volatile, uncertain, complex, and ambiguous) world on steroids, and future businesses and workers must be prepared to be adaptable, resilient, and innovative while not knowing what these megatrends mean for them. Of course, the exact nature of megatrends will evolve and change through time. Embracing the access economy for the C-suite will give organisations a better chance of succeeding in these environments than orthodox employment by harnessing the right skills at the right time.

This chapter starts by discussing some examples of megatrends and how these are influencing the future of work, along with some developing themes which we see in response to recent events. I then focus on how C-suite executives are beginning to want to work and how this will change further in the future, alongside the challenges facing organisations to maintain growth throughout constant turbulence.

The megatrends

There isn't a definitive agreed list of megatrends from futurists and academics. For this book and illustration purposes regarding their impact on society and the future of work, I have chosen to focus on globalisation, digitalisation, automation (including artificial intelligence (AI)), sustainability and decarbonisation, and demographic changes (including ageing).

There are also numerous definitions of the future of work, and I have selected the following description by Gartner: "The future of work describes changes in how work will get done over the next decade, influenced by technological, generational and social shifts" (Gartner, 2023, para. 1).

Globalisation

The Oxford English Dictionary defines globalisation as:

> In a general sense, the increasing worldwide integration of economic, cultural, political, religious, and social systems. Economic globalization is the process by which the whole world becomes a single market. This means that goods and services, capital, and

labour are traded on a worldwide basis, and information and the results of research flow readily between countries.

(Oxford Reference, 2023, para. 1)

The reduced cost and increasing ease of transportation of goods, technology advancements enabling 24/7 communication, national boundaries made irrelevant by social media, smartphones allowing shoppers to access a global virtual marketplace, and new electronic payment systems facilitating and increasing international trading are just some examples of developments which encourage organisations to go global, and earlier in their life stage too.

However, globalisation has consequences and complexities. For example, in *The shift*, Lynda Gratton (2014) refers to globalisation driving the developing countries of India and China to become the low-cost innovators of the future and talent pools of the world with their large populations. She predicts further urbanisation as a disproportionate number of our most talented and educated people gravitate towards mega-cities. Yet a regional underclass will emerge in the developed world as swathes of populations fail to keep up with technological advances and gain access to the skills to thrive in our increasingly polarised world of the "haves" and the "have-nots."

Digitalisation

Digital transformation involves products, services, business systems, and processes becoming digital. Traditional business models risk becoming defunct as their value chains contract to incorporate digital products and services. Examples include the digital transformation of the music industry as it moves from selling physical compact disc (CD) products to personal online music streaming services such as Spotify. Netflix replaces Blockbuster videos and TV networks. Digital cameras and smartphones oust Kodak, Uber has become the biggest global taxi firm yet doesn't own any taxis, and Amazon replaces physical bookstores and many other traditional retailers. Online banking using apps forces the closure of high street branches. The list goes on (Crofts & Thompson, 2018).

This disintermediation of value chains using digital technology is everywhere. We now can access services digitally with a personalised interface at our fingertips and on the move, and the more we experience, the more we want and expect this service across all parts of our lives. If we look ahead, this digital megatrend is only going to increase.

Automation (including AI)

Embracing new forms of technology is a strategic lever for competitiveness, reducing costs and risk, and producing better products and services that improve stakeholders' influence.

In the future, further technological advances will change how work will get done by humans, automation, or in partnership, essentially using a hybrid workforce. We will still need humans for judgement, insight, and collaboration, but we will replace and augment some human activities. Work will be redesigned and assigned to humans with automation. We will have to cope with the resultant culture change and give people the work they are good at doing. The issue for the C-suite will be to develop the most appropriate operating model and lead the organisational change.

All work will be within scope. There will be an impact on everything. It will be a question of when not what.

We already have experience of this. Robotics are replacing humans with self-drive cars, and they can do brainwork too, making decisions, not just physical work.

The evolution of technology, its economics, and social implications are holding us back from replacing humans with automation. It will become less expensive over time but will the drive for profitability override the social implications, perhaps forcing governments to intervene?

From a future of work perspective, our biggest issue will be how this automation will affect organisational cultures incorporating a commitment to people who have redefined jobs. The future C-suite will need to understand what work will create value and address the economics of using humans and automation in partnership to create jobs of the future through reskilling and redefining. They will need to develop a transformation roadmap that aligns with technology to invest in people moving into the right roles, focusing on innovation that will be ever-present.

Sustainability and decarbonisation

The climate change imperative is upon us. The sustainability and decarbonisation megatrends mean we need to source more energy from sustainably produced electricity and other clean alternatives in the future.

Throughout the industrial revolution, the utilisation and burning of fossil fuels have created enormous wealth. Collectively as a human race, and predominantly in the West, we have reaped the rewards with our living standards increasing significantly, yet the time has come to pay for these actions. We are not only depleting the earth's resources, but we are also polluting our shared environment. There is a significant concern among the scientific community that we are perilously close to the point of no return, and the earth is heating up to a level beyond our control. We could be entering unknown territory regarding the stability of our planet. The race is on to decarbonise and create a sustainable environment for future generations. We must reduce our oil, gas, and coal usage by finding replacement clean energy alternatives.

The conflict between Russia and Ukraine and the resultant scarcity of energy across Europe, as these countries move away from sourcing from Russia, has already educated much of the world on the importance of energy security. Traditional fossil fuel energy has become scarce and expensive and increased the urgency with which countries wish to transition to renewable sources under their control. This energy transition will provide a massive opportunity for investment into new technologies and business models to power our lives cleanly going forwards. The resulting revolution, this time renewable energy, will bring economic winners and losers as countries and organisations vie to transform themselves into the powerhouses of our post-industrial, digital world.

Demographic changes (including ageing)

Globally we are ageing. Populations go through a series of four stages (assuming net migration is zero): the pre-industrial age, when populations grow slowly due to high birth and death rates; the second stage of rapid population growth, when death rates decline due to advancements in economics and society, particularly in the food supply and healthcare; the third stage, when birth rates drop, and population growth slows; and the fourth stage, when birth and death rates are low, and the population size stays constant (Jefferies, 2005).

In general, in Western society, we are living longer. A child born in the West in 2007 has a greater than 50 per cent chance of living to more than 104 years old, compared with just one per cent back in 1914 (Gratton & Scott, 2016).

This trend of ageing populations and the increased length of our lives has enormous implications for society and the future of work.

On a macro level, the countries with declining and ageing populations face challenges of how their future workforce will be able to fund the care and demands of their older inhabitants.

In the developed West, the job for life is gone. We will likely have a multi-stage life with multiple careers characterised by breaks and transitions to retrain and reskill. People will work well into their 70s and 80s in new jobs augmented and partnered with AI. With a much longer working life, we must rethink our finances to support us through extended retirement post-work. We will prioritise healthcare to ensure we can stay fit enough to work for longer, and our relationships will change (Gratton & Scott, 2016).

In her book, *Couples that work*, Jennifer Petriglieri (2019) reviews how couples have stereotypically adopted the path of one partner working to pay the bills and support the family lifestyle and the other staying at home to bring up the children and then in later life, care for ageing parents. We have seen this change over the latter part of the twentieth century, with more dual-career couples. This desire for both parents to have careers and a family, combined with a longer working life, requires us to reassess the traditional family setup. We are reframing our thinking to align our ambition at work with our aspirations for relationships with our partners, parents, children, siblings, and friends. Petriglieri shares a future where couples carefully coordinate and plan their lives holistically to support each other through career transitions. Each one takes turns to step back from demanding roles to retrain and be ready for the next stage or care for their family, while their partner focuses heavily on work at critical points for their career advancement. This constant juggling and rebalancing, combined with a longer-term work horizon, enables couples to keep their careers and relationships on track.

A longer working life with multi-stage careers means moving from the conventional three-stage life of education, employment, and retirement characterised by the industrial age into one more flexible (Gratton & Scott, 2016). We will likely have multiple careers to keep pace and stay relevant. We will take time to invest in our skillsets and mindsets to reset and explore new perspectives.

Human resources within organisations will need to reframe their thinking of age being synonymous with the career stage, as we see post-60-year-olds investing in skills and moving back into education to kickstart their fourth or fifth career. There will be generational complexity as the lockstep of the three-stage life disappears (Gratton & Scott, 2016).

We will require regulatory and legislative changes to ensure the opportunities for re-education and development of the ageing Western workforce are accessible to all.

The megatrends of technological advancement and longevity of life interact to pose many questions for our global society. Scott and Gratton (2020) put forward three principles of Narrate, Explore, and Relate in their book, *The new long life*, to outline the steps needed to adapt to our increased time horizons. However, many questions still need to be answered about how the future of work will unfold.

Responses to the megatrends

What do these megatrends mean for the future of work, particularly how C-suite professionals will work going forward?

Concerning the short term, there are several responses and developing themes regarding our attitudes to work emerging from recent world events in the context of the megatrends.

Covid-19 and the new normal

The once-in-a-lifetime pandemic of Covid-19 brought about many changes to how we work. The McKinsey Global Institute predict the following three trends will stick with us as part of the new normal after the pandemic recedes (McKinsey & Company, 2021):

1. Virtual collaboration and working remotely will likely continue, albeit less frequently than they did at the pandemic's height;
2. Automation and AI may be adopted more quickly, particularly in occupations requiring a lot of physical closeness; and
3. The range of jobs may change, with low-wage jobs seeing little growth.

These three trends may play out, but some microtrends or themes have become apparent in our immediate responses to the pandemic. Particularly in the Western world, workers, especially those in professional roles likely to have more options, have begun to rethink how, when, and even why we want to work. The pandemic has caused us to question work's role in our lives for the first time. The real threat to our health and loved ones has made us reflect on what is important to us. As a result, we prioritise relationships, mental health, and our environment over our career progression and finances. Yes, we must make ends meet and make a living, but do we have to consume so much? Can we slow down and appreciate life and experiences more? This rethink, with the backdrop of the megatrends, has led to the following microtrends emerging:

Remote and hybrid working

During the pandemic, the professional workforce had no choice but to embrace remote working. We thought it was impossible initially, yet we realised that if we used technology wisely, only some of our jobs required us always to be onsite. The restrictions placed on us regarding social mixing also helped us appreciate our environments much more, and we started prioritising outside space and access to nature. This topped the wish list of our home environment, and we saw many of us move out of cramped apartments and properties in big cities and into the countryside. We deserted built-up conurbations, and local out-of-town high streets became the new hotspots. We even realised we could travel and work from different countries with the right technology.

Globally, as we continue to control the impact and spread of Covid-19, we are moving back to our offices for collaboration and social stimulation but not to pre-pandemic levels. We have finally welcomed the experience of being forced into working from home, not having to commute daily, and being more available for our families. We have had a taste of flexible working and want it to continue. Organisations not offering hybrid working find it hard to recruit the best talent. It is becoming a standard and hygiene factor for candidates.

Flexible working has always been available to C-suite professionals in the access economy. Finally, and slowly, the corporate world is catching on that many elements of roles can be done remotely. There are times when we are at our most productive, working quietly at home without the constant interruptions of the office environment. Of course, there are times we need to collaborate to innovate and learn, and it is this distinction that roles aren't homogeneous that Covid has helped us understand. There is also a switch required from measuring inputs to outputs. If we trust our teams to get the work done to standard, do we need to watch over them constantly? Strategy and leadership as Service provided by C-suite professionals has already turned this outdated thinking on its head. However, again, the world of employment is only just starting to realise this can be the case.

One significant advantage of the pandemic for access economy services is that it has normalised this way of working, i.e., CEOs and senior teams have finally realised, through experiencing it themselves, that being onsite every day in the office is not necessary to perform at our best and get the job done. Before the pandemic, C-suite professionals providing part-time services were the "odd ones out" as they were only onsite periodically, say one day per week or two days per month. Very few professional and office-based workers were onsite during the pandemic, and as the pandemic recedes and hybrid working comes to the fore, most employees in these sectors now work this way.

The Great Resignation

The Great Resignation is the name given to a growing trend of employees choosing to resign from their jobs or considering doing so because of the changes to work and life caused by the Covid-19 pandemic.

> The Great Resignation, also known as the Big Quit and the Great Reshuffle, is an ongoing economic trend in which employees have voluntarily resigned from their jobs en masse, beginning in early 2021 in the wake of the Covid-19 pandemic. Among the most cited reasons for resigning include wage stagnation amid the rising cost of living, limited opportunities for career advancement, hostile work environments, lack of benefits, inflexible remote-work policies, and long-lasting job dissatisfaction. Most likely to quit have been workers in hospitality, healthcare, and education.
>
> ("Great resignation," 2023)

Gallup reports regularly on the percentage of the global workforce engaged at work. At just 21 per cent in 2021 and rising to 23 per cent in 2022 (Gallup Inc., 2023), it is no wonder that the life-changing impact of Covid-19 leads to individuals re-evaluating whether their work is fulfilling and supporting their well-being, resulting in them leaving the workforce in droves. There are no signs that the record number of people who have quit their jobs since the pandemic began will decrease. Globally, almost one in five workers intended to leave their jobs in 2022, and more than two-thirds said they wanted a job that gives them more fulfilment (Ellerbeck, 2022; PricewaterhouseCoopers, 2022). What's more, a year on, 26 per cent of workers (up from 19 per cent in 2022) say they plan to leave their job in the next 12 months and 44 per cent of those feel over-worked (PricewaterhouseCoopers, 2023).

This is a global phenomenon. Australians are quitting six-figure jobs with nowhere to go, choosing unemployment over job dissatisfaction, and even leaving the nation because they don't think they can ever advance. Australian workplaces are about to undergo a profound shift that should terrify employers (Sharples, 2022).

The Randstad Workmonitor global survey in 2022 reveals that nearly half (48 per cent) would choose not to work at all if money were no object and most (58 per cent) claim that if they believed a job would negatively impact their work-life balance, they wouldn't accept it (Randstad [Work-monitor], 2022).

These trends show that we are rethinking why we want to work and what is essential to us if we do work. Well-being and fulfilment at work are climbing the agenda.

Quiet Quitting

Another trend emerging post-pandemic, originally after a TikTok video went viral, is that of Quiet Quitting (Zaid, 2022), which can have several meanings. Some refer to it as having a healthy work-life balance while still giving 100 per cent to our jobs. Others refer to it as doing the bare minimum requirements of our jobs and giving no more time, effort, or enthusiasm than is absolutely necessary (Daugherty, 2023). Most people agree that it does not mean quitting our jobs. Harter (2022), writing for Gallup, reported that Quiet Quitters make up at least 50 per cent of the US workforce, with the most affected being Millennials and Generation Z workers, all below the age of 35!

The global tragedy of the pandemic has brought into sharp focus what we want from life and why we work. Before the pandemic, we did not question going above and beyond without compensation to "get ahead at work," yet now, having lost or nearly lost those dear to us, we want more quality time with our loved ones. We expect to work flexibly, not have to commute daily and be there for our family at breakfast and bedtime. The climate crisis and increasing cost of living post-pandemic encourage us to live more for the moment and the here and now.

Meaning in and at work

The megatrends and fallout from the Great Resignation and Quiet Quitting post-pandemic bring me to the question of why we work as I search for clues into how we will work in the future and the role the access economy will play.

We work to pay our way and support our lifestyle and dependents. Nevertheless, what would persuade us back to full engagement at work if we have alternative income sources or can dial down our time commitment to work and still make ends meet?

We all accept decent pay and security are essential, yet meaningful work may be even more crucial (O'Brien, 1992). Work as a source of meaning and purpose is described in "Fostering meaningfulness in working and at work" (Pratt & Ashforth, 2003). Their research argues that meaning through our work can come from "in work," doing a specific type of work that is our calling where we have autonomy and freedom to redesign it; or "at work," where meaning comes from our membership in the organisation, our belonging; or "transcendence," a connection to something greater than oneself, an integration of the various aspects of oneself into a coherent system, and self-development. Creating an organisation as a container for transcendence requires the following ingredients: providing a cosmology or set of beliefs which connect and explain

> who one is (identity) and who belongs (membership), what matters (values) and what is to be done (purpose), how and why things hang together … to constitute 'reality' and 'truth' (ideology), how one is embedded in that reality and connects to what matters and what is to be done (transcendence),
>
> (Ashforth & Vaidyanath, 2002, p. 361)

the necessity of an environment of psychological safety, and enacting with integrity, where leaders have congruence between words and deeds, as shown in Figure 2.1.

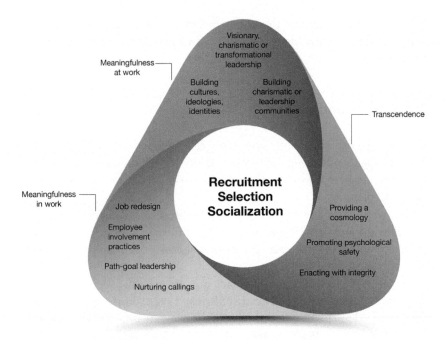

Figure 2.1 Organizational practices that foster meaningfulness

Source: Adapted from Pratt and Ashforth (2003, p. 316). Used with permission of Berrett-Koehler Publishers from *Positive organizational scholarship: Foundations of a new discipline*, Chapter 20 "Fostering meaningfulness in working and at work" by Michael G. Pratt and Blake E. Ashforth, 2003; permission conveyed through Copyright Clearance Center, Inc.

The three shifts

Gratton (2014) states our future way of working requires three shifts as follows:

1. From shallow generalist to serial master;
2. From an isolated competitor to an innovative connector; and
3. From a voracious consumer to an impassioned producer.

These shifts tie in with gaining meaning in and at work. A serial master is a specialist working in their flow in their area of expertise which they consider their calling. An innovative connector will be well networked and belong in their community using the power of many to find, win, and keep work. The impassioned producer will be doing work that matters and giving back.

Executive freedom

In *Executive freedom* (Mills & Daw, 2019), which describes why C-suite professionals choose to become self-employed in the access economy for professional services, the research from over 300 executives also reinforces the requirement for meaning in and at work and the three shifts.

The C-suite respondents articulate the overriding driver for working this way as freedom, i.e., they regain control over their career and lifestyle choices to decide with whom they work, when, and how. This freedom to design their roles gives them joy in their work. It ticks the boxes for becoming serial masters with autonomy and control, allowing them the flexibility to create appropriate work-life balance.

In addition, these C-suite professionals want meaning at work by being part of a community. They do not want to be outsiders to their clients. They want to be part of their clients' teams working "on the inside," which is why, despite being self-employed and fractional, their mindset is one of being integral to their clients. However, they also have the added benefit of being part of the community of C-suite professionals of their C-suite firm. Belonging to a large and diverse community of C-suite specialists aligned around making a difference to entrepreneurs and business owners provides them with a ready-made network for support, backup, knowledge, and camaraderie. They are never isolated and alone.

Lastly, by building a portfolio, they can become a producer and "give back" to their clients, continually operating in their specialism and challenging their intellect.

The dark side of the gig economy

Throughout this chapter and book, I refer to the team-based access economy business model as part of the future of work. It is also part of the gig economy, though very much at the privileged end.

The gig economy relies on individuals working on a contract basis or completing tasks that are paid separately rather than becoming permanently employed (Cambridge Dictionary, 2023).

The work has the reputation of being temporary, precarious, and unpredictable. At the low-paid end of the gig economy, it can undoubtedly be a hand-to-mouth existence with little security for the workers regarding employment rights such as sick leave, holiday entitlement, and redundancy pay. Zero-hours contracts mean organisations can refrain from engaging their workers or giving them protection when they are not needed. The work tends to be repetitive with a low skill requirement; hence the workers are commodities discarded at any time. Some workers have little choice but to put up with these conditions as they have few alternatives to make a living. Others are grateful for its flexibility and use it as a second or part-time job to fit alongside other life commitments such as studying, caring for family members, or starting their own business. As a result, there has been much scrutiny of the fairness to workers of the gig economy business models with various government interventions to introduce legislation for their protection.

At the C-suite level, the lens is different. Highly skilled individuals perform the work at a premium price point to deliver specialised solutions to clients in a flexible business model for the time required. Value-adding relationships for all parties determine longevity. Both C-suite professionals and clients embrace the flexibility of this style of working. The C-level executives can decide when and with whom to work, building in downtime for work-life balance. They actively enjoy not having the tie-ins and obligations of employment. They work on their terms with businesses they believe in, care for, and obsess over, which stretch and challenge them to make a real difference. The work is highly engaging and aligned with how they wish to live. I define this as the privileged end of the gig economy.

Future-proofing our careers

This chapter reviewed the megatrends facing our world and how they shape work's future. There are undoubtedly challenging times ahead for us. The microtrends emerging after the pandemic are depressing for the traditional world of work, and regardless of whether they continue in their current form, we need to take them seriously. In the main, organisations do not inspire us, and our jobs do not engage us. They are necessary for us to do what we want outside of work. We can imagine many of us lamenting, "The best bit about work is going home at the end of the day!" Surely this is an indictment of our society. There must be a better way.

I put forward that part of the solution for an improved, more fulfilling way of working for C-suite professionals is team-based working in an access economy.

This is a way to future-proof our careers and move from job security to income security. We will learn to find, win, and keep clients, so we can always access the market and work this way. By building client portfolios and belonging to a community of C-suite providers delivering Strategy and Leadership as Service, we can regain control over our lives, have freedom of choice, and build a work-life balance. The organisations we serve will gain the functional, emotional, and collective intelligence they need to grow.

As one respondent to the *Executive freedom* survey (Mills & Daw, 2019) summed it up, "I am helping a diverse group of businesses while being my own boss yet still very much part of a team."

The nine paradoxes

Finally, a different lens through which to view the future is the Paradoxes of our Times, described by Handy ([1994]2002). He proposed that while the future is chaotic, it must be treated as a series of paradoxes,

> like the weather, something to be lived with, not solved, the worst aspects mitigated, the best enjoyed and used as clues to the way forward. Paradox has to be *accepted*, coped with and made sense of, in life, in work, in community and among the nations.
>
> (Handy, ([1994]2002), p. 18)

While now, his work is coming up to 30 years old, his nine contradictions and simultaneous opposites of intelligence, work, productivity, time, riches, organisations, age, the individual, and justice, are still very much paradoxes society and organisations face today. He promotes federalism, characterised by twin citizenship and subsidiarity, as a way forward through these paradoxes.

Portfolio working fits neatly with federalism and twin citizenship, i.e., "I am independent working for myself, yet I belong to the clients I deliver my services to, and to the firm of C-suite providers I work with. The clients benefit from my local initiatives and personal relationships, and they gain from the wider skillsets and knowledge base of the community of which I form part."

Subsidiarity, as described by Handy ([1994]2002), means reverse delegation and that we focus on relationships of mutual confidence and work in small teams to deliver our services, again dovetailing well with team-based portfolio working.

From this, it is possible to see how an access economy business model for team-based portfolio work can provide a platform for the future of work.

References

Ashforth, B. E., & Vaidyanath, D. (2002). Work organizations as secular religions. *Journal of Management Inquiry*, 11(4), 359–370. https://doi.org/10.1177/1056492602238843

Cambridge Dictionary. (2023). Gig economy. In *Cambridge dictionary*. Retrieved April 1, 2023, from https://dictionary.cambridge.org/dictionary/english/gig-economy

Crofts, N., & Thompson, M. (2018). *Stealing from the future: And how you can stop it.* Holos Change Ltd.

Daugherty, G. (2023, February 25). *What is quiet quitting – and is it a real trend?* Investopedia. Retrieved April 1, 2023, from www.investopedia.com/what-is-quiet-quitting-6743910

Ellerbeck, S. (2022, December 8). *The great resignation is not over: A fifth of workers plan to quit in 2022.* World Economic Forum. Retrieved April 1, 2023, from www.weforum.org/agenda/2022/06/the-great-resignation-is-not-over/

Gallup Inc. (2023). *State of the global workplace report – Gallup: The voice of the worlds' employees.* Gallup.com. Retrieved August 13, 2023, from www.gallup.com/workplace/349484/state-of-the-global-workplace.aspx

Gartner. (2023). Future of work. In *Gartner human resources glossary*. Retrieved March 27, 2023, from www.gartner.com/en/human-resources/glossary/future-of-work

Gratton, L. (2014). *The shift: The future of work is already here.* HarperCollins UK.

Gratton, L., & Scott, A. (2016). *The 100-year life: Living and working in an age of longevity.* Bloomsbury Publishing.

Great resignation. (2023). In *Wikipedia*. Retrieved April 1, 2023, from https://en.wikipedia.org/wiki/Great_Resignation

Handy, C. ([1994]2002). *The empty raincoat: New thinking for a new world.* Arrow.

Harter, B. J. (2022, September 6). *Is quiet quitting real?* Gallup.com. Retrieved April 1, 2023, from www.gallup.com/workplace/398306/quiet-quitting-real.aspx

Jefferies, J. (2005). The UK population: Past, present and future. In *Focus on people and migration* (pp. 1–17). Palgrave Macmillan UK EBooks. https://doi.org/10.1007/978-1-349-75096-2_1

McKinsey & Company. (2021). *The future of work after Covid-19.* McKinsey Global Institute. Retrieved April 1, 2023, from www.mckinsey.com/featured-insights/future-of-work/the-future-of-work-after-covid-19#/

Mills, C., & Daw, S. (2019). *Executive freedom: How to escape the C-suite, create income security, and take back control by building a part-time portfolio career.* BrightFlame Books.

O'Brien, G. E. (1992). Changing meanings of work. In *Employment relations: The psychology of influence and control at work* (pp. 44–66). Blackwell.

Oxford Reference (2023). Globalization. In *A dictionary of economics*. Retrieved March 28, 2023, from www.oxfordreference.com/display/10.1093/oi/authority.20110803095855259

Petriglieri, J. (2019). *Couples that work: How to thrive in love and at work*. Penguin UK.

Pratt, G., & Ashforth, E. (2003). Fostering meaningfulness in working and at work. In *Positive organisational scholarship: Foundations of a new discipline* (pp. 309–327). Berrett-Koehler.

PricewaterhouseCoopers (2022). *PWC's global workforce hopes and fears survey 2022 | PWC*. PwC. www.pwc.com/gx/en/issues/workforce/hopes-and-fears-2022.html

PricewaterhouseCoopers (2023, June 20). *Global workforce hopes and fears survey 2023*. PwC. www.pwc.com/gx/en/issues/workforce/hopes-and-fears.html

Randstad [Workmonitor] (2022). *A new era in the #howwework revolution*. Randstad. Com. Retrieved April 1, 2023, from www.randstad.com/s3fs-media/rscom/public/2022-04/Randstad_Workmonitor_2022.pdf

Scott, A. J., & Gratton, L. (2020). *The new long life: A framework for flourishing in a changing world*. Bloomsbury Publishing.

Sharples, S. (2022, October 10). *Aussies quit 'hideous' six-figure jobs*. News. Retrieved April 1, 2023, from www.news.com.au/finance/work/at-work/the-great-resignation-aussies-prepared-to-quit-six-figure-jobs/news-story/3588a4c0b4dcdd54a4cd6884930a8bcd

Zaid, K. [@zaidleppelin]. (2022, July 25). *Quiet quitting. #work reform [Video]*. TikTok. Retrieved April 1, 2023, from www.tiktok.com/@zaidleppelin/video/7124414185282391342?lang=en

Part II

Access to the C-Suite through Psychological Ownership

The Rise of the Access Economy   **3**

The access economy

The access economy is still a relatively new phenomenon. Historically, the overriding method of use of an asset for the long-term has been through purchase and ownership: we buy our cars, we purchase the furniture for our house, we shop for the clothes we want to wear, and we acquire outright the music we want to listen to. We keep these assets for a relatively long period, often years, and they form part of our identity. We use these assets, but critically, a key point to note is that our interaction with them can be periodic, i.e., not 100 per cent of the time. Then when we have finished using the item, or we want to change to update to a newer model, we sell the asset. Alternatively, if the object isn't in good enough condition to sell, we might give it away and donate it to charity or throw it away. We have become accustomed to this way of living.

The Western post-second world war culture has been about achievement and success. The Baby Boomers' standard of living has risen significantly, resulting in them increasing their material possessions – a bigger and better house, another car on the driveway, the latest gadgets and home appliances (The MIT Press Reader & Higgs, 2021). We associate status with enduring and material ownership (Bardhi & Eckhardt, 2017). The value comes from the tangible fixed nature of the asset, its permanent and stable presence, which fosters loyalty, commitment, and feelings of attachment. These material items form part of our identity. We can express ourselves through our possessions. They help to shape and communicate who we are: "I have the latest model of car, so I am successful, I am doing well." Indeed, in Western societies, up until the focus on the

DOI: 10.4324/9781003368090-6

impact of our "make more, buy more, throw away more" culture on the climate, the consensus has been that more possessions are better for us.

However, there are disadvantages to ownership. It can become burdensome. Our sense of responsibility requires us to store the asset in a suitable place and to keep it in good condition, which could require an ongoing expense even when we are not using it. Cars require space to keep them, for example, on the driveway, in a garage, or outside on the street; we need somewhere convenient to park them. We need to insure, clean, and keep them maintained and roadworthy. We must find room to store our music collections safely at home. With our populations growing year on year globally and many Western societies suffering from a lack of affordable housing, owning and storing our possessions can be a problem that the access economy goes some way to remedy.

Business models have existed for many years before the rise of the access economy, which promotes using an asset through leasing or hiring, for example, renting cars or accommodation while on holiday. These business models meet the demand for temporary or short-term time frames, i.e., the holiday period.

The difference between the access economy business models that are popping up today and those that already exist to meet temporary demand is that access can now also provide a long-term alternative to ownership. We are moving away from solid, enduring, ownership-based, and material consumption to liquid consumption, which is ephemeral, access-based, and dematerialised (Bardhi & Eckhardt, 2017).

In their paper "Liquid consumption," Bardhi and Eckhardt (2017) highlight that access economy business models offer alternative value to material ownership. Their significance resides in the fact that they offer flexibility in service. They are often more adaptable, fluid, mobile, light, detached, and fast, placing more importance on use versus identity value.

While they are rising in popularity, and we see more and more of society move towards accessing goods and services by registering with the provider rather than physically owning them, adopting these access-based business models requires a different attitude from users. In general, drivers of early adoption are:

- The younger generation of Millennials and Generation Z who have grown up with increasing technological advances. Many access-based business models have new technology at their centre, which has appealed quickly to these age groups;

- Younger adults also have more concerns about climate change (compared to 56 per cent of those aged 55 and over, 70 per cent of Americans between the ages of 18 and 34 are concerned about global warming (Reinhart, 2018)). Many access-based business models deliver enhanced and efficient use of assets through sharing, which benefits the climate; and
- Necessity. There are also swathes of our population priced out of being able to own assets. The world is becoming increasingly polarised towards the "haves" and the "have-nots" (Gu & Wang, 2021). This second category of people might want to own assets but find that "paying-as-they-go" using an access model is their only option.

Access economy business models are gaining traction, whether by choice or need, and I share the following examples.

Owning a vinyl record or streaming music

Accessing music through streaming platforms such as Spotify or Apple Music and paying a subscription to the provider to listen on demand is an excellent example of digital services offered to the market using an access economy business model.

The music industry has undergone an enormous digital transformation since the late 1990s. Historically, individuals would purchase a vinyl record, tape cassette, or CD and consequently would have physical ownership of their copy of the music. Music lovers would likely have stored their records carefully and often on display for others to see and share, as music forms part of their identity (Frith, 1996).

The industry has moved to ownership through access facilitated by digital advances and abandonment of the original business model. We can feel as if we own the music through access to our music streaming account.

The advantages are that we can have almost unlimited choice in what we can listen to, anywhere, anytime, by logging on. We have access to a much larger volume of music than most of us could have hoped to buy in physical form. Given that this is a digital product, the music we listen to is shared with many others simultaneously, yet studies have shown that it does not feel like that to the user. Personalising our music accounts means it feels like the music belongs to us. Our sense of control over the music we access gives us feelings of PO (Danckwerts & Kenning, 2019).

Cars still provide status

Zipcar is an example of more traditional goods accessed rather than owned. There has been a move to accessing cars when we need them rather than having them sit idly on our driveways or outside our houses on the road, taking up space when we do not need them. Of course, it is not just the purchase price of the car that we are bypassing. It is the yearly insurance and the running and maintenance costs as well. There is most definitely a burden of ownership that some users want to offload. Zipcar users generally cite their green credentials and want to avoid tying up their financial capital in a depreciating asset as reasons to rent a Zipcar rather than buy a car. However, unlike music streaming services, studies found that Zipcar users do not have ownership feelings towards Zipcar or their vehicles (Bardhi & Eckhardt, 2012). Using a different vehicle each time, for relatively short periods and knowing someone else has just dropped off the car (and sometimes seeing signs of that) does not breed ownership feelings. Zipcar tried extensively but failed to build a cohesive community of users who identified with each other. The functional benefits of Zipcar are enough for this access economy business model to work. Zipcar would need to nurture the emotional connection with their cars or brand if they want to build deeper feelings of ownership.

Could this reluctance to forge feelings of ownership with what is, in effect, a rental car be determined by Western society's love of the motor car and its association with status, i.e., "If I own a car, I have made it?" Converting these individuals to the access model could be a challenge too far.

Development of an access economy ecosystem – Airbnb

The concept of renting out our homes or parts of our homes to others pioneered and scaled globally by Airbnb, is another example of sharing an under-utilised asset using the access economy. We have realised that we can better use our spare rooms or an annexe in our homes that we reserve for friends and relatives who only occasionally come to stay. We can make money from this asset when we do not need it. We can even offer out our entire home instead of it sitting empty when we are away or holidaying ourselves. We are happy to share someone else's home in this way too. We get a wide variety of choices in where we decide to go, the type of accommodation we can rent, and the time we need. Being welcomed by a host, made to feel at home, and even shown around or given guidance on what to visit adds to the experience.

Festila and Müller (2017) found that users perceive Airbnb as a functional and experiential practice. Factors such as good value for money, proximity to interest points, and access to residential neighbourhoods incentivise individuals to consider Airbnb as a viable alternative to traditional accommodation. However, users' value from the accommodation experience goes beyond functional benefits. The study also found that consumers constructed their identity with what they could access (Belk, 2014). Airbnb users value the feelings gained from the experiences of a resident and the community discourse (Festila & Müller, 2017), which contrasts with the findings from the Zipcar study where there was less evidence of a brand community (Bardhi & Eckhardt, 2012).

While the guests may feel at home when they stay away in an Airbnb, studies have shown that attachment to a platform firm like Airbnb plays a vital role in achieving a sense of PO for Airbnb hosts that ultimately influences citizenship behaviours toward the organisation as well as toward peer hosts (Lee et al., 2019).

The Uber of the C-suite?

I sometimes hear Strategy and Leadership as Service described as having parallels with Uber, and it is interesting to explore this and study the supply side of offering C-suite services and how it compares to Uber.

Uber started in California in 2009 and has since taken the world by storm, present in 1,200 locations covering 10,000 towns and cities worldwide (Duncan, 2022). It operates differently from traditional taxi services by connecting riders with nearby screened Uber drivers through technology, who provide rides in their private vehicles. Some Uber drivers treat it as a side hustle alongside other jobs and welcome its flexibility and the ability to control their schedule through self-employment. In contrast, others who choose or need to do it full-time to make ends meet would prefer it to include more benefits and security, like they would find in employment. Uber has developed an innovative business model which does not own taxis or employ its drivers!

The similarity of sharing C-suite services with Uber starts and finishes here. Yes, the services of the C-suite talent are provided to clients without employing them, like Uber using self-employed drivers. However, a significant difference is that the C-level talent chooses to be self-employed.

C-suite executives operate at the opposite end of the gig economy to Uber drivers, the privileged end. They select self-employment and exercise freedom of choice to decide the type of client they wish to work with, how many days a week they wish to engage, and the sectors or specialisms they want to focus on in their roles. They will work with a portfolio of clients who often require their skillsets for the long-term by delivering a premium service. They become deeply connected with their clients through meaningful relationships. In addition, through a portfolio of clients sharing the benefits of the C-suite professional, losing one client in the portfolio has a much lower impact than losing a full-time job. This way of working diversifies risk and replaces job security with income security.

In contrast, Uber drivers work at the commoditised end of the gig economy, often for low pay and long hours. They would not tend to have repeat customers and build meaningful relationships, but there would be plenty of variety. The C-suite executive does take the risk of not earning when not working, like the Uber driver, yet they consider this a positive rather than a negative. Most C-suite executives do not want to work full-time and wish to build flexible schedules to balance other life demands.

My research

Given the emergence of these new access economy business models and their similarity with Strategy and Leadership as Service, I wanted to explore them further.

The questions I was asking were:

- "Is the Strategy and Leadership as Service business model part of the access economy?"
- "What concepts do we know about already that might underpin the business model?" and
- "What research can I do to test and verify these concepts?"

By this point, I had understood enough from existing research to realise that there had yet to be any studies into an access economy business model focusing on the professional services industry, so mine would be the first of its kind.

In addition, PO could be key to moving the relationships between user and asset in the access economy, from uncaring and temporary with use value, to solid, enduring, long-term, and providing identity value.

This knowledge encouraged me to base my thesis for my masters in Consulting and Coaching for Change on investigating whether PO existed within the relationships between C-suite executives, their clients, and the firms of C-level professionals.

I began by increasing my understanding of the access economy and PO. I reviewed prior research in contexts other than professional services, namely car sharing (Bardhi & Eckhardt, 2012) and music streaming (Fritze et al., 2020). I sourced knowledge primarily from Google Scholar searches linked to HEC and Oxford University libraries and databases. I selected articles from top-ranking journals focused on the access economy, the sharing economy, and ownership (perceived and psychological).

Development of the access economy

Before I further decode the circumstances which foster access to substitute for ownership, i.e., the impact and presence of PO, it is important to review how the access economy has developed.

In this chapter, I introduce the various definitions of the access economy and distinguish between sharing, access, and ownership. I then highlight existing research on access substituting for ownership in different contexts. I review the growth, barriers, and drivers of the emerging access economy, and how it changes user behaviour, particularly for goods and digital services.

Finally, I summarise this chapter and its implications for Strategy and Leadership as Service. The study covered in this book tests the hypothesis that access can work with professional services. It is the first known study that uses PO to bridge the gap between access and employment. It suggests that organisational behaviour can change to engage C-suite executives and meet their needs through access while delivering better outcomes for organisations.

Access economy, access-based consumption, and access-based services

First, let us clarify the terminology used to describe the access economy. Many terms are used, other common ones being access-based consumption and access-based services.

Access economy

For this book, I have used the following definition: "The access economy covers a set of initiatives *sharing underutilized assets (material resources or skills) to optimize their use*" (Acquier et al., 2017, p. 4).

Access-based consumption

Access-based consumption (ABC) is a related term used to describe consumption in the access economy. I define it as "transactions that can be market mediated but where no transfer of ownership takes place" (Bardhi & Eckhardt, 2012, p. 881).

Access-based services

Access-based services (ABS) are an alternative and involve a consumer gaining access to products or services. If the transaction is market-mediated, they will pay a premium for that access (Durgee & O'Connor, 1995). Therefore, consumers pay for the right to access goods and services rather than owning them (Lovelock & Gummesson, 2004). ABS are "Services that let customers access goods" (Schaefers et al., 2016, p. 569).

ABS are like a rental experience, which has significant implications regarding ownership and consumers' relationships and feelings towards the product or service. The mode of consumption shapes consumer-product relationships, values, preferences, and desires (Bardhi & Eckhardt, 2012). For example, in an empirical study of experiential access to art via museums and galleries, there was a contrast between art collectors and visitors to art museums, suggesting the method of consumption determines consumers' perception of value reinforced by distinct consumer desires (Chen, 2009).

In summary, ABS provide a new method of consumption where consumers can gain access to a product or service that they otherwise cannot afford to own or that they choose not to due to other constraints, such as wishing to act more responsibly towards the environment (Bardhi & Eckhardt, 2012).

Throughout this book, I use both ABC and ABS interchangeably with the access economy. In broad terms, they all describe how users gain access to a product or service through necessity or choice.

Sharing versus access versus ownership – important definitions

Not only is it essential to be clear about the definition of the access economy itself, but it is necessary to distinguish it from sharing and ownership, as these are vital constructs to which it is a developing alternative.

Sharing versus access

The definition of sharing in this context depends on whether we define sharing use, access, or sharing ownership. In this research, the sharing economy predominantly refers to sharing use or access rather than ownership. Access is like sharing in that there is no transfer of ownership in either instance. The act and process of giving what we own to others for their use, and/or then receiving or gaining something from others for our own use constitutes sharing (Belk, 2007).

In summary, there is no transfer of ownership or joint ownership in access. Consumers simply access objects. Access can differ from sharing in that access is not necessarily altruistic or prosocial, as sharing is (Belk, 2010).

Access as part of the sharing economy

The sharing economy can be defined in many ways. At this relatively early stage in its development, there needs to be further clarity on its definition and more agreement in the academic and commercial worlds regarding its components and boundaries. In essence, it is too early to be definitive on this subject.

The description by Acquier et al. (2017) is the most useful for this research. In their definition, the access economy does sit within the sharing economy, an umbrella construct, which they describe as "a broad concept or idea used loosely to encompass and account for a set of diverse phenomena" (Hirsch & Levin, 1999, p. 200).

Their definition acknowledges that the sharing economy is a contested concept (Acquier et al., 2017). Without going into the debates surrounding the sharing economy regarding "what it is, what it fails to be, or what it should be" (Acquier et al., 2017, p. 3), they do come up with a simple-to-understand framework, which I found helpful for my research and which serves the purpose of acknowledging that the access economy can sit within the sharing economy. They describe the sharing economy as

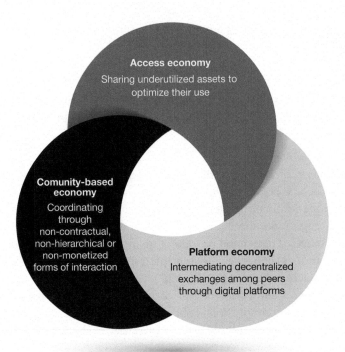

Figure 3.1 Three organizing cores of the sharing economy

Source: Adapted from Acquier et al. (2017, p. 4). Used with permission of Elsevier Inc. from "Promises and paradoxes of the sharing economy: An organizing framework," in *Technological Forecasting and Social Change* by Aurélien Acquier, Thibault Daudigeos, and Jonatan Pinkse, Volume 125, 2017; permission conveyed through Copyright Clearance Center, Inc.

having three foundational cores, and it is at the intersection of these three cores where the sharing economy ideal exists, as shown in Figure 3.1.

Ownership versus access

Ownership is the act or right of possessing something, whereas access can be described as an opportunity or right to use something or to see someone or something. Sharing, in contrast, is when we have, give, or use a portion of something jointly with another or others.

Bardhi & Eckhardt's study of car-sharing states that "Two of the major differences between ownership and access entail (1) the nature of the object-self relationship and (2) the rules that govern and regulate this relationship" (Bardhi & Eckhardt, 2012, p. 882).

The nature of the object-self relationship

The difference in nature of the object-self relationship in ownership and access contexts is precisely the point of this research: the importance of PO in access contexts is a way for users to feel ownership towards the product or service. In ownership, which tends to be for the long-term, possessions can become part of the extended self (Belk, 1988). Access is generally thought to be more fleeting and temporary, and therefore, the consumer-object relationship could be different (Bardhi & Eckhardt, 2012).

This research investigates the consumer-object relationship in accessing professional services and PO's effect in this context. Some research already supports the role of identity in access contexts, i.e., "the consumption experience is meaningful and self-enriching if consumers identify with the accessed consumption object" (Festila & Müller, 2017, p. 54).

The rules that govern and regulate this relationship

With ownership comes rules that allow the owner to control access and the right to use, sell, and work with the object as they please. It creates boundaries from others. In access, however, there is no such ownership of the object (Bardhi & Eckhardt, 2012).

Material ownership of goods has been society's default mode of consumption. We now see ownership and access competing in the same marketplace (e.g., CD ownership or music streaming; car ownership or use of Uber and car sharing). We are in a phase of transition between ownership and access. Which trend will prevail in each marketplace? Is access just a stepping stone to the future and a state we will pass through? These are questions we need to address.

ABS providers grant temporary access to a product or service in return for payment, with legal ownership remaining with the service provider (Schaefers et al., 2016). When we compare this to the firms who provide C-suite services, while they are the service providers, they do not employ the portfolio professionals. Instead, the firm has B2B contracts with C-suite professionals and clients.

There are also negative aspects of ownership, e.g., burdens of ownership (Schaefers et al., 2016), and ABS could be preferred (Bardhi & Eckhardt, 2017). Some research supports the notion that ABS relates negatively to ownership (Datta et al., 2018; Hennig-Thurau et al., 2007). Nevertheless, ABS is an alternative to the conventional consumption of material products through sole ownership (Bardhi & Eckhardt, 2012; Schaefers et al., 2018).

It is, therefore, possible to have access without ownership.

In conclusion, given that the sharing economy is still emerging with increasing numbers of new business models developing all the time and given its definition is much cause for debate, for this book, it is sufficient to assume that the access economy sits within the sharing economy.

Existing research

Existing research suggests the importance consumers give to owning material objects can be an obstacle to ABS (Kahneman et al., 1990). "Consumers do not experience perceived ownership and avoid identification with the accessed object of consumption" (Bhardi & Eckhardt, 2012, p. 894), which implies that the importance of material possessions for consumers relates negatively to their use of ABS.

In contrast, Fritze et al. (2020) found that acquiring PO, or the mental state of believing something to be one's own, through access-based services, may encourage users to access those services more frequently while avoiding material ownership and consumption. In addition, they found that access-based service providers can increase their clients' feelings of PO towards the service, which can then form a replacement for physical ownership and boost access-based service usage.

There is, therefore, evidence both ways as to whether users experience feelings of ownership for access-based services.

Growth and barriers to the emerging access economy

ABS could be the future for consumption and part of the sharing economy (Perren & Kozinets, 2018), a way to mitigate over-consumption, have more collaborative consumption (Botsman & Rogers, 2010), and build sustainability towards climate change (Eckhardt et al., 2019).

The access economy emerges when access to products or services becomes cheap, satisfactory, convenient, and reliable enough for the premium on ownership to disappear. However, ABS is in its infancy and emerging. High-profile tech giants like Netflix and Uber offering ABS are not the norm. It is still early days for Strategy and Leadership as Service. While the offering is growing in adoption and can be commercially successful for stakeholders, the concept is new, with enormous potential and opportunity ahead of it. Some access economy offerings, however, experience low consumer demand, with many providers struggling to scale and needing investment from outside funders (Cusumano, 2018). This is despite the total value of the worldwide sharing economy predicted to reach $600 billion by 2027 from $113 billion in 2021 (Statista, 2023).

To conclude, the widespread adoption of the sharing and access economy still has its barriers to overcome. Nevertheless, it is gaining momentum as it influences how we consume goods and services in the future.

Access economy emergence is changing user behaviour

As access becomes more widely available, we see fundamental changes in user behaviour. In San Francisco alone in 2015, Uber had yearly revenues of $500 million, three times higher than the city's taxi economy! Users are altering their behaviour to suit the highly elastic ride-sharing industry; why have a car sitting on the driveway at home or in the garage when you can "grab an Uber," which is now affordable and accessible (Van Romburgh, 2015).

Starbucks is another example. Their ambition has been to create a "third place", a term introduced by sociologist Ray Oldenburg in 1989, to denote a place to spend time between home and work. Customers receive an affordable luxury experience with a customised drink, but the main product isn't even coffee; it's a warm and welcoming space to meet friends and co-workers and from which to work. Over 30 years later, Starbucks is reimagining what this third place needs to be for the future (Peiper, 2022).

Access to new services and products has changed our behaviour, opening new markets.

Strategy and Leadership as Service is a prime example of this. Before offering part-time C-suite professional services, entrepreneurial business owners had the following choices, none of which met their needs:

- Employment of a full-time C-suite professional whom it did not need and could not afford. High-quality professionals were not attracted to these smaller roles;
- Employment of a more junior professional who did not have the skills or experience to perform the role;
- Using an outside consulting agency, e.g., an accountancy firm in the finance discipline, as a substitute for CFO services. These are not comparable services;
- Performing the role themselves, often not an option for most business owners who do not possess the required skillsets; or

- Making do without the skillset in their business, the most common way SMEs respond to the problem, often resulting in sub-optimal business performance.

Strategy and Leadership as Service has changed the behaviour of SME business owners who can now access the C-suite professional skillsets they need to grow.

Drivers of the access economy

The access economy is a phenomenon that has been around for a while. Access replacing ownership has existed for years, e.g., Hertz rental cars. However, why is it taking off now?

First, mobile technology is an enabler. We are physically connected. Second, we are seeing a generational shift where social capital is hugely important to the Millennials and younger generations. Being socially connected and more comfortable with on-demand access promotes this industry. They want experiences rather than ownership. Third, since 2008 and the global financial crisis, which caused an increase in wealth inequality, access has become the only viable option for some and the only experience the younger generations have known. Lastly, sustainability and a move to more collaborative consumption (Botsman & Rogers, 2010) to counteract over-consumption and promote a decrease in climate change mean some of us are choosing access over ownership.

The rise and emergence of ABS could be less about the dependency on non-ownership behaviour and more about the resulting emergent behaviour (Fritze et al., 2020).

However, while the premium on ownership might disappear, there's more to it than that. Ownership versus access is complex. On the one hand, focusing on lowering the importance of ownership is one approach. An alternative is to emphasise the benefits of access. One thing is certain, though, ignoring the long-established research that identifies the importance of ownership and possessions as a deeply rooted human preference is not an option (Beggan, 1992; Belk, 1988; Morewedge & Giblin, 2015; Pierce et al., 2001).

As humans, we still need to satisfy our needs of efficacy, self-identity, and belonging from our possessions (Fritze et al., 2020). Their study contends we can still satisfy these through PO feelings towards ABS.

Therefore, it could be more accurate to say that the premium for ownership disappears, and PO remains in its place and enables access to emerge. From this, we can imagine a future where we can choose access and PO as an alternative to ownership.

Conclusion

The access economy is gaining more and more traction worldwide. Global consumers are beginning to access goods and services rather than own them. In simple terms, the drivers of this are down to necessity, i.e., it is the only way some members of society can ever hope to be able to use these assets as ownership is just unaffordable, or it could be down to choice, i.e., the realisation that we do not need to own an asset to enjoy it and experience feelings of ownership.

Our world is changing, and technology, in some instances, is the enabler. It allows us to enjoy the benefits of ownership of an asset without the burden. By using technology to access digital goods and services like music and movies, we have become exposed and used to this concept of access versus ownership, which feels good!

There are many other goods and services we can enjoy this way too. Even for those of us who can afford to own an asset, it could be a way to free up cash and use it elsewhere while making better use of assets through sharing and hence being more kind to our planet and creating less wastage.

However, not all access economy business models are taking off. What is going on here? Why do studies show that some business models work better than others? Why do some users report feelings of ownership towards their access economy goods and services, which means they take care of the asset as if it was their own, yet others do not?

Some of these business models have PO present, and others do not. For access economy services to substitute for ownership, they need the routes and roots of PO and the appropriate ecosystem dynamics to thrive.

Moreover, I wanted to test the Strategy and Leadership as Service business model. Knowing that it was part of the access economy, I wanted to establish if PO existed between clients, the C-suite professionals, and the firms providing the C-suite services.

That is the subject of my next chapter.

References

Acquier, A., Daudigeos, T., & Pinkse, J. (2017). Promises and paradoxes of the sharing economy: An organizing framework. *Technological Forecasting and Social Change, 125*, 1–10. https://doi.org/10.1016/j.techfore.2017.07.006

Bardhi, F., & Eckhardt, G. M. (2012). Access-based consumption: The case of car sharing. *Journal of Consumer Research, 39*(4), 881–898. https://doi.org/10.1086/666376

Bardhi, F., & Eckhardt, G. M. (2017). Liquid consumption. *Journal of Consumer Research, 44*(3), 582–597. https://doi.org/10.1093/jcr/ucx050

Beggan, J. K. (1992). On the social nature of nonsocial perception: The mere ownership effect. *Journal of Personality and Social Psychology, 62*(2), 229–237. https://doi.org/10.1037/0022-3514.62.2.229

Belk, R. (1988). Possessions and the extended self. *Journal of Consumer Research, 15*(2), 139–168. https://doi.org/10.1086/209154

Belk, R. W. (2007). Why not share rather than own? *Annals of the American Academy of Political and Social Science, 611*(1), 126–140. https://doi.org/10.1177/0002716206298483

Belk, R. (2010). Sharing. *Journal of Consumer Research, 36*(5), 715–734. https://doi.org/10.1086/612649

Belk, R. (2014). You are what you can access: Sharing and collaborative consumption online. *Journal of Business Research, 67*(8), 1595–1600. https://doi.org/10.1016/j.jbusres.2013.10.001

Botsman, R., & Rogers, R. (2010). *What's mine is yours: How collaborative consumption is changing the way we live.* Harper Collins.

Chen, Y. (2009). Possession and access: Consumer desires and value perceptions regarding contemporary art collection and exhibit visits. *Journal of Consumer Research, 35*(6), 925–940. https://doi.org/10.1086/593699

Cusumano, M. A. (2018). The sharing economy meets reality. *Communications of the ACM, 61*(1), 26–28. https://doi.org/10.1145/3163905

Danckwerts, S., & Kenning, P. (2019). It's my service, it's my music: The role of psychological ownership in music streaming consumption. *Psychology & Marketing, 36*(9), 803–816. https://doi.org/10.1002/mar.21213

Datta, H., Knox, G., & Bronnenberg, B. J. (2018). Changing their tune: How consumers' adoption of online streaming affects music consumption and discovery. *Marketing Science, 37*(1), 5–21. https://doi.org/10.1287/mksc.2017.1051

Duncan, P. (2022, July 15). *The worldwide scale of the Uber files – in numbers.* The Guardian. Retrieved April 2, 2023, from www.theguardian.com/news/2022/jul/15/the-worldwide-scale-of-the-uber-files-in-numbers

Durgee, J. F., & O'Connor, G. C. (1995). An exploration into renting as consumption behavior. *Psychology & Marketing, 12*(2), 89–104. https://doi.org/10.1002/mar.4220120202

Eckhardt, G. M., Houston, M. B., Jiang, B., Lamberton, C., Rindfleisch, A., & Zervas, G. (2019). Marketing in the sharing economy. *Journal of Marketing, 83*(5), 5–27. https://doi.org/10.1177/0022242919861929

Festila, M. S., & Müller, S. D. (2017). The impact of technology-mediated consumption on identity: The case of Airbnb. *Proceedings of the 50th Annual Hawaii International Conference on System Sciences*, 54–63. https://doi.org/10.24251/hicss.2017.007

Frith, S. (1996). Music and identity. In *Questions of cultural identity* (pp. 108–127). Sage Publications.

Fritze, P., Marchand, A., Eisingerich, B., & Benkenstein, M. (2020). Access-based services as substitutes for material possessions: The role of psychological ownership. *Journal of Service Research*, *23*(3), 368–385. https://doi.org/10.1177/1094670520907691

Gu, Y., & Wang, Z. (2021). Income inequality and global political polarization: The economic origin of political polarization in the world. *Journal of Chinese Political Science*, *27*(2), 375–398. https://doi.org/10.1007/s11366-021-09772-1

Hennig-Thurau, T., Henning, V., & Sattler, H. (2007). Consumer file sharing of motion pictures. *Journal of Marketing*, *71*(4), 1–18. https://doi.org/10.1509/jmkg.71.4.1

Hirsch, P. M., & Levin, D. Z. (1999). Umbrella advocates versus validity police: A life-cycle model. *Organization Science*, *10*(2), 199–212. https://doi.org/10.1287/orsc.10.2.199

Kahneman, D., Knetsch, J. L., & Thaler, R. H. (1990). Experimental tests of the Endowment Effect and the Coase Theorem. *Journal of Political Economy*, *98*(6), 1325–1348. https://doi.org/10.1086/261737

Lee, H., Yang, S. B., & Koo, C. (2019). Exploring the effect of Airbnb hosts' attachment and psychological ownership in the sharing economy. *Tourism Management*, *70*, 284–294. https://doi.org/10.1016/j.tourman.2018.08.017

Lovelock, C., & Gummesson, E. (2004). Whither services marketing?: In search of a new paradigm and fresh perspectives. *Journal of Service Research*, *7*(1), 20–41. https://doi.org/10.1177/1094670504266131

Morewedge, C. K., & Giblin, C. (2015). Explanations of the endowment effect: An integrative review. *Trends in Cognitive Sciences*, *19*(6), 339–348. https://doi.org/10.1016/j.tics.2015.04.004

Peiper, H. (2022, September 13). *Reimagining the third place: How Starbucks is evolving its store experience*. Starbucks Stories. Retrieved April 2, 2023, from https://stories.starbucks.com/stories/2022/reimagining-the-third-place-how-starbucks-is-evolving-its-store-experience/

Perren, R., & Kozinets, R. V. (2018). Lateral exchange markets: How social platforms operate in a networked economy. *Journal of Marketing*, *82*(1), 20–36. https://doi.org/10.1509/jm.14.0250

Pierce, J. L., Kostova, T., & Dirks, K. T. (2001). Toward a theory of psychological ownership in organizations. *Academy of Management Review*, *26*(2), 298–310. https://doi.org/10.5465/amr.2001.4378028

Reinhart, J. R. (2018, May 11). *Global warming age gap: Younger Americans most worried*. Gallup.com. Retrieved April 1, 2023, from https://news.gallup.com/poll/234314/global-warming-age-gap-younger-americans-worried.aspx

Schaefers, T., Lawson, S. J., & Kukar-Kinney, M. (2016). How the burdens of ownership promote consumer usage of access-based services. *Marketing Letters*, *27*(3), 569–577. https://doi.org/10.1007/s11002-015-9366-x

Schaefers, T., Moser, R., & Narayanamurthy, G. (2018). Access-based services for the base of the pyramid. *Journal of Service Research*, *21*(4), 421–437. https://doi.org/10.1177/1094670518770034

Statista. (2023). *Value of the global sharing economy 2021*. Statista Research Department. Retrieved April 2, 2023, from www.statista.com/statistics/830986/value-of-the-global-sharing-economy/

The MIT Press Reader, & Higgs, K. (2021, April 20). *A brief history of consumer culture*. The MIT Press Reader. Retrieved April 1, 2023, from https://thereader.mitpress.mit.edu/a-brief-history-of-consumer-culture/

Van Romburgh, M. (2015, January 20). *Uber in SF is now three times bigger than city's entire taxi industry*. Biz Journals.com. Retrieved April 2, 2023, from www.bizjournals.com/sanfrancisco/blog/techflash/2015/01/uber-valuation-revenue-sf-taxi-industry-kalanick.html

The Role of Psychological **4** Ownership

If we accept my hypothesis that Strategy and Leadership as Service is part of the emerging access economy providing professional services, I needed to investigate why and how it worked. Through my research in different contexts, I found that some users experienced feelings of ownership towards their goods and services, and others did not. Why was that? What was present in some offerings and not in others to give these results?

Prior studies have focused on PO to explain these ownership feelings, and this is where I concentrated my research.

In this chapter, I summarise the key concepts and findings regarding the presence of PO in access economy business models and how it acts as a substitute for legal ownership.

I start by defining PO. There is much research in the field of PO, led by Jon L. Pierce, Tatiana Kostova and Kurt T. Dirks in their seminal papers "Toward a theory of psychological ownership in organizations" (2001) and "The state of psychological ownership: Integrating and extending a century of research" (2003).

Definition of psychological ownership

The concept of PO has developed over time. It partly originates from the work of James (1890):

A man's Self is the sum total of all that he CAN call his, not only his body and his psychic powers, but his clothes and his house,

DOI: 10.4324/9781003368090-7

his wife and children, his ancestors and friends, his reputation and works, his lands, and yacht and bank-account. All these things give him the same emotions. If they wax and prosper, he feels triumphant; if they dwindle and die away, he feels cast down, - not necessarily in the same degree for each thing, but in much the same way for all.[1]

(James, 1890, pp. 291–292)

Along with the work of Isaacs (1933):

... what is mine becomes (in my feelings) a part of ME.

(Isaacs, 1933, p. 225)

PO builds upon the extended self-theory by Belk (1988) that we believe possessions to be part of ourselves and was furthered by Etzioni (1991), who observed that ownership is a "dual creation, part attitude part object, part in the mind, part 'real'" (Etzioni, 1991, p. 466).

PO was then most famously introduced to social sciences by Pierce et al. (2001). They describe PO as:

That state in which individuals feel as though the target of ownership (material or immaterial in nature) or a piece of it is 'theirs' (i.e., 'It is MINE!'). The core of psychological ownership is the feeling of possessiveness and of being psychologically tied to an object.

(Pierce et al., 2001, p. 299)

These quotes illustrate the concept of PO, that a target can become part of the psychological owner's identity, and that possessive behaviour is present in every human society (Ellis, 1985).

Roots or motives of psychological ownership – why?

The roots of PO described by Pierce et al. (2001) underpin why the state exists. I describe them as follows in the context of Strategy and Leadership as Service:

---

1 I draw attention to the outdated and sexist language used in this quotation and others in this chapter. They were added to illustrate their conceptual relevance to psychological ownership (Pierce et al., 2001).

- *Efficacy*: for PO to emerge, clients and C-suite executives have to understand each other's needs, feel knowledgeable about the range of services offered, and be confident that the service and relationship are working to meet desired goals;
- *Self-identity*: possessions contribute to our sense of identity and self-definition. People use ownership to define themselves, express self-identity to others, and ensure the continuity of the self across time. In this context, C-suite executives and clients work together with shared identities and use them to establish and contribute to their own identities, fostering feelings of PO; and
- *Having a place*: individuals seek a particular territory or place, for belonging, and to call home and dwell (Ardrey, 1966). Working together enables C-suite executives and clients to be part of a group of like-minded people, contributing to their feelings of PO towards each other.

Routes of psychological ownership – how?

There are three major routes to develop PO, which are interrelated (Pierce et al., 2001):

- *Controlling the target*: the extent to which clients and C-suite executives can control and access each other impacts feelings of PO. This includes how accessible, approachable, and available they find each other;
- *Intimately knowing the target*: the more information and intimate knowledge the client and C-suite executive have about each other, the deeper the relationship between them, and the stronger the feelings of PO; and
- *Investing self into the target*: investment can take many forms - time, skills, ideas, physical and psychological, and intellectual energies. The more the investment, the more the individual feels connected to the target. An example here would be that the more the client and C-suite executive work together to co-create outputs, the stronger the feelings of PO.

Psychological safety – an additional route to PO

In addition to the work by Pierce et al., a meta-analysis study found through a review of existing research that psychological safety is a further emerging route leading to PO (Zhang et al., 2021).

All the roots and routes of PO, including psychological safety as a fourth route, were incorporated into my research to investigate their role in developing PO in the access-based consumption of professional services delivered through Strategy and Leadership as Service.

Targets of psychological ownership

The concept of PO requires a "target" of ownership. Research finds that there can be various targets for PO, such as work, work outcomes, territory, people, houses, ideas, and other creations (Pierce et al., 2003). While prior studies of PO have mainly addressed material possessions (Stoner et al., 2018; Peck et al., 2013) researchers have recently explored intangible entities such as services and digital goods as potential targets of PO (Peck & Shu, 2018).

Individuals can be considered as "extensions of self" (Belk, 1988, p. 156) and, therefore, a target of PO. This supports my thinking that PO is essential in building relationships between the C-suite executives, their clients, and their C-suite provider. Stakeholders of an organisation can feel PO towards C-suite executives who are self-employed in the access economy and vice versa.

Situational factors – structural and cultural

Situational factors strongly influence PO development. These can be cross-cultural differences and the work environment structure (Pierce et al., 2003). I conducted this study in the UK within one organisation, The CFO Centre. I noted structural and cultural factors when salient, yet they were not given particular focus during the study.

Individual factors

PO can vary in strength within individuals and over time. Individual factors such as personal values and characteristics, traits, and the role of identity will impact the roots and routes of PO (Pierce et al., 2003). In this study, I evaluated differences in individuals and made connections with the extent to which PO had developed.

Target attributes

The degree to which an individual will develop feelings of PO for a target will be affected by specific target attributes that influence:

1. The potential of the target to satisfy the roots of PO; and
2. The target's capacity to facilitate or impede the routes through which the feelings of PO emerge.

(Pierce et al., 2003)

Examples of attributes that influence PO include accessibility and openness.

My study investigated different CFOs and their individual ways of delivering CFO services and their impact on the PO established.

Process of PO development

Former research has shown that PO emerges through a complex interaction between roots, routes, target factors, and individual factors. Roots are complementary and additive; the more roots involved, the more intense the feeling of ownership. While routes are also distinct, complementary, and additive, they do not have a multiplicative relationship (Pierce et al., 2003).

What this told me, and I was eager to test in my research, is that there were likely to be many combinations of roots and routes which foster the development of PO rather than just one pathway. Is this the case for C-suite services? Prior studies focus on which routes are most effective. One of this study's main aims was to understand which routes and roots appeared most prevalent.

The amount of time it takes for PO to develop is also important. Cognitively it can be quick, i.e., we know the car is ours. However, the process may be lengthy, dynamic, and reiterative for the feeling to grow and blossom as an entire affective state fully integrated into the self (Pierce et al., 2003). In this case study, I reviewed young and well-established relationships to understand the role of time in PO development.

Deterioration of PO

Another critical point apparent from my research into PO was that it does not last forever and changes over time. Decoupling occurs through the same process as coupling, i.e., changes in the roots, routes, and characteristics of the target, individual, and interaction (Pierce et al., 2003). This is a significant point when delivering a professional service over time. Changes to the individuals involved and service delivery will affect the PO's strength. It also implies a requirement to put effort into maintaining, sustaining, and strengthening PO, or else it wanes, and it is possible to say that we cannot take it for granted.

I conducted the research for this book at a particular point in time. However, a longitudinal study of how PO changes over time within the same relationships would be further research to give insight.

Previous studies of psychological ownership in access-based services contexts

Appendix 1 illustrates existing research on PO in ABS settings. The contexts cover digital services such as music streaming, augmented reality holograms, social media, film streaming, car sharing, material objects, and Airbnb hosts. There was a range of findings, with many highlighting that PO is present in these ABS contexts.

The outlier is the car-sharing study by Bardhi and Eckhardt (2012), which found that access did not result in the sense of joint or perceived ownership.

Research into settings for delivering professional services was notably absent.

Is psychological ownership the key for access-based services to be solid and enduring?

A different lens through which to view consumption and use of goods and services is liquid or solid. Liquid consumption is ephemeral, access-based, and dematerialised, while solid is enduring, ownership-based, material and tangible (Bardhi & Eckhardt, 2017). It can be helpful to picture them as poles at either end of a liquid-to-solid spectrum.

Liquid consumption

At the extreme liquid end of the spectrum, consumers access, rather than own, digital goods and services in a temporal fashion. The relationship is fleeting, temporary, and desired. It is often particular to a specific context, representing their relationship to the objects or services. For example, Bellezza et al. (2017) argue that consumers don't take particular care of their phones, so they have an excuse to gain frequent upgrades, i.e., the consumer wants the relationship to be ephemeral.

The goods and services are accessed rather than owned. This could be down to the consumers wanting to avoid the burden or responsibility of ownership, wanting more variety and flexibility, feeling priced out of ownership, and environmental consciousness. As mentioned earlier, unlike most studies highlighted in Appendix 1, Bardhi and Eckhardt (2012) found in their Zipcar case study that car users did not express feelings of ownership towards the cars, i.e., there was low relevance to self. However, they do acknowledge that the design of the access system can affect this, i.e., when drivers can personalise their settings on the car, which can be preprogrammed into each vehicle they access, there can be a stronger sense of attachment to the accessed objects.

Dematerialisation means fewer and fewer materials deliver the same functionality (Thackara, 2005). The consumer desires this as they move towards using experiences to make themselves happier than owning material possessions (Van Boven & Gilovich, 2003). The extreme of dematerialised goods and services is digitalisation, also one of the world's megatrends we are experiencing.

Solid consumption

In contrast, at the extreme solid end of the spectrum, consumption relates to the more traditional ownership of goods and services purchased outright at the start of the relationship. They tend to be tangible items with high relevance to self (Belk, 1988), and given the construct of legal ownership, the length of the relationship tends to be longer.

PO as a substitute for legal ownership

In this study, I hypothesise that by substituting PO for legal ownership, access, defined by Bardhi and Eckhardt (2017) as liquid, can become enduring and a characteristic of solid consumption. Hence PO with access provides a route to bridge the gap between a transaction and a relationship, and we can use PO to help us gain identity rather than use value from liquid consumption.

Essentially, access with PO can bring the best of all worlds across the entire spectrum – short and extended use, flexible and fit-for-purpose, intangible feelings of ownership with genuine relationships. Essentially PO can enable stakeholders to enjoy the benefits of accessing the skills of C-suite professionals while having feelings of solid consumption.

Forced into liquid consumption

Liquid consumption, as described by Bardhi and Eckhardt (2017), is not to be celebrated in all contexts. It represents a novel concept, yet one which brings uncertainty and ambiguity. Suppose this is the new normal in our post-pandemic world, with the increased global disparity between rich and poor. In that case, liquid consumption could become the only choice for those forced to go there, i.e., the homeless and lower-income families. While solid values and possessions have become paramount in today's Western society, these people will have to forego the more stable solid consumption, which will become even more of a luxury. Those with money and space will characterise wealth.

Liquid characteristics of Strategy and Leadership as Service enhanced by PO

In the professional services market, situated at the privileged end of the gig economy, ABS allow service providers to hold client portfolios, and diversify their income streams and risk, as they transition from traditional job security to income security. For the professional, once they have a complete portfolio of clients, it is improbable they will lose their entire income stream overnight, compared to being in the wrong place at the wrong time when a market shock occurs and they are made redundant in a corporate restructuring – something I repeatedly hear from C-suite executives in permanent employment who are looking to join the portfolio world.

The access economy business model gives the C-suite professional agency. They control their destiny and can design their client portfolio to suit their skillset, personality, and capacity. This way of working has far more variety and flexibility, including a core element of balancing work with their lifestyle. Again and again, I hear from our C-suite professionals that they no longer miss their children's school plays or first sports matches due to work commitments, which was a regular occurrence in corporate. Working across a portfolio of organisations enables them to forward plan their diaries to accommodate these commitments while delivering superior value to their clients. The high performers recognise that if they obsess about their clients and put them first, they earn the right to have the flexibility and lifestyle that was never within their grasp in corporate.

This control over their schedules, workload, and designing the type of work delivered to each client enables job crafting (Tims & Bakker, 2010) and drives a real sense of purpose and meaning in their work. They can work in their flow with their clients, delivering real impact.

In addition, the fact that they work through a C-suite provider means they have access to and gain support from a community of like-minded individuals and specialists. They are not on their own, faced with having to learn how to build their portfolio of clients as well as having to deliver the work at the same time. The support and structure baked into the Strategy and Leadership as Service business model and the sense of belonging they feel towards the wider team means they get the best of both worlds.

The hurdle to overcome with clients and potential C-suite executives considering this new way of working is the same faced by other access economy business models emerging in the marketplace. It is not the norm. It is different from what we have traditionally done, and from talking to potential clients and C-suite professionals, some perceive it as a temporary solution. The barrier we need to overcome is seeing through the illusion of stability and security associated with ownership and legal employment.

We must actively choose liquid consumption with PO as a substitute for solid consumption

With PO present in access consumption, we can have the benefits of ABS while having feelings of solid consumption. The more we access goods and services, the more this way of consuming is normalised, making it acceptable and affordable for all and less divisive between "the haves" and "the have-nots." Indeed, it could control the consumption of our planet and enable us all to manage liquidity through feelings of solid consumption.

While this trend is just emerging, the direction of travel in the work environment is towards liquefying work through the rise of the gig economy. I argue that this more liquid service provision has the potential to be more enduring and solid with the awareness of what PO can bring, along with, of course, the appropriate regulation to address this new way of working adequately, particularly at the less privileged end of the gig economy in low paid roles.

Thus, liquid consumption could provide the longer-term safety and stability we crave by utilising PO.

The dark side of sharing

The fact that access economy business models enable more continuous usage of goods and services introduces the concept of sharing, even if the relationship between sharers is covert.

What I mean here is that sharing through an access economy business model is often mediated through a third party, so while sharing occurs, it is not apparent to the sharers, i.e., they do not see each other, know each other, or necessarily have a relationship with each other.

Take, for example, car sharing through Zipcar. Each car user will locate their car, have an access code or key to unlock it, get in and start their journey. They will know from their knowledge of the company that other users have previously used that car, but it is unlikely they will have any interaction with those other users. The vehicle should be cleaned and valeted between users to remove all traces of prior users.

The same goes for sharing music using Spotify. Everyone has an account and can log in to access their music of choice, curated by themselves. Users are aware that others, including friends, family, and people they know, also use the service and may even be listening to the same music simultaneously, but it does not feel like that to them when they use the service. It feels as if it is their music.

Having a third party mediate the relationships between users also introduces the opportunity for usage governance. It gives the user somewhere to go if there is a problem to resolve and a route to complain or provide feedback. It also offers a sense of structure to the service and communicates a set of standards to expect by holding the service providers to account. This is important if multiple individuals are using the asset. It ensures it is in the proper condition, ready, and waiting for its following user. It also eradicates any trace of other users, which helps to create the right conditions for feelings of ownership to grow towards the asset. A good example of third-party mediation is Airbnb, which connects property hosts with potential guests.

All users share goods and services, yet sharers do not necessarily have a direct relationship. It is likely that they will not know each other personally, which would typically happen in a more informal relationship of sharing, such as neighbours sharing the use of a lawnmower.

Sharing is a very positive behaviour. It is practical, as well as altruistic and prosocial, not to mention including environmental consciousness to prevent waste and unnecessary consumption.

However, there can also be a dark side to sharing which is worthy of consideration on how that can affect the optimisation of access economy business models. In their study, Zhang et al. (2021, p. 752) found that "PO produces not only altruistic employee attitudes and behaviors but also defensive employee behaviors (e.g., territorial behavior, territoriality, anticipatory defending behavior, and marking behaviors), which we refer to as the 'dark side' of PO". Feelings of ownership could also lead to territorial behaviour towards their possessions.

In addition, Malhotra and Van Alstyne (2014), highlight in their paper, "The dark side of the sharing economy ... and how to lighten it," other darker characteristics of the sharing economy to consider when developing and designing new business models.

In Strategy and Leadership as Service, the firm of C-suite providers mediates the relationships between business owners and their fractional C-suite professionals. Business owners using the service do not necessarily know each other, at least initially. However, to build a sense of community with knowledge sharing and thought leadership dissemination between business owners, the C-suite firm can host events and activities to bring these leaders together. This can promote feelings of PO from the clients towards the C-suite firms.

There are, of course, several ways of looking at this situation. Some business owners will indeed feel as if they are gaining here. They can see they have access to an immediate network of like-minded business owners and a vibrant community of knowledgeable C-suite talent who offer extra support. Another way of looking at this could be territorial, i.e., the business owner could feel threatened that they might lose their C-suite executive to someone else.

Understanding the dark side of sharing and its presence was included in my research. I specifically investigated whether The CFO Centre clients understood they were sharing their CFO, whether it felt like that, and if they had met other business owners serviced by their professional.

Other factors

This study is concerned with understanding PO's presence in ABS in the professional services environment. Context and other concepts and factors could influence the individuals' feelings of ownership in this study. I note some of these as follows. They are not exhaustive and could form the basis for further research to understand if and how they influence feelings of PO in the access-based economy.

Tragedy of the commons and sharing

"The tragedy of the commons" (Ostrom, 2008) arises when individual utility is more important to individuals than collective utility, as was found in Bardhi and Eckhardt (2012) regarding Zipcar services. Since clients share CFO services in this case study, this is particularly interesting, and I considered this concept. I was interested in understanding how the knowledge that a business owner was sharing the services of a CFO affected their treatment of the CFO and their attitude towards them. While it has been found in other contexts that a lack of PO leads to a lack of care towards the asset, I wanted to understand if knowledge of sharing impacted feelings of PO. I deliberately tested this in my research.

Mere ownership effect

"The mere ownership effect" (Beggan, 1992) finds that owners evaluated objects more favourably merely because they owned them. This concept refers to legal ownership, which is not present in the access economy. While comparing the effect of PO with the mere ownership effect of legally owned objects would be interesting, I did not cover this specifically in my study.

Psychological contract

A psychological contract (McFarlane Shore & Tetrick, 1994) is an exchange concept providing a broad explanatory framework for understanding employee-organisational linkages. The development of psychological contracts between C-suite professionals and their clients and the firm of C-suite providers may impact the feelings of PO across the system. I acknowledge that this could influence the expressed feelings of PO in this study. I did not specifically address this, and I recommend it as a topic for further research.

Conclusion

This chapter sets out the concept of PO with its roots and routes and a definition and review of the access-based economy's emergence. Some research supports the presence of PO within ABS, mainly for material goods and digital services (Fritze et al., 2020; Peck & Shu, 2018). Nevertheless, prior research also found that ABS tended to be ephemeral and transactional, i.e., liquid in character, rather than solid and enduring (Bardhi & Eckhardt, 2017). A review of car sharing in the Zipcar case study found that users lacked a sense of joint or perceived ownership (Bardhi & Eckhardt, 2012).

Therefore, existing research is only partially conclusive on PO's role in ABS. This is hardly surprising given the emerging and changing nature of the access economy business models, which are still a very new phenomenon. Outright purchase and ownership are by far the most common and understood ways to enjoy goods and services. The increasing polarisation of society into those with wealth and those without lends itself to access economy initiatives for more to enjoy goods and services. However, without PO, it may not feel the same, and a stigma could be attached in that it outwardly implies a lack of status and success. However, the move towards a more dematerialised liquid mode of consumption, preferred by those wanting a more circular and conscious economy, could well prevail over time and normalise access economy consumption with PO.

None of the prior studies attempted to investigate PO's presence in a different context, one of ABS for sharing professional services.

In addition, this book focuses on the role of PO in accessing professional services in the context of the future of work in the new normal, i.e., how working relationships could change as the future unfolds. I am particularly interested in the rise of the gig economy, with more virtual working and changed behaviours and attitudes towards delivering and receiving professional services through portfolio working in the post-Covid-19 environment.

References

Ardrey, R. (1966). *The territorial imperative: A personal inquiry into the animal origins of property and nations*. Atheneum Books.

Bardhi, F., & Eckhardt, G. M. (2012). Access-based consumption: The case of car sharing. *Journal of Consumer Research, 39*(4), 881–898. https://doi.org/10.1086/666376

Bardhi, F., & Eckhardt, G. M. (2017). Liquid consumption. *Journal of Consumer Research, 44*(3), 582–597. https://doi.org/10.1093/jcr/ucx050

Beggan, J. K. (1992). On the social nature of nonsocial perception: The mere ownership effect. *Journal of Personality and Social Psychology, 62*(2), 229–237. https://doi.org/10.1037/0022-3514.62.2.229

Belk, R. (1988). Possessions and the extended self. *Journal of Consumer Research, 15*(2), 139–168. https://doi.org/10.1086/209154

Bellezza, S., Ackerman, J. M., & Gino, F. (2017). Be careless with that! Availability of product upgrades increases cavalier behavior toward possessions. *Journal of Marketing Research, 54*(5), 768–784. https://doi.org/10.1509/jmr.15.0131

Ellis, L. M. (1985). On the rudiments of possessions and property. *Social Science Information, 24*(1), 113–143. https://doi.org/10.1177/053901885024001006

Etzioni, A. (1991). The socio-economics of property. *Social Science Research Network*. www.researchgate.net/profile/Amitai-Etzioni/publication/235363137_The_Socio-Economics_of_Property/links/582f5f6408ae004f74be5f69/The-Socio-Economics-of-Property.pdf

Fritze, P., Marchand, A., Eisingerich, B., & Benkenstein, M. (2020). Access-based services as substitutes for material possessions: The role of psychological ownership. *Journal of Service Research, 23*(3), 368–385. https://doi.org/10.1177/1094670520907691

Isaacs, S. (1933). *Social development in young children*. Routledge and Kegan Paul.

James, W. (1890). *The principles of psychology*. Holt.

Malhotra, A., & Van Alstyne, M. (2014). The dark side of the sharing economy … and how to lighten it. *Communications of the ACM, 57*(11), 24–27. https://doi.org/10.1145/2668893

McFarlane Shore, L., & Tetrick, E. (1994). The psychological contract as an explanatory framework in the employment relationship. In *Trends in organizational behavior* (Vol. 1, pp. 91–109). John Wiley & Sons Ltd.

Ostrom, E. (2008). Tragedy of the commons. In *The new Palgrave dictionary of economics*, (pp. 1–5). https://doi.org/10.1057/9780230226203.1729

Peck, J., Barger, V. A., & Webb, A. (2013). In search of a surrogate for touch: The effect of haptic imagery on perceived ownership. *Journal of Consumer Psychology, 23*(2), 189–196. https://doi.org/10.1016/j.jcps.2012.09.001

Peck, J., & Shu, S. B. (2018). *Psychological ownership and consumer behavior*. Springer. https://doi.org/10.1007/978-3-319-77158-8

Pierce, J. L., Kostova, T., & Dirks, K. T. (2001). Toward a theory of psychological ownership in organizations. *Academy of Management Review, 26*(2), 298–310. https://doi.org/10.5465/amr.2001.4378028

Pierce, J. L., Kostova, T., & Dirks, K. T. (2003). The state of psychological ownership: Integrating and extending a century of research. *Review of General Psychology, 7*(1), 84–107. https://doi.org/10.1037/1089-2680.7.1.84

Stoner, J. L., Loken, B., & Stadler Blank, A. (2018). The name game: How naming products increases psychological ownership and subsequent consumer evaluations. *Journal of Consumer Psychology, 28*(1), 130–137. https://doi.org/10.1002/jcpy.1005

Thackara, J. (2005). *In the bubble: Designing in a complex world.* MIT Press.

Tims, M., & Bakker, A. B. (2010). Job crafting: Towards a new model of individual job redesign. *SA Journal of Industrial Psychology, 36*(2), 1–9. https://doi.org/10.4102/sajip.v36i2.841

Van Boven, L., & Gilovich, T. (2003). To do or to have? That is the question. *Journal of Personality and Social Psychology, 85*(6), 1193–1202. https://doi.org/10.1037/0022-3514.85.6.1193

Zhang, Y., Liu, G., Zhang, L., Xu, S., & Cheung, M. W. L. (2021). Psychological ownership: A meta-analysis and comparison of multiple forms of attachment in the workplace. *Journal of Management, 47*(3), 745–770. https://doi.org/10.1177/0149206320917195

Part III

The C-Suite Industry Players

The C-Suite Professionals **5**

The C-suite professionals have decided to leave employment, transition to portfolio working, and become self-employed. They then take one of two pathways, either going it alone or joining a firm of C-suite providers and working as part of a team.

Part-time, portfolio work for the C-suite is in its infancy and is a niche market. There is little prior research regarding why these individuals make this change and what they are moving away from and gravitating towards. *Executive freedom* (Mills & Daw, 2019) shares research gathered from 300 C-suite professionals who participated in a survey to identify the types of individuals working this way, what attracted them, what issues they were most concerned about, and what kept them engaged for the longer term. These responses, along with 30 in-depth interviews and experiences over the years, prompted the development of a "Magic Triangle" see Figure 5.1 which comprises:

1. Eight categories, "Key Personas" of individuals who are attracted to team-based portfolio work;
2. Six "Personal Virtues" these individuals display; and
3. Six "Attraction Magnets" which draw these C-suite professionals to this way of working, and two significant "Turn-offs" that were their concerns.

A thorough review of the Magic Triangle for this book highlights that the personas, virtues, attraction magnets, and turn-offs are still valid. More is known about these concepts now. This chapter describes them in detail to give a complete and up-to-date picture of the C-suite executives working in this industry and includes the latest thinking.

DOI: 10.4324/9781003368090-9

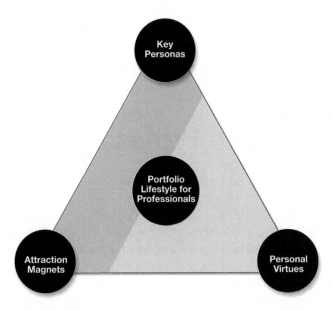

Figure 5.1 Team-based portfolio working: The Magic Triangle

Source: Mills and Daw (2019, p. 14). Used with permission of Colin Mills from *Executive freedom: How to escape the C-suite, create income security, and take back control by building a part-time portfolio career*, 2019.

The key personas

The key personas have been extended from eight to ten to include female and male personas for the Freedom Seeker and Seasoned Veteran, as these are the personas most adopted by new joiners and have gender differences regarding their drivers and concerns. In this chapter, I share a brief biography of each persona for the C-suite finance discipline at The CFO Centre. There will be some differences for other professions. Nevertheless, the drivers to move towards portfolio work, the issues these executives face, and the worries and objections they must overcome are broadly the same regardless of their discipline.

Valencia "The Freedom Seeker – female"

Valencia has always put her career first. She's a dedicated finance professional with extensive overseas experience in well-known corporates. She knew she wanted to work with larger organisations to take advantage of their comprehensive training and extensive learning and development programmes and build her network in her specialism. She's finally made it to Group CFO roles in multi-nationals and is still relatively young.

She also wanted to have a family, and after meeting her partner through friends, she married in her early 30s. Her employers were generous with their maternity leave. Yet, she ensured she was back at work well before it formally ended to keep up the momentum regarding her career progression. She has been rewarded for this approach by being fast-tracked to roles with extra responsibility and status. When Valencia reviews her career to date and her employer, on the face of it, all is going well. She likes her co-workers, her work is challenging and varied, she relishes being a leader, and her 360 feedback has been a good balance between giving her a reality check on areas to improve and reinforcing she's on track.

Then why is she feeling overwhelmed?

Her partner also has a demanding job, and to start with, they found a nursery nearby for their children. This was stressful, though. The five o'clock pick-up time felt like the middle of the day, resulting in rushing home for tea, bath, and bedtime and then resuming work into the early hours to finish everything. After a while, they took the plunge and hired a full-time nanny to ease the burden. Life is still hectic. It almost always falls to Valencia to be the primary carer at home responsible for family organisation and household chores, and that's before spending any quality time with their children.

She's starting to resent her partner for putting his work first, her children for being so demanding, and her employer for not understanding the pressure she is under. She's talked about it to her boss, who cares, but puts it down to the stage of life "We all go through that phase!"

Valencia is starting to ask herself if this is the case. Life is a whirlwind. Holding down a job and being there for her children is challenging. She feels she needs to be a superwoman to make it all work. It is making her miserable. She's not enjoying life, and something needs to change.

Is it possible to have it all? Quality time for her family and a progressive career?

Ideally, she would like to keep her career going. She loves working, and she knows she's good at it. She wants more flexibility and balance, though. It's hard to get time off to be at important moments for her children. She's always the mum who rushes in at the last minute and must return to work afterwards. She's aware her children are noticing as they ask her the dreaded question of why she can't pick them up from school like their friends' mums. She misses them, and when she sees her nanny taking them off for fun days out, she silently asks herself why that isn't her.

On the flip side, she's conscious of her hard work and the milestones she has achieved in her career. She can see how impressed others are when she talks about her employer and accomplishments at work.

If she takes the leap into portfolio work and starts supporting SMEs, how will she feel without the backing of the big corporate brand? Will she lose credibility and status?

What if she can't do the work? There's no guarantee that her skills will translate to the entrepreneurial world. Yet if she could, she would have a much better lifestyle, with meaningful work under her control. She can balance being there for her family with delivering value to others and feel like she has it all.

Jonathan "The Freedom Seeker – male"

Jonathan grew up in a family of accountants. He could see the benefits of becoming one. It is a well-respected qualification, providing a solid business grounding with a guaranteed career path. He started with the Big Four and then moved into industry, taking up multiple CFO roles. He carefully planned his route to the top, ensuring he gained broad industry experience and the full suite of operational challenges expected of a CFO.

Now in his mid-40s, he is married with two young children. He loves spending time with his family and is confident in his CFO capabilities.

There's a problem, though. Daily life in a corporate is wearing him down. He is disillusioned. He travels constantly, and life on the road, living out of a suitcase during the week, is taking its toll. He is asking himself, "Why am I doing this?" Until he started his family, each corporate priority was a new and exciting challenge to conquer, but now, it never ends. There is always another crisis to solve.

Most days, when he's not travelling, he leaves home before his children wake up and returns after bedtime. He fills any spare time at the weekend with activities with his children. He knows his relationship with his partner is suffering.

Not only that, but he also needs to watch what he says at work. Office politics are ever-present, and while he wants to be himself, he feels safer if he bites his tongue and is more guarded. He's aware this might not be for the good of the organisation, but he's scared of any negative repercussions, and now he has a family, he has responsibilities at home to keep the money coming in.

Taking time to reflect, he feels something is missing from his work life. He wants to be himself at work, make a difference, create an impact, and, most importantly, gain more agency and control over his work life.

He dreams of controlling his schedule to have breakfast before school with his children and be back for some time with them before bath and bed. Not having to return to his laptop after dinner but spending time with his partner must also become the norm, as does less overseas work travel.

But what alternatives does he have? If he steps away from corporate, won't he lose his earning potential and career development opportunities? How will he gain income stability to support his family, continue his career development, and enjoy family life?

Sanjay "The Independent Who Wants to be Part of Something"

Sanjay has been an independent portfolio CFO for owner-managed, entrepreneurial businesses for several years. Before that, he had held senior corporate CFO roles. When he hit his late 40s, he became disillusioned with corporate life and office politics. He knew he had enough experience to "give back" and help small and medium-sized businesses, so he took the leap and set himself up on his own.

To start with, it was frantic and exhilarating.

He had an excellent personal network which, once mined, gave him plenty of roles. He started working with his first few clients and loved it. However, he found it difficult to service his clients and keep up his networking to bring in the next ones. He was busier than ever! After a while, he just stopped marketing to get ahead with his client work, but when he needed to pick it up again, he found it harder to gain momentum. How can he build a full portfolio and balance marketing and servicing clients?

At this point, he started picking up project work to keep the money flowing but turning these into long-term relationships took a lot of effort. He had to keep doing projects or drop down to do some lower-level financial controller roles with his existing clients to continue earning but at a lower price point. How else was he going to get a complete book of clients?

This was different from the way he thought it would work!

While he had lots of variety, his other issue was loneliness. He loved his clients but missed having colleagues who would advise him about client problems, challenge his ideas, and guide him in his work. He was also worried about where he would go for support if his clients needed expertise outside his skillset.

He wanted structure, support, and belonging alongside his independence and freedom. If only he could belong to a group of fractional CFOs like him. He would feel supported and part of something. He could learn how to build long-term relationships and use their marketing expertise to keep his portfolio topped up while still having freedom of choice regarding which clients he worked with.

Nyasha "The Post-Kids Career Woman"

Nyasha is married with three children. They are now becoming more self-sufficient, and she's considering returning to her career as a CFO.

Getting to this point has certainly been a rollercoaster.

Before her children, she had qualified as a Chartered Accountant and then moved into industry and worked hard to get into CFO roles. She took full maternity leave with her first child and returned to work four days a week, putting her son into a nursery for three days and asking her parents to cover the fourth day.

It felt doable, but it didn't quite work out like that.

The reality was that she carried on with a workload of five days, accommodated in evenings and weekends, but was only paid for four, which just about covered her childcare costs! Determined not to be beaten, Nyasha put up with it. However, when child number two came along, something had to give.

She decided to put her career on hold and take a break. Child number three arrived, and she extended her time not working.

Roll on ten years, and Nyasha still hasn't returned to work. She is grateful for her time with her children at home but now wants back some of her old life. Part-time work would be ideal.

Looking through the jobs on offer, Nyasha is getting nervous. She doesn't have a network anymore, technology has transformed the working world, and while she knows she is well qualified, she asks, "Can I still do this? Am I good enough?"

She wants support to help her transition back into CFO roles and learn new skills to build a portfolio of local clients. The flexibility of portfolio work could be ideal. She can regain her confidence and identity as a professional, competent CFO and be mum.

She's looking forward to regaining control of her life.

Daniel "The Professional Interim"

Daniel is a well-rounded and experienced CFO. He was made redundant immediately after the global financial crisis and took an interim role as a stopgap. Wind on 15 years, and he has been an interim CFO ever since.

He loves the variety and being able to develop his knowledge and skills in different sectors and functional challenges – restructuring, systems implementation, raising finance, mergers and acquisitions, and covering for illness and career breaks. He has gained vast experience working with pre-revenue start-up organisations that require seed funding to mid-tier firms and large multi-national conglomerates. There are few situations he hasn't experienced or types of business leader he hasn't come across over the years.

He is now in his mid-to-late 50s, and he's wondering if he should continue working as an interim until his retirement, which is on the horizon. Working as an interim does have its downsides. He's starting to get tired of the on-off nature of the work. It's feast or famine.

He has used this to his advantage in the past by taking extended holidays between roles. Yet inevitably, these are cut short when he receives an urgent call to start a new engagement. Not knowing when the next one will arrive, he almost always takes it. This unpredictability and expectation that he will relocate to fit in with each role are beginning to take their toll.

He also wonders what it would be like to finish a job and see its longer-term impact. How would it feel to build long-lasting relationships in an organisation and see the fruits of his work make an enduring impression? It's also lonely working solo, going from job to job. He builds good relationships everywhere he works, but then he must break them off to go to his next assignment.

He thinks it is now time for a change. A portfolio lifestyle would fill all these gaps. He can gain flexibility on an ongoing basis rather than in between roles. He will build relationships with businesses for the long term, and he will have a support group of colleagues and belong to a team.

Jessica "The Rising Star"

Jessica is still relatively young for a CFO. She is in her late 30s. When deciding which career to adopt, she was attracted to accountancy because the skills are recognised globally and would provide a solid platform to work and live overseas one day.

She comes from a family of entrepreneurs and remembers how stressful it was when money was tight, and their businesses needed funding. She knows how much her parents struggled with the finances and was determined to learn the relevant finance skills to help other entrepreneurs succeed.

Jessica likes to stretch herself and go outside her comfort zone. She's a learner and loves personal and professional development. Working her way up through the ranks, she always sought out mentors to ensure she was learning from the best. She was thrilled to gain the opportunity to become a divisional CFO in a mid-market corporate. Yet it wasn't quite what she expected. The bureaucratic culture and protocol were restrictive. She felt a long way from the sharp end of the business. Everything moved very slowly. She wondered why she was doing this, just going through the motions of reporting, month in, month out. It was also taking up far too much of her time. She was constantly working late and at weekends, but for what purpose? This wasn't what she was looking for.

A portfolio career working with entrepreneurs, seeing the impact of her endeavours immediately and being part of the decisions that affected their lives seemed far more suited to her. She'd relish the flexibility, and she would be learning all the time, too, from her clients and her CFO colleagues, who had heaps of real-world and technical experience. Of course, if it doesn't work out, she'd have to return to corporate, but the risk seems worth it.

Christoph "The Scale-Up Enthusiast"

Christoph has always been a very ambitious CFO, craving new challenges and loving the pace and excitement of innovative businesses. He has worked in both small and large organisations, learning what it is like to "feel" big and what it takes to get there. He has gathered extensive experience with businesses looking to scale quickly; this is his passion.

He has a strong reputation within the investor community and is known for getting things done at scale and working well with ambitious entrepreneurs who are going places.

He loves variety and rapid growth. He particularly excels in raising strategic funding for the latest tech innovation through to proof of concept, commercialisation, and eventual exit, as the business goes mainstream. He's good at managing stakeholder expectations and sensing market timing. He is always active and energised to achieve an impact, often evidenced through some sort of transaction.

He doesn't like it when things slow down, take too long, go quiet or need steady state management. That becomes boring for Christoph, and he loses interest quickly. He knows this is a risk in the businesses he works with. Only a few of them make it. Picking a winner can be challenging.

Recently he's started to wonder how he can fill his working life with the excitement and pace of scaling businesses and minimise the chances of steady-state or markets turning unexpectedly. He's heard of portfolio work and is curious. By having a portfolio of clients, he can undoubtedly gain variety and challenge through working with a range of clients, not just one at a time. He would have fellow team members who might be more suited to the steady state management, and he'd love help finding these potential unicorns to work with. He's only ever been employed before and never had to sell himself, so a supportive, structured environment to help him perform this way would be ideal.

Delphine "The Seasoned Veteran – female"

Delphine has had a very successful career as a corporate CFO. After qualifying in industry, she rose rapidly through the ranks and has been rewarded by working for larger and more complex organisations ever since. She's always had ambition, so she only took standard maternity leave even when she had her children. She's never had an extended career break.

Helped by her parents and full-time nannies, she, and her partner, who also worked throughout, just about coped as a family when their children were young.

Now, in her mid-to-late 50s, with children in their 20s, Delphine has come up for air. She's loved her career, but she's recently started asking herself if she needs or wants to keep up this pace of work. Their finances are secure, and she can see retirement beckoning if she looks ahead.

She's looking for a change, a sense of purpose, to feel valued and appreciated. The last thing she wants is to feel irrelevant, yet she's beginning to ask herself, "What was the point of working all these years? Isn't it time to enjoy what I've worked for?" She's not ready to retire and wait for the grandchildren to come along, but she's wondering if she can change her career to find something fulfilling and purposeful while slowing down to weave more balance into her life.

Some of her friends have already retrained for their second career in their later years, and she's intrigued by what this could be for her. She's sure she still needs a community and somewhere to belong. She prefers being surrounded by like-minded people. She's excited to learn new skills, spend more time with her children as they start their families, and enjoy life a little more.

Simon "The Seasoned Veteran – male"

Simon has had a great career as a corporate CFO. He's moved organisations a few times, with his efforts rewarded with progression in every firm he's joined. Now in his mid-to-late 50s, it's the first time he's stopped to think about what might be next. The word "retirement" has been mentioned, and he's struggling to come to terms with it. It feels far too early for him, yet if he's honest with himself, another role the same as before feels like Groundhog Day.

Looking back, he acknowledges that he's spent a lot of time at work and little time with his family. He doesn't regret doing this, but they have all paid the price for the financial stability that work has given them. He's worried that life will pass him by if he doesn't make changes now. A part of himself is excited to see if he can regain some work-life balance. He most definitely still wants to contribute and make an impact. He has always been driven and aims for success. He's still in good health and has plenty of energy, but the thought of yet another few years of the same corporate world is demoralising.

It's time to put himself and his family first. He has considered starting his own business, but that feels daunting. He has seen how much it takes to build a business from scratch, which feels like a step too far.

He'd love something where every day is different. He would like the opportunity to work with a variety of people, businesses, and cultures, all with their challenges. He's seen most things now and feels he has accumulated skills and knowledge that will make a real difference to others. He's looking forward to being valued and feeling appreciated too. He wants an enjoyable lifestyle where he can fit in some activities for himself and his family and to feel like he's running his own show.

Sarah "The Work/Care Balancer"

Sarah has been a large corporate CFO for many years. She's held senior finance positions in multi-nationals and enjoyed every moment. Her experience has been wide and varied. She particularly enjoyed integrating smaller entrepreneurial organisations into the larger corporates she worked for. She feels this has given her insight into how these SMEs operate and why they are attractive targets for bigger businesses.

She's travelled extensively in her roles. Being single, she has leapt at the chance to experience different countries and has built up a wide group of friends from her time abroad. She's even taken up a few roles overseas and has thoroughly enjoyed them.

However, Sarah now has a problem she needs to reconcile.

Both her parents are now elderly, and her mother is in ill health. She sees her father struggling to cope on his own, and given she is an only child; they are now expecting her to be more available to help. She's moved closer to them but struggles to be on hand when they need her and give her full time and attention to her big corporate job, which still involves lots of travel. Her work needs to be more flexible. She feels distraught when she's away from home, and her parents call expecting her to be able to pop around. She's distracted from her work, anxious about the next 'phone call, and deep down, feels she is abandoning her parents when they need her most.

Sarah would like things to change. She wants to maintain her CFO career and be more available for her mum and dad. Having spent a lot of time integrating SMEs into larger businesses, she's confident she can support growing, owner-managed organisations, especially those who want to exit to a corporate buyer. She also likes the sound of building a portfolio career with local clients, which she could flex around her commitments to her parents.

She knows their needs will change over time, so something she can dial up and down would be perfect. All of this would give her the control she needs.

Why do CFOs join The CFO Centre?

The research for *Executive freedom* (Mills & Daw, 2019) revealed six Attraction Magnets which draw portfolio professionals to join a firm of C-suite providers. These were freedom, the ability to work with a variety of SME businesses, flexible working and work-life balance, an open and fair business model, a sales and marketing machine that delivered results, and being part of a team.

Updated research in 2022 corroborates these findings. The CFO Centre commissioned in-depth interviews with over 40 CFO team members. Their reasons for joining are summarised as follows:

1. Lifestyle – "Sometimes, I want to be able to go for a walk at 3 pm."
2. Purpose – "I want to give back."
3. Excitement – "The variety of clients is amazing."
4. Structure – "I didn't have to start my business on my own. It's a soft landing."
5. Belonging – "I have a community of CFOs rather than the lonely life of a CFO of a company."
6. Control – "I get to choose." "You can design your own life."
7. Support – "The sales and marketing machine solves the feast and famine."
8. Impact – "I can have a meaningful conversation in the morning and execute in the afternoon."

Overall, the context for joining is freedom. All the reasons given support that. Freedom to choose with whom they work, when and how, with fulfilling, varied and purpose-driven work which makes a real difference is paramount. They want to be part of a structure that provides support and belonging yet feel in control over their lives.

The personas also reveal the importance of couples working together to coordinate and plan their individual career paths within the context of their shared lives (Petriglieri, 2019). While embarking on a portfolio lifestyle is a big change and requires investment in time and energy, it can ease the pressure on dual-career couples by providing flexibility for one partner to support the other at critical times to achieve their work ambitions.

What are their fears?

Executive freedom (Mills & Daw, 2019) found two significant concerns, the Turn-offs. These were the uncertainty of income stream and getting used to this way of working. The research in 2022 and updated personas highlight these issues remain with an additional concern from The Rising Star persona regarding fear of missing out on learning and development.

The personal virtues

Lastly, the recent research revisited the characteristics of a portfolio CFO from The CFO Centre. *Executive freedom* (Mills & Daw, 2019) identified the personal virtues required to succeed in portfolio working as being:

1. Humble – "You need to leave your ego at the door."
2. Givers – "Those who give without expectation of return are more successful in the long run."
3. Networked – "Building an authentic professional network really helps."
4. Relationship-focused – "It's all about the relationships."
5. Learners – "Anyone who thinks they are too old to learn is probably not a good fit for this type of work."
6. Hungry and active – "You need to be constantly on the lookout for more things to do, more to learn, and more responsibility to take on."

The recent research reinforced these findings and gave more detail as follows regarding the characteristics of who is best suited to becoming a high-performing portfolio C-suite professional:

- *Motivation*: The CFOs were motivated by building long-term relationships with their clients. This gave them a strong sense of purpose and making a difference, alongside creating a lifestyle that worked for them with flexibility and balance;
- *Emotional intelligence*: They were emotionally intelligent, with good listening skills. They had empathy, were caring, and supportive of their clients and team members;
- *Professional mindset*: Professionally, they felt it was important to act like an owner. This helped them empathise and be considered a peer with their clients. It was crucial to be strategic, systematic, insightful, and value driven. They also could see the merit of being hands-on and adaptable to client situations. They were team players and generous with their time and knowledge;
- *Professional style*: Concerning their style, they have broad business experience and can be a mentor for their clients. They like communicating through storytelling and are practice orientated in their work; and

- *Personal mindset*: Being passionate, optimistic, and confident were common traits balanced with humility and being approachable. They are candid with their clients and open to learning. They embrace being in an environment where they can be themselves.

Conclusion

The professionals are key players in the access economy for the C-suite. They have significant drivers for moving into the industry and making it work. Joining a firm of C-suite providers provides plenty of structure and support, yet it's not for everyone, some prefer to go it alone.

The remainder of Part III looks in detail at the enlightened clients already embracing this concept and taking advantage of its benefits and the firms of C-suite providers.

References

Mills, C., & Daw, S. (2019). *Executive freedom: How to escape the C-suite, create income security, and take back control by building a part-time portfolio career.* BrightFlame Books.

Petriglieri, J. (2019). *Couples that work: How to thrive in love and at work.* Penguin UK.

The Clients

6

This chapter shares four case studies of clients of The CFO Centre already using the access economy to give their businesses the C-suite skills they need. The clients cover a range of sectors, sizes (from SMEs to large multi-nationals), and geographies. They highlight the diversity of needs the model can meet and the benefits and outcomes it can deliver. These real-world illustrations show how the model operates with smaller organisations through predominantly working with an individual C-suite professional from a C-suite firm to a team approach which offers flexible and agile solutions for more complex and larger organisations.

Holos Change, UK – Neil Crofts, CEO and Co-Founder

The Holos story

Holos is an interdependent, leadership, and culture change consulting organisation that operates globally with hubs in the UK and Europe, Singapore and Hong Kong, and North America. With an international faculty of over 150 members, Holos focuses on working predominantly with large multi-nationals and seeks to expand into political and educational establishments and bodies. Coaching, consulting, events, and digital learning empowers their transformation for sustained success in a disrupted environment (Holos Change, 2022).

Holos was founded in 2014 by Neil Crofts (CEO) and his co-founder. They had a shared passion for purpose and authentic, driven leadership and realised that the global change context had already developed further than teaching in the sector. They decided to conduct some research

DOI: 10.4324/9781003368090-10

and set up Holos to help organisations transform through an approach that integrates and brings together a post-conventional strategy for dealing with the three (often disparate) issues of leadership, culture, and change.

The Holos faculty members are world-class experts in their field. They are self-employed, operating at the partner level and come together to work on client projects, as required, united in their purpose to help these organisations develop the capability for sustained success (Holos Change, 2022).

The post-conventional philosophy

Holos is a global, growing, entrepreneurial business which focuses on helping larger organisations to change and adapt to the megatrends disrupting their environments and become what Neil calls "post-conventional."

Even though Neil recognised that he would need C-suite skills to help Holos grow, he knew he didn't want to employ anyone to do these roles. That is because Holos role models the cultures it promotes and is post-conventional.

No one is employed at Holos, not Neil, his co-founder, their faculty, and refreshingly none of the internal team. Neither does the business have any offices. The whole team works from home or their clients' premises. This was a conscious experiment by Neil and his co-founder to structure Holos differently. It allows the business to scale up and down painlessly and remain agile and lean, always having the right resources at the right time.

Strategy and Leadership as Service is a disruptive approach to engaging with professionals. It aligns with the Holos post-conventional philosophy that organisations don't need to employ their people to have a fully committed, engaged, and productive team.

Neil firmly believes that not employing his people (both his client-facing faculty and internal support team) contributes to them being the best versions of themselves and capable of building healthy interdependent relationships, leading to superior results through collaboration.

Let me explain.

Employment immediately creates dependency. As soon as individuals become dependent on a system, they become compromised. Neil refers to *Radical candor* (Scott, 2017), which is about getting people to be honest with each other. Through his work and research, he has found this is very challenging in employed situations. The difficulty comes when there is a dependency on the business and colleagues, too, because it is hard to give honest feedback when your job, work environment, and livelihood are riding on the relationship.

The same is valid at the organisational level. Working flexibly with the Holos faculty, who don't want to be employed, helps Holos to be honest with its clients and confront them when needed, rather than being so dependent on them that this feels dangerous and puts the engagement at risk. This contrasts with conventional consulting organisations, who might find challenging clients more difficult to achieve, given they have a monthly payroll to meet and office buildings to fund.

Since Holos is structured as it is and does not employ anyone, connecting with a part-time CFO from a post-conventional model like Strategy and Leadership as Service seemed like a perfect fit. Zara Skinmore from The CFO Centre became the part-time CFO at Holos and slotted seamlessly into the team, just like anyone else in the business, becoming integral to the organisation. She also has the advantage of being part of the larger structure of The CFO Centre and can bring access to additional knowledge and experience to Holos as needed.

Neil describes how Holos works with Zara and others within the organisation as collaborations. He believes that thinking employment gives business owners more control over individuals is a myth. He explains:

> The people we have the most control over are ourselves, yet even that is hard. If we cannot control ourselves fully, how can we control others? Control is just an illusion; at best, we can influence others. We would be better making a paradigm shift and moving from a model of employment based on dependency and control to one based on developing interdependency and collaboration.
>
> (Crofts, 2023)

The challenges

When I asked Neil about what is difficult regarding working with Zara without employment, his first response was that he was tempted to say "nothing."

On reflection, he shared that to make this type of relationship work as a business leader; you must accept a degree of vulnerability, i.e., a lack of control. He explains further that if he asks someone not employed to do something, they will do it if they want to and if they can. He has no coercive methods to make them do it, which might make him feel vulnerable because he does not know he has backup when needed. That might be a challenge to work in this way. However, Neil countered this line of thought by admitting that we don't have control even in dependent (employment) relationships. We still have the vulnerability of asking others to do things and run the risk of them not doing them.

Neil thought the answer was that we needed to plan. He can't guarantee that Zara will be available at 4 pm on a given day. If he wants something done, he needs to prepare for it, or if it is an emerging issue he cannot foresee, he needs to go "cap in hand" and ask her to help at the last minute. A solid and positive relationship with Zara will count here and give him a better chance of getting what he needs. Nevertheless, the reality of delegation is that we need to plan because even in employed situations, regularly asking staff to do things at short notice will rub people up the wrong way and damage long-term relationships.

Neil concluded that nothing specific was challenging about working with Strategy and Leadership as Service. It was good as it forced better behaviour because fewer options were available.

The advantages

Neil shared that the significant advantage for Holos of not employing its faculty is that it provides access to a potentially unrestricted pool of talent of coaches and facilitators with whom they can collaborate. He can see a future where Holos can access infinite talent, build teams flexibly, and create dynamic solutions for their clients.

Coaches and facilitators form a segment of the market who are already very used to working independently. As Strategy and Leadership as Service gains traction and more C-suite professionals move to independence, the same could become a reality for the C-level industry.

Another advantage highlighted by Neil is that Zara has exposure to many other businesses through her broader portfolio and can bring that learning and knowledge to Holos. Neil reflected that just working with someone who doesn't work for anyone else means their learning would be limited, and they would be less likely to spot new and different things than someone engaged with a portfolio. Additionally, when he asks Zara something that she doesn't immediately know she has the backup of her community, which is very reassuring.

Finally, with ownership (or employment) comes responsibility, which can become a burden (Schaefers et al., 2016). By not employing anyone at Holos, Neil can have a different relationship with his team, one which isn't so tied to feeling wholly responsible for them but is interdependent, with everyone in the system taking responsibility for themselves. All team members have freedom of choice regarding their engagement, and overall, the relationships feel lighter and healthier.

Neil is keen to stress that not feeling the burden of responsibility should not be interpreted as he doesn't care. He cares deeply about his people and ensures he looks after his team, being there for them when needed. He also pays equal attention to their concerns, whether they are shareholders, faculty, or internal team members.

Holos does things differently; it lives and breathes what it believes in. It proves that access can be a credible alternative to employment with real advantages. It forces us to focus on authentic relationships with our people and clients. It enables us to be flexible, agile, and lean, building dynamic teams to tackle issues. It promotes interdependency with freedom of choice and fosters radical candour, honest conversations, and healthy debate for better outcomes.

Soundmouse, UK – Kirk Zavieh, Co-CEO and Co-Founder

The brotherhood

Long-time friends, studying together at school and at Cambridge University, Kirk and Charles were passionate musicians and songwriters and founded Adelphoi Music, which became a leading music production company in the mid-late 90s.

They were also both technological (much of their production used the latest computer systems) and observing the issues and complexity of music royalties within the music industry, saw the opportunity to build a technology platform that improved the music royalty registration and collection process for audio-visual content for composers and artists.

They formed Soundmouse with their first client in Channel 4 in 2001.

Over the years, they grew their business to include BBC, Discovery, ITV, Sky, and others, attracting highly talented developers to build a leading pattern recognition technology that automatically matched music on tv, radio, and the internet, a system they patented, and that now powers music royalty payments at scale on platforms across the world.

With a staff of almost 400 people and offices in London, Bulgaria, Seoul, Sri Lanka, Taipei, and Tokyo, Soundmouse connects broadcasters, programme makers, collecting societies, distributors, labels, publishers, and musicians (Paine, 2023).

Their software reports music usage to broadcasters and collecting societies to identify music usage across radio, TV, online, and other media (PRS for Music, 2022). With long-term contracts with media giants such as the BBC and Sky, it has become the industry standard.

Like all entrepreneurial experiences, it hasn't been straightforward building Soundmouse to be the industry benchmark. Kirk and his partner have had their fair share of ups and downs. Negotiating long-term contracts with the big broadcasters can be tricky and managing cash and resources has been a constant balancing act.

Their original driver for creating Soundmouse was to establish a global and valuable enterprise to solve the music and broadcast industry's challenges around disjointed data flows. Yet the demands of running a technology business at scale with ever growing needs are extreme.

Soundmouse was just one of the businesses Kirk and his partner invented. The original Adelphoi Music is still prospering – Adelphoi stands for brotherhood in ancient Greek and sums up their philosophy about sharing and fits well with Soundmouse's intention to unblock value for music users and creators.

The professionals

While it was never about selling, the founders did want to secure some freedom. They knew they had something special in Soundmouse. When would they be able to realise some of its value, but in a way that kept them engaged and continuing to build the industry? There's still a long way to go in the market. The proliferation of media globally means the requirement to track down and report music usage in new environments is a constant challenge and never ends.

Kirk and Charles recognised that they would need to professionalise the business to attract investment for further growth and development. Kirk is the first to admit that he is unsure about bringing in "professionals." He would only accept them if he thought they brought significant additional skills to the highly experienced existing management team. That's not an arrogant statement; Kirk observes that these individuals need to be top-notch experts who know their stuff and can free the existing teams up to add value to the business in other ways. At this point, Kirk knew all the numbers inside out, daily. While it comforted him and helped him feel in control, he knew he could do with releasing some time to scale the business.

At that stage, it was clear to both founders that, as an SME, they needed the skills and experience of a first class CFO to steer them through the next few years, deal with the incoming expressions of interest from across the industry, and realise their ambitions. From working with gifted software developers, they knew that one good person at the top of their game is streets ahead of a team of lower-level talent. A high-quality fractional or part-time CFO was going to be the answer, and through my relationship with Kirk (we had been fellow members of a peer networking organisation in the UK for some time together), he knew he could reach out to me.

Raymond Yager joined Soundmouse four years ago as their part-time CFO, averaging two days per week with them over the years.

The skills

Together, Kirk, Charles, and Raymond built a solid working relationship and developed a shared obsession with priorities of:

- Continually protecting the business;
- Raising funds for growth;
- Bringing in the right advisors to get it into shape to scale; and
- Making it attractive to investors.

Of course, the main goal, with Raymond's guidance, was to work together to form an ambitious financial plan to take Soundmouse into the next chapter of growth and to provide some liquidity to the co-founders.

Raymond used his black book of contacts within The CFO Centre to bring in the full suite of professional advisors they needed to make Soundmouse investable and complete the transaction. Kirk acknowledges that having the right relationships in place and ready to go, i.e., knowing who to bring in and when was vital in keeping on track. That and Raymond's ability to present the business to investors were crucial.

The relationship

When I ask Kirk about his relationship with Raymond and why it worked so well, he talks about Raymond being able to get along with anyone, like a chameleon. Kirk refers to him as someone focused on priorities and knowing what to do, with whom, and when.

Moreover, Kirk finally felt comfortable with Raymond on board and in charge of the numbers to let go of monitoring the daily cash levels. That was a big step.

Though working part-time and often off-site through Covid, gaining access to Raymond was never a problem. He was always available for Kirk, whether evenings, weekends, or holidays; he consistently made time, and it felt to Kirk that he was Raymond's only client; he never felt as if he was in a queue or not a priority. This helped Kirk feel in control.

The freedom

In January 2023, the US music tech platform Orfium acquired Sound-mouse, and Kirk and his partner Charles partially divested.

Kirk had his freedom and a role going forwards with Orfium to continue with his team.

It was the best of all worlds.

Group Five, South Africa – Anthony Clacher, Group CFO

The rescue

It was December 2018, and Anthony Clacher, a seasoned CFO with significant experience in well-known, large African corporations covering manufacturing, distribution, construction, and energy sectors, was considering his next role.

He was headhunted to join Group Five, a public company listed on the Johannesburg Stock Exchange in South Africa, as Group CFO. Group Five provided global construction, project management, and supply in infrastructure, energy, resources, toll road construction, operations and management services, property development, and manufacturing. Anthony wanted to gain first-hand exposure at a large publicly quoted organisation, as he had previously worked at a subsidiary level for listed entities.

What he didn't realise at this point, though, was that not only would he tick this box for his CV, but Group Five would add so much more to his experience and knowledge.

The CFO role at Group Five came up due to the resignation of the former CFO. Anthony knew the organisation was in some financial difficulty when he joined, but he wasn't aware of the extent and scope of the problem and nor did he know, at this point, just how much this role would change his life.

Within a few weeks of walking through the door, he saw that Group Five could not pay its debts as they fell due. It had borrowings of some ZAR 5 billion, and it couldn't make the short-term commitments coming up on its bridge financing due in full in a couple of months. Only certain of the current projects were profitable, and calls had been made on performance bonds which had a material impact on the Group's liquidity position. Due to reduced infrastructure development in South Africa, Group Five's pipeline contracted, which had knock-on effects for a business geared towards growth. It was exacerbated by its lenders not providing further support to curtail their growing exposure.

During this time, the Group CEO also resigned, and a non-executive director stepped in as an interim CEO for a few months. Anthony, being new to the Group, was faced with an insurmountable task of navigating the way forward, which included:

- Delivering lenders' weekly requirements, including detailed cash flow forecasts, which were not being achieved. Additional requests for funding were not supported by the lenders;
- Ensuring stock exchange compliance and providing related announcements for the looming reporting deadline for the December interims;
- Adopting the role of major shareholder interface to support a proposed rights issue;
- Investigating alternative financing sources which required an assessment;
- Dealing with group auditor resignations which were retroactive to the beginning of the financial year June 2018, covering the majority of 179 subsidiaries spanning 38 countries, on the back of the resignation of key senior financial incumbents;
- Getting up to speed with various streams and management of material assets disposal processes which had commenced before his appointment; and
- Developing revised strategies for each business unit which in many cases required a deep drill down to the core drivers and included retrenchment programmes, cost reduction strategies, and the buy-in of remaining management under severe trading circumstances.

The list is not exhaustive and paints a broad picture of the Group's challenges.

The Board had no option but to place the major trading subsidiary into Business Rescue or face liquidation.

Business Rescue is a formal legal process in South Africa designed specifically to rehabilitate financially distressed organisations. It operates as follows: a temporary moratorium (or stay) on the rights of claimants (for example, creditors) is imposed, before the company, its business, and property are placed under the temporary supervision of a Business Rescue Practitioner (BRP). Finally, the rehabilitation process is facilitated by developing and implementing a Business Rescue plan, which, if approved, restructures a company's business, property, and management of its affairs (Hart & Mello, 2022).

Business Rescue could either result in an entity's rehabilitation or place the creditors in a better position than they would achieve under liquidation.

Shortly after the appointment of the BRP, the majority executive and non-executive directors of Group Five resigned, leaving Anthony as the only remaining director at the listed entity level and brand new to the company and the role. Business Rescue has the effect that the practitioners ultimately "step into the shoes of the directors."

With reporting deadlines fast approaching in February and an understaffed finance team facing the prospect of a lengthy Business Rescue process, Anthony had to make a critical decision.

Should he stay and see the Business Rescue through or quit now and find another role? After all, none of this was his making, and it would be understandable if he decided it wasn't for him.

Anthony could see that the Business Rescue process would be lengthy and complex. Group Five was a listed multi-national organisation. It employed close to 6,000 people, with annual revenue of ZAR 7 billion per annum, and just before its collapse, it had a market value that peaked at ZAR 7 billion. The Group incurred financial losses of approximately ZAR 800 million in the year ended June 2017 and further losses of ZAR 1.3 billion in the year to June 2018. More losses and significant negative cash flows were predicted going forwards. The Group's bankers and shareholders had declined further funding, making Business Rescue the only alternative to liquidation.

Anthony had never been involved in a Business Rescue before, and certainly not as high-profile as this. He could see it would take years with enormous ramifications for thousands of people. If he could work with the BRP to gradually wind down the business and sell off the profitable entities, he would gain invaluable experience and new skills and make a difference to many lives.

Against the odds, he took the courageous decision to stay.

The plan

In March 2019, Group Five was still listed. It had total creditors and contingent creditors of approximately ZAR 7 billion, with 2,300 individual creditors. It had over 100 active construction-related projects on the go, investments in property or property-related assets, and close to 100 litigation and legal matters underway.

Word of the crisis was also starting to spread: the appointment of a BRP was headline news, and consequently, the best employees were being poached by more stable construction businesses. It was becoming increasingly challenging to continue.

The rescue plan, led by experienced Business Rescue practitioners, being specialists in their respective fields, involved delisting from the stock exchange, raising post-commencement funding for the rescue, actively engaging with clients to proactively manage the portfolio of construction projects, selling profitable businesses and restructuring or terminating the failing subsidiaries, realising value from other financial assets, saving as many jobs as possible, and returning significantly more to creditors than would have been received under liquidation. Ultimately the organisation needed to be wound down.

The team of peers

After deciding to rise to the challenge, Anthony needed the best finance team around him to execute the Business Rescue plan's financial aspects.

He knew he needed high-quality, committed people, just like him, who were used to delivering under pressure at the top level, with a wide range of skills to meet the complex and demanding roles of the rescue.

There was just one problem. He went to the market to attract people and drew a blank.

No one wanted to join him. The rescue had been covered extensively in the press, and the CFOs he approached who were looking for full-time permanent roles wished to avoid the uncertainty of not knowing how long the position would last nor what the outcome would be.

Then, Anthony engaged the services of The CFO Centre, which he had explored for himself several years earlier. By bringing in a team of highly committed, experienced CFOs from The CFO Centre, who are used to working together, he could engage with individuals who needed minimum oversight and operated at his level as peers. These CFOs are experienced and have had careers where they know how to cope with working under high pressure.

Anthony selected the CFOs to work with from The CFO Centre to ensure they were the right fit and then assigned workflows and structures to them to start executing the rescue plan.

He describes the team of CFOs he worked with and the benefit to him as follows:

> They are on the same page; they are chartered accountants who are like-minded and understand tax implications and the accounting requirements regarding compliance standards. Furthermore, they oversee resources for the nuts-and-bolts work to complete the accounts and direct the processes. It gives me time to start looking at the other side regarding managing the key aspects to support the rescue plan. This included focusing on essential opportunities and cash flow drivers, managing external relationships, implementing cost reduction initiatives through centralisation of functions, and outsourcing other aspects of the support services, developing an overall matrix of the deliverables for the CFOs, which facilitated weekly updates, resource planning, changing internal control requirements as the Group downsized, and delisting the Group.
>
> (Clacher, 2023)

The beauty of the peer solution for Anthony meant he had access to a team of CFOs, all pre-vetted by The CFO Centre, and he could be sure they had the experience he needed. The CFOs are used to working this way and getting up to speed quickly to tackle new issues. Each had specialisms so that he could place individuals with the most relevant expertise for each role.

Anthony ensured the CFOs were fully integrated into Group Five, gradually finishing all the work. He defined the scope of the roles and established an open-door communication policy with weekly and sometimes even daily meetings to discuss progress and keep things on track.

The flexible nature of this way of working also meant that he could flex up and down the time requirements to fit the roles as needed. Over the last four years, this arrangement has worked so well that he reflects he has "lost count of the number of times he has renewed the engagement!"

The outcome

Despite the complex and extensive nature of the rescue, which also had to be conducted throughout the pandemic, Group Five's Business Rescue has been an overwhelming success. It is considered a case study of how one should be done.

Significant achievements include only 13 per cent of employees being retrenched, and all had full statutory retrenchment entitlements. Some 68 per cent of employees were transferred to new employers or remained employed by Group Five. Secured and concurrent creditors gained significantly, with core funders repaid and the organisation was successfully delisted from the stock exchange.

It was recognised as Business Rescue Transaction of the Year 2021 (DealMakers, 2022).

Significantly, Anthony can stand back and be proud of deciding to stay with Group Five and see the project through to the end, knowing that he has made a difference.

Soben, UK – Scott Smyth, Founder and Group CEO

Creating a vision

It was 2011, and Scott was the happiest he had been for a long time, despite having just been made redundant!

His employer, a large contracting business, was a casualty of the global financial crisis. It had over-extended its borrowings, entered the residential construction market at the wrong time, and now had to cut back significantly.

With a technical background in quantity surveying, Scott saw the gap in the market to set something up of his own, focusing on combining professional consultancy with commercial contracting knowledge – his sweet spot of experience. He knew this offering had the chance to be a real winner. The giant global developers and contracting businesses worked on wafer-thin margins. Cost management is the key to success. Scott could see that the industry was in dire need of professional consulting experience to manage this risk and ensure projects came in on time and within budget. However, the approach needed to be grounded in practical, real-world, commercial experience delivered by those who lived and breathed this industry and knew just what it was like from the perspective of the construction site. It couldn't be theoretical.

Building a business which offered this different and refreshing value proposition gave Scott his route out of employment and into the entrepreneurial world.

When he discussed this with his wife, he had already done the household numbers and worked out it was doable. Surely, he could make enough to cover what they needed to live? Yes, they would have to tighten their belts, make some sacrifices, and forego that extra holiday for a few years. Still, he was motivated by the freedom it could bring, and he had had enough of not feeling in control of his destiny.

It didn't take long to come up with a name for his new venture; Soben stems from his children's names, Sophie, and Ben. He was soon up and running with his first client.

The growth story

Initially, growth was steady, and Scott could see his idea gaining traction and credibility in the market. From their Glasgow base, Soben successfully expanded throughout the UK between 2011 and 2020. They moved to the United States, Mexico, Chile, and Germany a year later. Soben's APAC office opened in Singapore in January 2022, and Australia in April 2022, and the company plans to expand throughout the region to match Soben's capabilities with ongoing client demand (Soben, 2022).

However, during Covid and over the last two-to-three years, Soben's real growth kicked in. Acceptance of using Teams for a first call with new prospects quadrupled their business development efforts. They no longer had to take a whole day to travel to meet a prospect for an initial consultation, and that was when it was in the UK. For overseas clients, it took even longer and was a significant investment. They had to look further afield than Scotland to find meaty contracts with major clients. Everyone knows everyone in this industry, and client advocacy is critical to success. Building a business with the skills and ability to secure high-profile projects with global players was top of mind. Being forced online was the game changer for Scott because his team became more productive, and the elapsed time for converting their new business pipeline contracted significantly. Soben doubled in size to 280 people and aims to reach 1,000 people by the end of 2027.

Scott's approach to leading his team and keeping them as a cohesive unit is finding the best people he can and empowering and supporting them to make his vision a reality. This was a long way from the environments he had worked in throughout his corporate career, and he was determined to create a culture at Soben that was one of inclusivity and sharing.

This combined with listening to clients carefully regarding their issues, wants, frustrations, and desires, has helped shape and design Soben's offering further. With 15 global locations, Soben is now present and visible in its clients' markets, but this rapid growth brings complexity. Maybe a little too late, Scott recognised that his business needed more strategic C-suite capabilities to design and drive the scale he was looking for.

Soben's wider workforce

Scott started with marketing. He'd already had the foresight to educate himself on scaling Soben and attended a strategic growth programme for entrepreneurial businesses. Through this, he engaged a coach who became his non-executive director. An introduction to The Marketing Centre (a member of the Liberti community) made him realise he was "playing at marketing" and needed to get serious. At first, he baulked at the cost. A price tag of £1,000 per day seemed too much, and he settled for a more junior freelancer who could work more at £400 per day.

He soon found out this was a false economy and a big mistake. He needed those higher-level skills and experience to design, build, and deliver the marketing strategy for his growth vision. Someone who had done this before and knew what they were doing and what was needed to get to "big." Scott soon realised that this was an investment, not a cost. He found that engaging with a top-notch fractional Marketing Director was a revelation. They achieved more than he could have hoped for and combined with a lower-level resource to support strategy implementation, he was able, after 12 to 18 months, and with the Marketing Director's help, to hire one full-time employee to continue their work.

This strategic part-time marketing support was just what Soben needed. Scott now had the bit between his teeth. He could see how to use this fractional, access economy business model to bring in all the strategic skills he needed to set up and design his critical functions and, at times, to help him solve the more complex problems he faced. They could be his wider workforce, with the expertise and capability he needed, on tap, at those pivotal moments in Soben's growth where a business-as-usual approach just doesn't cut it. This could get him through those strategic step changes for sustained success. Over time Scott brought in further fractional C-suite professionals to cover other disciplines.

Scott's learnings

Soben has benefitted significantly from engaging with Strategy and Leadership as Service, and Scott shares his learnings which form part of his blueprint for growth, as follows:

- Don't pay half price with a less skilled and experienced resource to get double the time! Pay a fair fee for this high-quality, fit-for-purpose expertise. These professionals are at the top of their game and will deliver what you need. It's an investment, not a cost;
- Don't wait until there is an urgent need and rush into engaging with a resource that might be available but doesn't have the knowledge and skills you require. Scott wished he had thought further ahead and engaged with his wider workforce earlier;
- Spend time ensuring the individual fits commercially and culturally for your business. For an entrepreneurial business, it is important to have C-suite professionals who have big company experience but are commercially savvy and can relate to the practicalities and pace of the SME business environment;
- Do your homework. Get references on the proposed C-suite provider and professional, particularly to establish how they dealt with any performance issues. You want to know that the provider will react positively to a challenging situation and support a resolution if things go wrong; and
- Use a third party, i.e., a firm of C-suite providers, to mediate the engagements. This enables oversight, account management, pre-vetting, access to different skillsets for specialisms and extra capacity while facilitating knowledge share between team members for continuity of service.

Ultimately, access to fractional C-suite professionals through Strategy and Leadership as Service has allowed Scott to bring in the high-level skills he needs to design and build out Soben's business functions for growth. Scott's approach is that once built, these roles can be backfilled with permanent employees for business as usual. However, given his ambition and plans, he knows the next challenge or opportunity is always around the corner, so he tends to keep this wider workforce as part of his armoury. That way, they are always on-hand, available, and working in a light-touch oversight way or on ad-hoc projects. He can call on them to take on the next new initiative when needed. They've always got his back.

References

Clacher, A. (2023). *Group Five: Case study.*

Crofts, N. (2023). *Holos Change: Case study.*

DealMakers. (2022). *The 2021 DealMakers annual awards.* DealMakersSA. Retrieved May 1, 2023, from www.dealmakerssouthafrica.com/2021-awards

Hart, D., & Mello, L. (2022, April 26). *A beginner's guide to business rescue in South Africa.* Knowledge | Fasken. Retrieved April 30, 2023, from www.fasken.com/en/knowledge/2022/04/26-a-beginners-guide-to-business-rescue-in-south-africa

Holos Change (2022, October 24). *Who we are – Holos Change.* Retrieved April 10, 2023, from https://holoschange.com/who-we-are/

Paine, A. (2023, January 16). *Music tech platform Orfium acquires music reporting service Soundmouse.* Publishing | Music Week. Retrieved April 10, 2023, from www.musicweek.com/publishing/read/music-tech-platform-orfium-acquires-music-reporting-service-soundmouse/087247

PRS for Music. (2022). *Soundmouse.* Retrieved April 10, 2023, from www.prsformusic.com/what-we-do/who-we-work-with/soundmouse

Schaefers, T., Lawson, S. J., & Kukar-Kinney, M. (2016). How the burdens of ownership promote consumer usage of access-based services. *Marketing Letters, 27*(3), 569–577. https://doi.org/10.1007/s11002-015-9366-x

Scott, K. (2017). *Radical candor: Be a kick-ass boss without losing your humanity.* St. Martin's Press.

Soben (2022, September 23). *Our history – Soben.* www.sobencc.com/about-us/our-history/

The Firm of C-Suite Providers   **7**

Introducing the Liberti Business Model

History of the Liberti business model

Liberti's business model evolved over many years. It didn't start life as it is now. Indeed, neither did it have the Liberti name.

It originated from The FD Centre (FDC), founded in 2001 by Colin Mills, now executive chair, and his wife, Julie. FD stood for Finance Director and was more commonly used than CFO back then. FDC grew as a UK business and then overseas, offering the same part-time and fractional FD or CFO services to SMEs in each country. In 2022 all the CFO and FD businesses united under one brand name, The CFO Centre.

Over time, the FDC business model was adopted by the Liberti community of independently owned and run businesses offering part-time C-level services in other disciplines. Our former CFO and my husband, Andrew Daw, chose the Liberti name, representing our desire to have freedom from corporate life.

It started as an idea

Colin was a corporate CFO working in larger organisations, and back in 2001, he realised that he had reached the end of the road in working for

DOI: 10.4324/9781003368090-11

these types of businesses. His life wasn't his own. He was always required to surrender to his boss's and their bosses' needs and follow the corporate agenda. The breaking point for Colin came after he missed his youngest son scoring the winning goal in an important football match because he was yet again travelling for business. Waking up in another European city on the corporate treadmill focused his mind. He had had enough. He decided to leave. His father had also recently died, compounding Colin's determination to be more available for his family.

He saw the gap in the market that owner-managed, entrepreneurial organisations, typically with revenues between £2 million and £100 million or equivalent, didn't have access to the strategic financial skills they needed to grow.

Yes, they often had a bookkeeper who could do the data entry and keep a set of books. Yes, they sometimes even had a financial controller who could put together the management accounts and show how the business had performed for a certain period. Some also had an external accountancy firm that compiled a set of yearly statutory accounts. Yet they needed access to the skills to drive growth strategically, from the inside out, putting a solid financial strategy in place to support the overall business plan and take responsibility for finance within the organisation.

These SMEs either went without this finance skillset, or sometimes, the business owner would have a go themselves, even though they were often not qualified or trained or didn't have the time to do this role on top of leading the business and everything else they had to do.

These businesses needed access to an FD skillset but couldn't afford it full-time. At six-figure salaries, these talented individuals were out of the question. After all, the business owners didn't even pay themselves this much at this stage of their business growth. They also only needed the skillset part-time. While the finances of these organisations might seem complicated to those untrained, to a highly qualified and experienced FD at the top of their profession, the FD skills required for a growing entrepreneurial organisation can competently be delivered in a smaller amount of time.

With a limited amount of money invested by his wife, Julie, which allowed Colin to leave behind his well-paid corporate CFO job, they started FDC. The idea was to provide FDs to growing, entrepreneurial organisations who didn't want, didn't need, and couldn't afford a full-time FD but recognised they needed the skillset on an ongoing basis or as the need arose.

Colin saw this opportunity for demand in the market. In the UK, there were many SMEs. The market was large and growing. There was also no other solution to this problem for SMEs. It was a real problem to solve.

He started offering his FD services to SMEs part-time. While Colin wanted and needed to work full-time, each organisation he worked with would only need his services on a fractional basis, anything from half a day a month up to three or four days per week, depending on the size and complexity of the company.

Colin would deliver his FD skills fractionally to a portfolio of clients, possibly between three and ten. Yet a vital factor of the offering was that he would work with these organisations on a self-employed basis and for the long-term, just like a full-time, permanent, and employed FD would do for a larger corporate.

He started searching for clients to work with and tells this story of how he found and began work with his first few clients:

> In September 2001, my older sister introduced me to her boss. He was struggling with cash flow, so she pitched my services, 'My brother has just set up a business to help entrepreneurs like you with these types of issues. I think it would be a good idea to chat with him.'
>
> We met, and I sorted out his cash flow. My sister helped me secure our first client. I remember the excitement of solving his problems and receiving our first payment. Holding that cheque tightly in my hand was a great feeling but also presented a problem, as I didn't have a bank account.
>
> I'm always keen on a referral, so I asked my neighbour about his relationship with his bank. My neighbour ran a successful business, so I knew I could trust his judgement; he gave me a glowing endorsement and made an introduction for me.
>
> So, I go with a cheque to see the business banking manager at the local bank. We got talking, and I explained my background and the sort of ways I could help businesses. He told me the corporate banking team upstairs would be interested in what I did and asked if I had any marketing literature to share. I told a little white lie that I did have some material but not with me and said I'd drop it in the next day.
>
> I quickly said my goodbyes and rushed off to the nearest printers. I asked for a pen and paper and then began scribbling out the content of the tri-fold leaflet.

I picked up my 'promotional dynamite' the next day and dropped it into the corporate team at the bank. By Friday of the same week, a member of the corporate team, who had a longstanding client whom he thought I might be able to help, gave me a call. The business owner had a company that he wanted to build, develop, and then sell.

I remember my first meeting with this entrepreneur like it was yesterday. I can still feel the potholes as I drove over them in the car park of the modest office building in the middle of the countryside. A smiling receptionist greeted me with a very, very growly dog – I must tell you this was a million miles away from my corporate days of flying to meetings and plush hotels. I chatted with the receptionist and bravely patted the dog on the head.

What I didn't realise was that the wife of the owner's business partner was sat in the corner of the room while I was chatting to the receptionist. I found out later that she sent a message upstairs to say I was ok, nice to the dog, and friendly with their receptionist. She had effectively given them the thumbs up that I would be a good cultural fit.

The business owner opened up about his business ambitions, and I shared how we could work together to support his journey. He didn't look convinced and said, 'I think I need to speak to my partner first.' I quickly spotted the objection and offered to invest in the relationship. I suggested I undertake the first two days' work at 50 per cent so that they could experience what I was capable of and the value I could bring.

I presented the potential client with a no-lose scenario, and it worked, and he signed the purchase order there and then.

I saw the 50 per cent fee as a way to invest in building a relationship, an opportunity to build trust, and a cost of sale. It also gave the client the experience of a part-time FD – a new concept. It was the best way to get inside his business. We all know that we can only influence from inside a business. We have no say or sway if we're on the outside.

The business owner saw my value and appointed me as his part-time FD; those first two days led to a relationship that blossomed over the next seven years. We became a winning partnership and worked together to build each other's businesses.

It became a relationship based on trust and belief in our part-time FD proposition. As the business grew, so did the need for a dedicated

FD. This was when I brought our first FD, Richard Walker, into our team.

Richard and I worked on the two trading entities, eventually leading to the sale of both – the sale of the first was for more money than they thought they would secure for both businesses combined. This meant that the sale of the second was an absolute bonus.

The business owner invested the profits of these sales into other businesses. Because of our approach, he continued to partner with us and use our services in those companies.

Not only that, but he was a member of a small group of entrepreneurs locally and introduced us to another business owner, a close friend with whom he had built a strong relationship over many years. I started with this business owner as his part-time FD in 2004, and he is still a client today.

I'd love to say I was smart enough to have made that happen, but my first client asked me how my business was going. He wanted to know why I hadn't asked him for any referrals. He was surprised that I hadn't! Focusing on his company meant I had almost missed the chance to grow my own. He gave me a list of three people he knew and asked if I would like him to call them. And that led to the introduction to my next client.

One thing that is as clear to me today as it was then, is building a business is all about understanding your client's needs, how they feel, and creating a genuine relationship.

Also, people love to help. Just remember to ask them!

As Colin built his portfolio of clients in those early days, he proved that the idea worked.

Joining Colin

My story is similar. Joining Colin a few years later, I was also seeking freedom from corporate life alongside balance so I could raise a young family. I was grappling with the common problem of furthering my career as an FD and being a mum. By this point, I had qualified as an accountant, specialising in corporate finance. I had also worked in a large corporate, completed an MBA, and helped build and run an entrepreneurial training and coaching business. Nevertheless, I was at a loss regarding how to mix work with motherhood.

My husband was working full-time, and I wanted to work and progress and be available for our children. I had just about managed to hold down a full-time role after our first daughter was born, yet what was manageable with one was tricky with two and impossible by the time our third daughter came along. I also decided to move to be self-employed, with the vision of working locally with several regular clients, each needing my services part-time.

> Don't you hate someone getting onto your plane with a crying baby? We've all been there. When you spot a mum and baby coming down the aisle, you are sitting in your seat, getting ready for take-off, and wishing all the other passengers would hurry up and board quickly. Mum is flustered. She has too many bags. She drops bottles under seats, bumps into other passengers, and the baby yells.
>
> And you keep your eyes down, don't you? You are willing her not to sit next to you.
>
> Well, listen, I was that person: not the one in the seat, but the one with the baby.
>
> It was May 2003, our first daughter was almost one, and we were taking our first solo flight together. I was desperately searching for somewhere to sit and someone friendly to sit next to.
>
> But no luck. Everyone had their eyes down.
>
> And then, an older woman jumped up from her seat with a big smile. She asked me to sit with her and happily took my daughter out of my arms and started playing with her, allowing me to pack our bags away and settle in.
>
> We got talking. She explained she had a portfolio career as a non-executive director, sitting on several UK PLC Boards – some of the nation's biggest retailers.
>
> Now we all know the FTSE companies' objectives regarding female representation on their Boards – yet this was almost 20 years before that! What this told me was that this woman was a rather remarkable business person.
>
> And I'd never heard of a portfolio career before. It got me thinking.
>
> This was a life-changing moment for me, though I didn't realise it then. At the end of the flight, she gave me her number, and we connected. We became friends, and she inspired me to think differently about the direction I could take my career.
>
> At that time, and I probably haven't shared this with many people, I was stuck, lost, and frozen.

I had already left good corporate roles because I felt I couldn't be myself in those environments for some reason. I had plenty of qualifications, and I wanted to use them. I wanted a career. I knew I was good, yet I had lost confidence and couldn't figure out how it would all work. How on earth could I balance a growing family with a fulfilling career?

Up until this point, it just seemed impossible. From this chance encounter and encouragement from my husband, I started to piece together a way forward that balanced building a career with motherhood.

It might be possible to step away from the traditional employment route and have a portfolio career as a self-employed FD. I could build a portfolio of local SME clients that I could work with part-time. Working locally was a big attraction for me. I didn't want to have to commute to London daily and work extended hours, as had been the case in the corporate life I had left. I was going to hire a nanny to help with childcare, yet I still wanted to work part-time, probably two-to-three days per week, and I also wanted a flexible role. By the time our second daughter arrived, I was determined to find a career where I could still spend time with our young daughters by flexing my agenda to take them to some of their activities as they grew up. I wanted to be in control.

Being a part-time FD seemed a perfect way forward, so I set myself up.

There was just one problem.

I liked being part of a team and was concerned I would be lonely. I was also aware that I would only know some of the answers for my clients, and I wanted some support and backup from other FDs. My husband suggested I see who else was doing this type of work, so I started looking around, and it took only a short time to find Colin as it was such a new concept.

We met up. I liked the idea of FDC and joined quickly, keen to start building my client portfolio.

Given that I only wanted to work two-to-three days per week, I only needed a few clients and built up my portfolio of three clients rapidly within six months.

What surprised me most about working with SME businesses was how understanding my clients were of my family situation. Many were in the same boat and saw balancing family commitments with work as normal. Don't get me wrong, I focused on delivering what my clients needed, ensuring they were happy. That was my main priority. However, they were genuinely interested in me and wanted to know about my family. Finally, I was in an environment where it was ok to talk about my children and home life rather than pretend I didn't have one.

The best example is when I became pregnant with our third daughter. I asked my clients if they wanted a replacement FD from FDC while I took a few weeks of maternity leave after her birth. They responded, 'No, we will wait for you, and if we need anything, we'll come to you rather than you having to travel to us.' And this is what they did! I clearly remember my client carefully holding our youngest daughter at my house when she was just a few weeks old while I spoke to the bank on his behalf!

Becoming a UK business

What was incredibly encouraging in those early days was that even then, there were other senior executives and C-suite leaders like Colin and me, and just like Nadim and Tara. The more we spread the word, the more they gravitated towards us. We were onto something.

By 2005, we were a small team of former corporate FDs looking to live and work differently.

We had proved that SME business owners wanted to use our services. We all had full portfolios. We were developing our marketing channels and doing a lot of networking which started to attract other FDs. We had a lot of interest from FDs wanting to change their lives. There were plenty who were, like us, disillusioned with corporate.

Over time, we transitioned from a collection of individuals building our portfolios of clients under the FDC brand name to becoming a UK business.

Future-proofing our careers forever

I didn't know it then, but over the years, I realised that working this way provided a fast route to future-proofing our careers forever! If we all learn the skills to find, win, and keep clients, we will always be able to access the market and work with a portfolio of clients. It is possible to work full-time in this model and earn significantly well or work part-time and balance with other interests. In addition, when we reach the stage of life where we want to retire, we can slowly wind down our portfolios over an extended period as the clients naturally come to an end, rather than retiring from corporate life, which often involves going from full-time work one day to nothing the next.

Portfolio working is a change of career

This is a crucial point. When C-suite professionals first consider working this way, we need to explain that working fractionally in this self-employed model differs from working full-time for one employer, even though the discipline is the same. Working with a portfolio of SME clients is very different. It is a career change. C-suite professionals must invest time and money to make the change to learn how to find, win, and keep clients.

First, if our focus is SMEs, we must transition from working with more mature businesses to owner-managed, growing companies. An entrepreneur runs these organisations, and while the functional content of the C-suite roles will likely be straightforward for us to deal with, the lack of resources in these smaller businesses and the ability to emotionally connect with the entrepreneur can be challenging.

Before the Covid pandemic, the fact that we weren't present in our clients' offices daily like traditional employees meant we had to put extra focus on this to ensure we were considered part of their team. Covid has normalised this now, with more and more businesses operating a hybrid model between working from home and the office.

Portfolio work also requires us to learn new skills. We need to know how to find, win, and keep clients. These are often very different skills from those we've developed to be the expert in our C-suite function, and they take time and commitment to learn.

Good communication skills are vital for this type of work. We are often remote when our clients need us, and it is unlikely they will have worked with a service like ours before, so communicating early and well regarding our focus, work, and outcomes are key. It also requires a mindset change for some of us, as shared by one of our CFOs who recounts:

> When I started as a part-time CFO, I thought it was all about me and getting the lifestyle I wanted. I would work with my clients but became agitated and annoyed if they tried to contact me outside of

my office hours. Then I wondered why some of the relationships weren't going so well! I realised they valued me and needed my help when they called me. I began to see this as a way to deepen the relationship rather than resent it. Since then, my client relationships have got longer and longer.

Lastly, because it takes time to build our portfolios when we first start, most of the investments in time, money, and learning are at the front end, which is different from interim work, with which C-suite professionals were more familiar when FDC started.

Early adopters

In those early days, most FDs coming forward to join were at that point when they weren't ready to retire, but they didn't want to stay in corporate. They were jaded from all the travel and the 24/7 nature of the roles.

There were also a few female FDs whose children were more self-sufficient and realised they could combine working as a part-time FD with the flexibility to be around at home for them. This was a route back into work.

Both categories of FDs coming forward were interesting because they could afford to transition to part-time work. Given it can take up to a year to establish an entire portfolio of clients, they had enough financial runway to build their portfolios. Later in their careers, the former had paid off their mortgages, and their children had left home. The latter often had a partner still working full-time, and this was a move back into work from looking after the children full-time.

Part-time versus interim versus external consultancy

It is important to distinguish between part-time portfolio work, interim work, and external consultancy.

For the former, the service provider delivers a permanent part-time C-suite service to each client every week, month, and year, usually with a regular time commitment from half a day per month up to three or four days per week. Hiring a full-time resource or interim provider has been the traditional route if a business requires more than four days per week of involvement over a long period. Now clients also have the option to move to a team approach using Strategy and Leadership as Service. The key benefit of fractional portfolio working is its flexibility in time commitment, i.e., clients can flex time up and down in line with their needs. Regarding earning potential for C-suite professionals, they start from zero and gradually build up as they bring on more clients. The goal is to build a portfolio of clients which matches the number of days per week the executives want to work. Once they complete their portfolio, it can be relatively stable. A portfolio also diversifies their risk, as it is unlikely they will lose their whole client base overnight. C-suite executives will foresee any changes to their portfolio, for example, if a client sells their business and the acquiring company fulfils the role. They can plan to bring on a new client when the gap in their portfolio arises. This is a move from job security (when a professional holds down a full-time job with just one company) towards income security, where the professional receives income from a portfolio of clients, thus spreading and limiting the risk of losing income if something negative happens to one of the organisations in the portfolio.

The downside of portfolio working is that it takes time to establish, and the C-suite professional must learn and implement the skills to find, win, and keep clients. This is all part of the training built into the business model, yet it still isn't for everyone. What's more, the executive needs some other form of income (savings, redundancy, or backup from others) to support themselves through the period of building the portfolio, which can take up to a year. Of course, as the Strategy and Leadership as Service industry gains momentum with wider acceptance, the elapsed time to get going will improve.

In contrast to part-time, interim providers typically deliver full-time services to complete a specific project with a start and end date. Due to the intense and full-time nature of these roles, individuals who offer this service can only work with one client at a time, and they move from one full-time interim position to the next, taking holidays and breaks between roles. Businesses that generally require these temporary services are mid-to-large corporates rather than SMEs. Interim providers tend to be self-employed, and they only earn when they are working. Professional interim executives at the C-suite level enjoy the variety of working with different organisations, using the roles to pick up a great deal of experience in functions and sectors. After a while, however, some interim professionals get fed up with the feast and famine, the on-off nature of the work, and the unpredictability of the role and location begin to take their toll. They want to belong somewhere permanently rather than feel like a business nomad, always moving to the next assignment. It is at this point that interim providers sometimes make the switch to fractional work.

External consultancy does have a place in the SME business community. Organisations that provide this service deliver expert advice, e.g., management consultants, external accountants, and taxation advisors for the finance function. Engagements are usually project-like rather than continuous services. Consultants work from an "outside-in" perspective, never taking on a business position akin to C-suite portfolio professionals. They are also often traditionally employed by the consultancy business.

Regional directors (RDs)

As FDC grew with more FDs joining, we started looking at how to organise ourselves.

We realised that we needed two different skillsets within the business. Of course, we needed the skillset of our C-suite professionals (FDs back then) to deliver the services to the client. This was crucial.

Yet we also realised that we required another role in the organisation, that of the RD. We recognised that we needed individuals who could lead our teams of C-suite executives locally in each region, bring new members into the team and ensure they were happy working with our clients and vice versa. We needed RDs with team leadership skills and an ability to build relationships to find, win, and keep clients and team members. In those days, we also thought it was important for them to have a background in the relevant C-suite discipline.

It was our early adopter FDs initially who became our RDs. I focused on building our first-ever region in the Thames Valley in the UK, bringing together a small team of FDs living locally to service clients across the territory.

Having a local presence for our clients and team members was important. We could regularly get together physically as a team and support each other as we built our portfolios. This sense of belonging became a crucial part of our strong growth. Because while our FDs wanted to maintain an element of independence through being self-employed, they also wanted to belong and have a community to gravitate towards for support. Our structure gave them the best of both worlds.

We started to build out FDC in the UK in this way. We divided the country into regions, finding an RD to lead each one and then attracting FDs into their teams.

I became increasingly interested in building the business rather than delivering FD services and started focusing on finding new RDs. Through this approach, we quickly built-up national coverage.

Because this was a new service back then, and we were creating a new market, we have always had to spend a lot of time educating the SME population and market of potential FDs about our service. Our model has always been one where we create demand as we go. We have never had a strong pipeline of clients waiting for our services. Instead, we involve everyone in the business in finding, winning, and keeping clients through various marketing channels and convert the work as we go. Our model has always involved using our C-suite executives as integral to our regional marketing. We train our team and help them learn the skills to build a portfolio of clients, and then we support them to do so with the help of the RD and other team members.

Developing partnerships

Another critical aspect of our strong growth in those early days was our desire to partner with other professional services firms. We were already finding clients and new team members through active networking, which was going well. Yet we thought there could be a more coordinated way. We began forming deep partnerships with organisations that served our potential client base. We wanted to build a network of trusted partners we could rely on to deliver complementary services to our clients. We took advice from specialists on how to develop strategic partnerships and rolled the approach out across FDC. We performed many roadshows around the UK, introducing it to our team and incorporating it in our induction for all new joiners. It was a defensive strategy in that if a partnership firm was working with us and it was going well, why would they go elsewhere? It was also progressive because it was a good way to gain access to many potential clients. We introduced this approach in 2006 and it doubled our growth in the following years.

Buying a competitor

In 2008, we had the opportunity to buy our major competitor. This was an exciting time for us and emphasised some critical points about the market we were servicing. Like us, this organisation started in 2001. By 2008, the company had a core of C-suite executives with clients. Its strategy to gain new clients up to this point was an above-the-line approach using traditional marketing, PR activities, and the resourcefulness of the core of "natural" part-time FDs.

After being approached by them, we took the opportunity to acquire them. This was a significant move for us as we immediately increased the size of our team, and the outside world saw it as a surprise move. Our lower profile and guerrilla, direct marketing approach combined with our partner strategy meant we weren't a well-known brand, just to those clients and partners with whom we worked. We were bigger than our competitor in revenue, the number of clients, and people, but their slick advertising and PR campaigns meant they appeared to have more scale.

Going global

By 2009, we had created a national UK business, and our sights started wandering overseas. We were ambitious and excited by what we had created.

The global market potential for SMEs was huge. Owner-managed entrepreneurial businesses were facing the same issues in many other countries. They needed a strategic financial skillset to help them grow but didn't want, didn't need, and couldn't afford it full-time. In tandem, more and more CFOs wanted to work this way.

We realised we were creating a movement, with CFOs wanting to build a career doing the work they loved, with the people they liked, and earning the money they needed.

We knew that there would be other countries which would welcome this concept.

Through mutual contacts and a CFO from our UK business deciding independently to emigrate to Perth, we set up in Australia. While it was a long way away, we were encouraged by having close contacts from our partner network who were happy to give us a soft landing and help us connect with individuals, businesses, and other professional advisors who might be interested in our concept. We carried out a few fact-finding trips and set up the business shortly afterwards. We used the same structure in our overseas territories as at home, with the addition of a Country Leader to lead our team of RDs, CFOs, and support team members.

Australia was quickly followed in 2010 by South Africa, and in 2011 we opened in Canada.

Our criteria for choosing a country were initially decided by it being English-speaking and as culturally aligned to the UK as we could find.

We wanted a substantial SME population and CFOs with drivers to live and work differently. Our business model also needed to work, i.e., it is acceptable for C-suite professionals to provide services to clients on a self-employed basis, and we were keen that the country had a recognised accounting qualification for CFOs.

From 2011 to 2019, we focused on aggressively building our footprint globally, opening at least one new country annually, including Singapore, Netherlands, Hong Kong and Greater China, India, USA, Belgium, New Zealand, Ireland, and Italy.

Taking our business global like this meant that we were starting to be able to offer a whole new level of service to SMEs who wanted to go international. Going global is more accessible now but still complex, and with our teams in many countries worldwide, we began to help our clients become multi-national too. We can also provide contacts to our clients in other geographies, helping them establish supply chains or new markets – with our growing team of CFOs and our breadth and depth of knowledge, we can always get the answer for our clients, and our CFO team feel fully supported as they also know that someone in our team will be able to help them if they don't know the solution. Critically, our overseas expansion has given us first-hand experience of the challenges facing SMEs when going global. This growth path has taught us countless lessons, and we are still learning.

As the Covid-19 pandemic began to recede, we opened Germany in 2021, and we plan to continue our strategy of one new country per year going forwards.

The CFO Centre

As we grew internationally, we used branding for our name, which seemed most appropriate in each local geography, e.g., FDC in the UK, Ireland, and South Africa, and CFOC in other countries. In 2022, we decided it would benefit the business to operate globally under a single brand name, so all our FD and CFO businesses united as The CFO Centre.

Liberti

We could see the opportunity for other C-suite disciplines to work this way. From 2011 onwards, we developed the Liberti community of independently owned and run businesses to offer part-time C-suite level services to further C-suite domains. These businesses are UK based and beginning to expand internationally. Importantly, they often engage the appropriate fractional C-suite services from the other disciplines within the Liberti community to help scale and accelerate their growth.

The new agents for portfolio workers

The Strategy and Leadership as Service business model has similarities with the "New Agents" for portfolio workers described by Charles Handy ([1994]2002) in *The empty raincoat*. He foresaw that for portfolio workers to thrive, they would need somewhere to belong. He proposed that new intermediaries, like the C-suite firms, would develop to provide a home for this new movement of professionals. Somewhere they could gather, learn, share, and enhance their knowledge. He saw them as clubs, not employers, but organisers and places to convene. This is how the Liberti business model has developed: a new breed of organisation which supports and provides a home for these workers of the future.

References

Handy, C. ([1994]2002). *The empty raincoat: New thinking for a new world*. Arrow.

Part IV

Evidence for C-Suite Access

Testing the Concepts   **8**

This chapter sets out how I tested the concepts to establish whether PO is present within the relationships between:

- C-suite professionals and their clients;
- The firm of C-suite providers and their clients; and
- The C-suite professionals and the firm of C-suite providers.

I draw on over 20 years of experience by basing my study on the most significant and longest-established C-suite provider in the Liberti community, the UK business CFOC, which provides part-time CFO services to owner-managed entrepreneurial enterprises.

The three relationships in the study are fundamental to accessing C-suite services for clients. I wanted to establish why and how this business model worked, i.e., "What is present in these relationships to ensure they thrive and continue for the long-term? Does PO underpin these relationships to ensure they are enduring and, if so, to what extent in each relationship?"

Differences between employment and access

First, it is helpful to highlight some key differences between traditional employment and access to C-suite services. There are limitations to the employment model, which prevents it from working in a way the market of clients and budding portfolio C-suite professionals desire, making it unfit for purpose in this context.

DOI: 10.4324/9781003368090-13

Contractually, the relationships for access are all business-to-business between the C-suite individual, the firm of C-suite providers, and the clients.

This is a key point.

Clients want access to the C-suite on a fractional basis and the ability to flex up and down in line with their needs. They want instant access when needed and the C-suite team member to be available at the end of the 'phone, by email, or even in the client's offices at short notice in urgent situations. They want to avoid having to pay for the time of their C-suite when they aren't using it or don't need it. Most SMEs want to grow and are immature organisations. They are on their journey towards sophistication and gaining scale. Resources are scarce and used wisely. They can't afford to pay for idle resources. It's slightly different for larger organisations in that they want dedicated skills at specific times for particular roles. Still, the outcome is the same. They only want to pay for this service when they are using it. Determining the exact input they need is challenging for both types of clients. It can fluctuate significantly in line with business changes. They want an on-demand, fit-for-purpose service; always there when they need it and not paying for it when they don't.

Traditional employment doesn't work in this context

Employing a C-suite individual to do this directly is possible, but it is tricky because of the rapidly changing needs and patterns of use required by these clients. It could be feasible to be employed directly by a small number of steady-state clients and work part-time for each. Perhaps for one or two clients. However, their needs would have to be stable, and these situations, in my experience, are relatively rare. When more clients are added into the mix, and their demands change over time, the direct employment model starts to break down. It becomes too restrictive and inflexible to be agile and difficult to work for different clients from one day to the next, and certainly not hour-by-hour, which is often the case when working fractionally for multiple clients.

An excellent example of how an on-demand business model solves the complexity of meeting the ongoing needs of a portfolio of clients is how to deal with daily client requirements.

It is difficult to manage multiple clients simultaneously and be able to keep on top of all their daily demands and needs and plan for the medium and longer term. This is one of the most frequently asked questions from new joiners: "How do I manage my diary, and how do I deal with requests from other clients in my portfolio when I'm with a different client?" CFOC encourages team members (called Principals) to develop these skills early on and invests time in sharing best practices with them when they join. There isn't just one answer here. There are various ways of dealing with daily demands from clients. Whether a chosen method works depends on ensuring that all clients in the portfolio understand how the individual Principal prefers to manage their time and signs up for that approach. It will work if the Principal communicates clearly and every client understands and adopts it.

Katrin's approach

Katrin was an early adopter of working as a fractional CFO. She has a longstanding portfolio of loyal clients. She takes great pride in giving her clients complete attention when working with them. Her approach to managing all their needs means she switches off her 'phone as soon as she enters their premises. She also doesn't answer messages from other clients when she is with each client. The client she is with is her priority.

This only works because Katrin has spent time educating her clients on how she manages her time. When starting with a new client, she talks to them about this. She explains that she will be available for them every day before 9 am, at lunch, and after 6 pm when she's not working that day for them. She will check her 'phone and email at these times and respond immediately. Because all her clients are treated the same way and know how to contact her, and she's quick to respond when she says she is available, all her clients feel heard and cared for. They understand and appreciate the dedicated and uninterrupted time they receive from Katrin when she is with them in person.

Rajiv has a different approach which also works well for him:

Rajiv's approach

Rajiv works with some very fast-paced tech clients. He enjoys the rapid pace of change, which keeps him on his toes. He also likes to keep in close contact with their business owners, so he's up to speed with everything happening, even when he's not there. The way he likes to do this is the equivalent of an open-door policy. He says to each of his clients:

"Call me any time, and if I am available, I will speak there and then, and if not, I will get back to you as soon as I can and definitely, that day."

This means that his clients will call him when he is on-site working with another client. If he's busy, he will often quickly message the client to say he knows they want to speak and let them know when he will get back to them. This is important. Business owners often want reassurance that their C-suite professional knows and is dealing with their issue. They might not need the answer there and then.

He will take the call if he has the time to talk, even when spending the day with a different client. He's careful not to spend too long with the calling client, but he feels it is important to talk and get a brief understanding of what the client needs and set expectations for anything he needs to do. Now this might seem like the client he is with that day is losing out, but not at all, because this client knows that they too can call Rajiv anytime when he is at other clients, and he will respond.

Like Katrin's approach, the key is to ensure all the clients work with Rajiv the same way. That way, they all benefit from having instant and immediate access to him.

When CFOC engages with these SME businesses, it is often the first time they have experienced a skillset like this, and the clients rely on the team to educate them on how best to use the service for specific functions and over certain periods. The experience CFOC has built up over the years means it can quickly educate the team on typical situations to expect and share knowledge and support to ensure they hit the ground running with new clients.

The Covid-19 pandemic brought a new dimension to portfolio working and how CFOC interacted with clients. As it wasn't possible to physically visit most clients during this time, all communications went online, and the team spent their days working across their whole portfolio through online tools like Zoom and Teams. The time spent working with each client shifted from days at premises to hourly timeslots. The team worked with every client most days and became even more accessible and available, paradoxically giving clients increased feelings of closeness and connection when the whole world was forbidden to be physically together.

In tandem, post-pandemic hybrid working means that clients' employees are now working remotely more often, which has helped normalise the Strategy and Leadership as Service business model.

The C-suite team will also want to know that they have the optimum number of clients in their portfolio and fill any gaps so that they work as much as they want yet have sufficient time to service each client. This is important. Finding one part-time role is possible, sometimes two, but maintaining them over time and adding to them as required means the team need to develop skills in finding and winning clients while also servicing their existing clients to keep them for the long-term. Marketing and capacity management are skills to master.

A C-suite professional can do this without working through a third party, but it is tricky. The problems come when they have exhausted their network in finding their first couple of clients. They get busy with work and need help finding the time to develop a broader network to fill up days three, four, and five in the working week. This is a widespread issue. Often, I see independent C-suite professionals forced to dumb down their skillsets to fill gaps in their existing clients by performing lower levels of work to keep busy. This typically ends badly because either the C-suite professional must reduce their rate as it is a lower level of work, thus not working to their full earnings potential, or, if not, the client quite rightly realises they are overpaying and terminates the assignment. It is also lonely for the C-suite executive. They feel they need someone to bounce ideas off or help them solve problems in their clients where they have a gap in experience. The clients are also limited to the one set of skills of the C-suite professional, one set of contacts, and one set of time, which means they may struggle to have all their needs met.

Lastly, the C-suite executives themselves don't want to be employed. This is the most compelling reason to move to a non-employment model. They have had enough of being at the beck and call of their employer during their corporate careers. Instead, they encourage their clients to call them outside of normal working hours. There is an important yet subtle difference here. They may be working the same or even more hours than when they were employed, but they have chosen to be available compared to it being at the discretion of their boss and coming from a position of power rather than equality. They know that being available for their clients outside of normal working hours helps to build better relationships with them. They want to move into roles where they are experts sharing their accumulated knowledge and delivering their hard-earned skills to make a real difference to business owners' lives. They want to give back. They want to be appreciated and valued for their services and to have a degree of distance and independence from their clients, which gives them the confidence to challenge without feeling psychologically unsafe and that they might lose their job if they overstep the mark. If done well, this sets the foundations for healthier relationships between C-suite individuals, the C-suite provider, and their clients. The relationships become interdependent, and there is evidence, as can be seen from the findings in this book, that such relationships can become even more intimate and meaningful than employment relationships.

For all these reasons, C-suite professionals are self-employed. Neither the firm of C-suite providers nor the clients employ them; all parties are happy with this arrangement. Employment relationships usually bring a set of legal conditions which need to be met by each party. The critical point of difference here is that employment relationships are generally considered the default way to engage individuals and provide the gold standard model to be emulated. Employment is thought to be long-term, with other types of contracts being more temporary – that's certainly not the case for the relationships underpinned by Strategy and Leadership as Service. This access economy business model can provide the conditions for some very long-term relationships lasting 12 to 15 years or even longer, in my experience. Moving the debate and emphasis from the contractual relationship to the human relationship can provide another perspective on how we can work differently, now and in the future.

My approach

Qualitative before quantitative

I was aware that my research topic could lend itself to quantitative research because a theory already exists that when roots and routes of PO are present, they can contribute to feelings of PO towards a variety of objects, both material and immaterial (Pierce et al., 2003).

In "Access-based services as a substitute for material possessions: The role of psychological ownership," Fritze et al. (2020) found that PO attained through ABS can lead customers to increase their service use and forego material ownership and consumption, acting as a psychological substitute for physical ownership. This quantitative research focused on consumers using digital and material goods.

While a valuable piece of future research could be a quantitative study for accessing professional services, a qualitative approach with a smaller sub-set of portfolio C-suite professionals and their clients would provide a solid foundation for initial research in this new context. This would yield further data and build the case for quantitative analysis later on. As a result, I designed and conducted semi-structured interviews with samples of CFOs and clients.

My case study

I wanted to test if and how PO is felt within the system of the C-suite firm, its clients, and its professionals. I compared PO levels and the influence of roots and routes between the different sets of relationships, which resulted in three categories of interviews for each pairing of CFO and client, as follows and shown in Figure 8.1:

1. PO of CFO towards the client;
2. PO of the client towards CFO; and
3. PO of CFO towards CFOC.

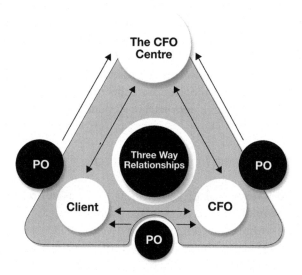

Figure 8.1 The Strategy and Leadership as Service relationships for The CFO Centre

For this study, my main objective was to understand the influence of PO on the relationships both ways between the client and the CFO. In addition, I studied the relationship of the CFO towards CFOC.

I didn't focus on the relationship between the client and CFOC because when CFOC began many years ago, the initial goal was to ensure clients had access to a CFO who could deliver the skills they needed part-time. Over the years, CFOC concentrated on giving as many organisations as possible the opportunity to use this service. As a result, to start with, most of the clients had just access to one CFO rather than the whole team. The clients knew CFOC had a growing group of CFOs, and they understood that their CFO would use the wider team to ensure they got the best solution. Occasionally, clients would work with more than one team member.

More recently, as CFOC has grown, the business acknowledges that clients' needs change over time; they are complex and cross geographies, sectors, functions, and skillsets. Consequently, through a team approach, CFOC can provide an even better, more comprehensive, and longer-lasting solution to partner with clients in their growth. Given this approach is relatively new and ongoing, at the time of this research, I knew there was only a limited relationship between clients and the wider CFOC. Therefore, while I asked clients about their relationship with CFOC in the interviews, I didn't focus the discussions on this area.

I designed the case study to be comparative, ensuring that the CFOs selected had experience in short, medium, long, and extended client engagements. This allowed me to understand how PO can influence the length of relationships.

When analysing the results, my approach was not linear but one of careful iteration between theory, data collection, and review over eight months. I share my research approach in Appendix 2.

Number of CFOs and clients selected

I selected and interviewed 22 CFOs. Initially, I was curious about how many clients would agree to participate. I wanted at least four CFO and client pairings within each comparison set to cover CFOs with experience (before Covid-19) across the full spectrum of client relationships (short, medium, long, and extended). Therefore 22 potential pairings provided some headroom. In total, 17 clients agreed to participate, giving the desired minimum of four pairings per comparison set. In total, I conducted

61 interviews. This included two CFOs who interviewed regarding two of their clients (both recorded as just one interview).

My interviews

These centred around understanding if the roots and routes of PO were present in the relationships I was investigating. Through a thorough review of existing studies in different contexts, I developed sets of questions as shown in Appendix 3.

For illustration purposes, I now share the lead question for each route and root for the client's interview regarding their feelings of PO towards their fractional CFO.

Exploring roots of PO – characteristics of the service offering

The roots are the motives which need to exist for PO to be present and explain why it might be.

1. *Efficacy relating to intimacy*
   E.g., To what extent does your part-time CFO understand your needs? (Scale 1–5)
   I included questions to establish whether the service works for both parties regarding the relationship and achieving desired goals. Essentially, is the service fit-for-purpose, did it work to meet the needs identified at the outset and is it working ongoing? More detailed questioning digs deeper to gauge the level of understanding of the broader services offered and the knowledge acquired about the services. Ultimately this indicates intimacy between the parties.

2. *Self-identity relating to identity*
   E.g., To what extent does having a part-time CFO help you to achieve the identity you want to have? (Scale 1–5)
   Humans use possessions to help form identity. These questions help us understand the importance of having a part-time CFO to develop the client's identity. For example, some clients believe that having a fractional CFO sends a message to the outside world that their organisation is professional and mature, which is the identity they wish to portray. Given that before this service was established,

a small business couldn't have a CFO, having a part-time one means the client can immediately look bigger and more sophisticated in the market.

3. *Having a place relating to communal identification*
    E.g., To what extent does using a part-time CFO allow you to be part of a group of like-minded people? (Scale 1–5)
    Prior research explains that belonging to groups helps foster feelings of PO. Humans want to "have a place." These questions focus on asking the clients how much they feel like part of a group of like-minded people, i.e., the other users of part-time CFOs. The questions focus on understanding clients' activities with the broader community of fractional CFO users. Do they meet up? Do they share common problems? Do they feel other users are like-minded? Do they share some common identity with the wider group of users of these services?

Exploring routes of PO – activities users undertake in response to the characteristics

The routes are how individuals feel ownership and how PO develops.

1. *Control*
    E.g., How much control do you feel you have over your part-time CFO? Objectives? Actions? Time? Input? (Scale 1–5)
    These questions relate to control. They establish the level of control the client feels they have regarding the CFO services. I included questions to cover the accessibility, availability, and approachability of the CFO. Was the CFO easy to get hold of quickly? How responsive was the CFO if they had to leave a message? When available, was the CFO easy to talk to? I also wanted to understand the client's control over the context and content of the CFO's work and the time the CFO allocated them.

2. *Knowing intimately*
    E.g., How intimately do you feel you know your part-time CFO? (Scale 1–5)
    This was a fascinating set of questions regarding the depth of intimacy in the relationship between the client and the CFO. I asked them how much they knew about each other. I asked further questions about the amount of time they spent together and the types of activities they did – related to work or other. Would they consider themselves to be friends outside work? How would they describe

their feelings towards each other? How comfortable are they spending time together? This was designed to get an accurate picture of the depth of relationships and their intimacy level.

3. *Psychological safety*

    E.g., To what extent do you feel psychologically safe? (Scale 1–5) The questions regarding psychological safety were there to understand how candid and open parties felt they could be towards each other in groups. Did they feel safe raising delicate issues and discussing them sensibly, or did that make them feel unsafe and fearful of negative repercussions?

4. *Investing self*

    E.g., To what extent do you feel that your part-time CFO is part of, a member of, or belongs to your organisation? Would you say your part-time CFO is your CFO? (Scale 1–5)

    Individuals can feel PO towards each other when they invest time and effort in working together and co-create things. I designed these questions to understand the level to which this was happening as an indicator of PO. How does the client introduce their CFO to others? How do they describe them and their services? Whether they feel the need to defend them if criticised also gives clues to the level of feelings of PO.

Following these initial questions on the roots and routes of PO, I also included questions on the following:

Client archetypes

On a scale of one to five, where one is introverted and five is extroverted, where would you say you sit on the scale?

I was interested in investigating whether it was possible to identify and develop client archetypes from my study, so I included a question on the individual's awareness of their introversion or extroversion.

Drivers

On a scale of one to five, where one is profit or income-focused, and five is purpose focused, where would you say you sit on the scale?

I initially included this question to understand how focused the individual was on financial rewards compared to a higher purpose for being in business. When conducting the interviews, I found that the discussions which developed from this question led to a better understanding of the overall identity and drivers of the individual, and the responses weren't just profit or purpose related but included some further drivers, for example, creating a social impact or looking after the people in their organisation.

Sharing

> What level of usage do you have of other sharing services or products? E.g. Airbnb, Uber, Spotify? (Scale 1–5)

Accessing fractional C-suite services involves sharing assets, i.e., the part-time C-suite professional. I wanted to include questions in my research to understand the level to which clients knew they were sharing and their attitude towards this concept.

I started by asking them about their experiences of sharing assets or services in other contexts, e.g., Airbnb, Spotify, and Netflix and how they thought this was similar or different to sharing the services of their CFO. I then asked them if they understood they were sharing their CFO and how they felt about it. I wanted to know if they had met and knew the other clients who worked with their CFO and their commonalities and differences. I also asked how they felt about introducing other business owners to their CFO to engage their services.

There is a dark side to sharing, some users develop territorial and protective behaviours towards their targets of PO, and I wanted to investigate the extent to which this was happening.

Substitutive value

> To what extent is having a part-time CFO a good substitute for employing one? (Scale 1–5)

Did they think the service was a direct substitute for employment?

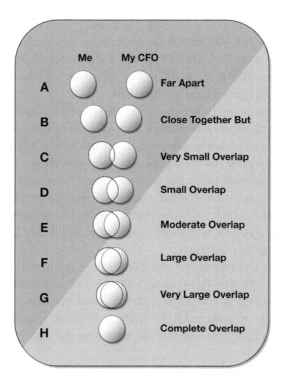

Figure 8.2 Degree of feelings of psychological ownership towards my CFO

Source: Adapted from Boivie et al. (2011, p. 575). Used with permission of *Academy of Management Journal* from "Me or we: The effects of CEO organizational identification on agency costs" by Steven Boivie, Donald Lange, Michael L. McDonald, and James D. Westphal, in Volume 54, No. 3, 2011; permission conveyed through Copyright Clearance Center, Inc.

Ownership

This question was critical to establish the level of feelings of PO. I asked directly for the client to describe, by using Figure 8.2 adapted from Boivie et al. (2011, p. 575), their degree of feelings of PO towards their CFO.

Clients chose the option that best represented their feelings of PO towards their CFO.

Mediator role

> *How would you describe your relationship with The CFO Centre?* (Scale 1–5)

I included this to understand clients' relationship with CFOC rather than the individual CFO. I expected clients to have limited feelings towards CFOC at this stage because it has only been a recent development of CFOC to concentrate on building deeper client relationships directly. Most clients still needed to experience this.

It was a good opportunity to talk to clients and to investigate if they would like a relationship with their firm of C-suite providers and what they would like it to involve. Clients were encouraged to share ideas about how this relationship could add value to their businesses. What do they think they could gain from the firm of C-suite providers? What other value could it give to them? What are they currently missing in their business and industry which would help them? What perspective could a firm like this bring that they now don't have? How would they like to engage with any suggested offerings?

This section also included a question to the client about their interaction with their RD. The RD's role in CFOC is to lead the team of C-suite executives in a region and manage the relationship between CFOC and the client. They are responsible for finding, winning, and keeping clients in their geographical area and ensuring they have the right group of CFOs to deliver to clients.

In summary, I developed my approach to test for feelings of PO between the client and the CFO and the CFO towards CFOC. The findings to which I now turn were rich and informative. They gave great insight into the level and extent of PO feelings and the particular roots and routes in place.

References

Boivie, S., Lange, D., McDonald, M., & Westphal, J. D. (2011). Me or we: The effects of CEO organizational identification on agency costs. *Academy of Management Journal, 54*(3), 551–576. https://doi.org/10.5465/amj.2011.61968081

Fritze, P., Marchand, A., Eisingerich, B., & Benkenstein, M. (2020). Access-based services as substitutes for material possessions: The role of psychological ownership. *Journal of Service Research, 23*(3), 368–385. https://doi.org/10.1177/1094670520907691

Pierce, J. L., Kostova, T., & Dirks, K. T. (2003). The state of psychological ownership: Integrating and extending a century of research. *Review of General Psychology, 7*(1), 84–107. https://doi.org/10.1037/1089-2680.7.1.84

Insights from C-Suite Access **9**

In this chapter, I set out insights into how I find PO feelings present within the relationships between CFOs, clients, and CFOC.

My analysis of the data has three levels. Initially, I look for first-order concepts, i.e., the most apparent patterns. From here, I develop some second-order themes, i.e., themes within the first-order concepts. Lastly, three overarching aggregate dimensions emerge through a back-and-forth process between the raw data and the second-order themes.

For each aggregate dimension, I share the first-order concepts and second-order themes that led me there and my rationale for arriving at the dimension, along with a detailed analysis.

I also use quotes from the semi-structured qualitative interviews with CFOs and clients to illustrate the findings.

Overall insights

While this is not a quantitative study, in all interviews, I ask my interviewees to score their responses to support their reasoning and indicate the strength of the roots and routes of PO, which could be present in their relationships. These subjective scores may be interpreted differently by each interviewee.

From these scorings, detailed in Appendix 5, I discover the following:

- *PO is present at relatively strong levels within each relationship, i.e., the client towards the CFO, the CFO towards the client, and the CFO towards CFOC.*

DOI: 10.4324/9781003368090-14

This is a significant finding. It highlights the important role PO can play in non-employment settings. It doesn't mean that PO isn't present in traditional employment relationships. I expect it to be. However, this indicates that it exists in these non-employment, access economy relationships and could therefore contribute to the glue that holds them together for the longer term. More research is required, yet this is a positive and early indication of PO's influence.

- *In all three categories: the PO feelings experienced increase in line with the expressed increase in the strength of roots and routes of PO.*

   This finding indicates that we can manage PO levels by creating environments for roots and routes of PO to develop. By focusing on fostering conditions and encouraging behaviours between players for roots and routes to take hold, plus designing a business model which allows them to flourish, it could be possible to increase levels of PO across the system and keep it in balance. Ultimately this means optimum conditions for access economy business models can be managed and sustained over time.

- *Overall, the scores illustrate that the CFO towards CFOC exhibits the highest levels of PO, followed by the client towards the CFO, and then the CFO towards the client.*

   There is a hierarchy of PO levels in the relationships in this research. I discuss the reasons for this in detail in this chapter.

I develop three aggregate dimensions from the research:

- *Feelings of PO* – factors influencing feelings of PO are the matching of the CFO and client, CFOC organisational norms, CFO skills, and the personal context of the CFO.
- *Ecosystem PO dynamics* – factors in the system can positively and negatively adjust the PO balance within it. Several first-order concepts drive these enabling and disabling dynamics; and
- *PO pathways* – lastly, different pathways to establishing PO through many combinations of roots and routes are evident. There isn't a set or preferred way to create PO. Instead, it could arise through many variations of the three roots and four routes.

This chapter analyses these aggregate dimensions in detail, explaining the critical influencers for developing PO feelings, creating the optimum ecosystem for PO, and understanding the different pathways to develop PO through various combinations of roots and routes.

Discussion of aggregate dimensions

Feelings of psychological ownership

Figure 9.1 shows the first-order concepts and second-order themes which lead to Feelings of PO emerging as an aggregate dimension.

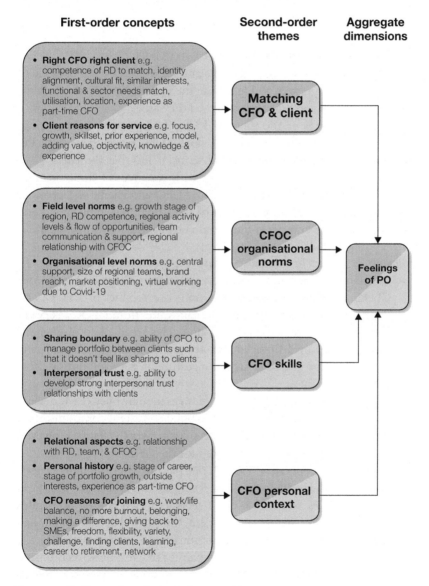

Figure 9.1 Feelings of psychological ownership

The key factors influencing the feelings of PO are matching the CFO and client, CFOC organisational norms, CFO skills, and CFO personal context.

Matching the CFO and client

I consider two areas of matching: first, the matching of PO levels in the relationship between the CFO and the client, and second, the matching of identity between the CFO and the client.

MATCHING OF PO BETWEEN THE CFO AND CLIENT

Given that interviewees score the roots and routes of PO, it is possible to understand the strength of PO felt. I use the scoring by CFOs and clients as a lens to understand how well-matched they are.

I rank the pairings of the client and CFO by how well their scorings of PO towards each other match, i.e., does a CFO's overall score of PO towards their client match the overall score of PO that the client gives towards the CFO? I investigate pairings with variances of three or more between the roots and routes scorings by CFO and client, as I consider these to indicate less of a match. Out of the 17 pairings, nine are a good match based on the criteria, and there are eight mismatches as follows:

Product or market fit mismatch: There are two product or market fit mismatch relationships. The first relates to a client engaging with CFOC as an interim contract, a non-core product of CFOC, and the second is a client too small to gain value from CFOC's services and where the model is not working. This small client disengaged through the Covid-19 lockdown, and the CFO continued providing ad hoc support free of charge as a gesture of goodwill during these challenging times.

Covid-19 impact mismatch: The CFO of an extremely busy client dealing with the pandemic found it hard to build consistent communication and interaction with the client and shares lower PO levels. However, the client exhibits high PO feelings for the CFO.

Interpersonal trust mismatch: There is one pairing where an unusual incident led to the breakdown of interpersonal trust between the client and the CFOC team. The client feels let down and demonstrates low levels of PO. Before this incident, the client shared that they had high PO levels. The CFO does not mirror the low levels of PO.

Length of relationship mismatch: One pairing is a very new relationship of five months, and the CFO is more cautious in assessing feelings of PO towards the client who feels higher levels of PO. The relationship is positive, and the CFO feels PO will grow with time.

Roots and routes of PO mismatch: The other three relationships which show a mismatch are due to variances in PO's roots and routes. Two clients disengaged from CFOC during the lockdown due to the business downturn. One of these clients resumed their engagement as business improved.

Note: *There are seven situations where I only interview the CFO. In those cases, it isn't possible to establish if there is a match of PO between the CFO and the client.*

IDENTITY MATCHING BETWEEN THE CFO AND CLIENT

The identity alignment between the client and CFO is a first-order concept and a significant pathway towards creating PO feelings. I compare the identity scoring between CFOs and clients. During the interviews, I ask the client and CFO about their focus as a proxy for identity. I acknowledge this is quite a crude measure and only a guide. Yet, in general, the initial findings suggest that CFOs with a customer-focused identity are most likely to create good alignment with their clients to help them achieve their chosen identity, whatever that may be. Also, those CFOs who articulate a different focus or identity to their client and are not customer-focused generally show more misalignment of PO.

CFOC organisational norms

Field and organisational level norms, i.e., the way the teams of CFOs are set up, supported, and structured throughout CFOC both locally in the region and centrally, are first-order concepts influencing the second-order theme of CFOC organisational norms.

CFO skills

SHARING BOUNDARY

CFOs who can create high PO levels in client relationships are also very careful in managing the boundaries between clients. This means their clients do not feel like they are sharing their services with other clients. While the CFOs work for several clients simultaneously, they have highly developed organisational and communication skills. They can ensure each client feels as if they are their only client. All clients interviewed knew their CFO works with other businesses; some have met and even interacted with the other clients in the CFO's portfolio through introductions and events. Yet when experiencing the CFO service, the clients feel they are the only client of the CFO.

One CFO describes this well:

> That's the only thing which counts, that they feel as if I am the full-time CFO.

The increase in working from home due to Covid-19 made it easier for CFOs to work simultaneously with clients across their portfolio, quickly transitioning between meetings with clients on Zoom.

Managing the sharing boundary is a vital skill for CFOs and a significant contributor to developing feelings of PO in their client relationships. This is part of training new CFOs when they join CFOC and a specific conversation topic to ensure they understand how it can work best for them and their clients. There are various ways to do it, as shown by the following CFO quotes:

> The people I work with know that I've got other clients. I have an upfront conversation with them ... if I get a call from another client, and it would be the same for them if I was somewhere else and got a call from them, I would take the call if I could, and if it were a quick answer, I'd answer it. ... if it were more complex, I would agree to 'phone them back at another time.

> I always point out that I'm not taking on more than I can cope with, so I'll always have time for them ... I will get back to them on that day without fail.

> I try hard not to interrupt the day for anything else ... I try and create the illusion that I am their full-time CFO ... I try to be very responsive ... I'll make sure I go back to [them] at least that evening.

> If I have to change the diary at very short notice ... as long as I'm communicating, and people think that it's fair ... if I drop them one week, then ... they get me to change my diary in their favour another week ... and ... keep everybody aware of the value that I am adding more generally.

THE DARK SIDE OF SHARING

I didn't find any instances where clients are territorial towards their CFO. The clients are keen to learn from their CFO's experiences with other clients (confidentiality respected) and only regard sharing their CFO as an upside rather than something of concern. Therefore, I found no evidence that clients experience the dark side of sharing (Pierce et al., 2003), demonstrating that the CFOs manage the boundary between clients.

This is articulated well by one client interviewed:

> [N]ot possessive over him at all ... if anything, it enriches ... because you feel that they're constantly being exposed to things, which means I've always got someone who is relevant.

Another client put it very succinctly when referring to other clients in the CFO's portfolio:

> I don't give them a second thought. I know he has three to four others. I love [that] we can 100 per cent up-flex and down-flex ... I know we pay a premium for that.

INTERPERSONAL TRUST

CFOs and clients mention interpersonal trust when asked what is most important to them about their relationships.

Clients:

> Trust in this kind of environment, where everything is so critical, and teamwork is so important, is more important than performance ... you'd rather give up some performance in exchange for reliability and trust.

> ———————————

> Trust, I trust her implicitly. I hope she trusts me.

CFOs:

> I am integrated with them, feel part of the family, a trusted advisor and partner ... driven by the same motivations that they have.

> ———————————

> He can trust me and ... he can call me anytime ... and discuss the issues with the business or where they're going.

CFO personal context

The stronger the CFO's relationships with their RD, CFOC, and wider team, the stronger the feelings of PO. Other influencers are the CFO's personal situation, i.e., whether they have different or external interests which compete for their attention, their career stage, their experience as a fractional CFO, and the extent to which they have developed their portfolio of clients. Generally, the more time and commitment the CFO dedicates to building and managing their client portfolio, the higher the levels of PO they experience.

Drivers for joining also play a part. The stronger these are, and the levels to which they are met and aligned to client engagements, contribute to the development of PO.

Ecosystem psychological ownership dynamics

PO dynamics are paramount to sustaining a balanced system over time, as shown in Figure 9.2.

Enabling dynamics
OPTIMUM PO

My findings indicate that it is possible to optimise PO between CFOC, the CFO, and the client, to manage and develop a sustainable system.

I find PO levels are strongest between the CFO and CFOC. CFOC provides the overall structure and scaffolding for CFOs to serve clients, so it makes sense that this relationship has high and continuous PO levels. It will be the relationship that survives individual client relationships.

There are no relationships in the study between clients and CFOs with low PO levels longer than two years old, indicating that higher levels of PO are needed for relationships to endure and get past this stage. One CFO illustrated this by having low PO levels towards their client. The CFO was unhappy and unfulfilled in the relationship, seeming to keep it going at a transactional level from a "sense of duty" of initially being engaged by another member of the business owner's family, who the CFO connected well with and wanted to help. The following quote from the CFO illustrates the much weaker relationship with the business owner:

> [H]e's not particularly bothered about engaging, and he's quite difficult to pin down ... he'd often cancel days at quite short notice.

The system works best and is sustainable when the levels of PO between CFO and CFOC are the strongest, and there are significant levels of PO between clients and CFOs, i.e., between moderate and very large overlap.

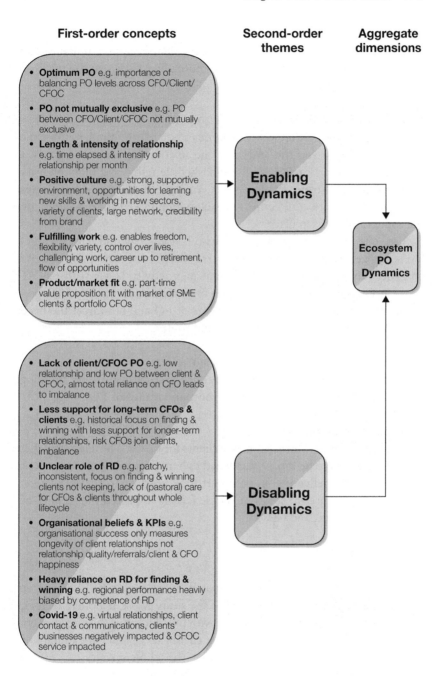

Figure 9.2 Ecosystem psychological ownership dynamics

PO IS NOT MUTUALLY EXCLUSIVE

This study shows it is possible to hold many relationships simultaneously with high levels of PO. Thus PO is not mutually exclusive in the relationships in this system.

LENGTH AND INTENSITY OF THE RELATIONSHIP

The findings indicate that PO contributes to increasing the length of the relationship. However, the length of the relationship isn't necessarily a determining factor for PO. Well-established, lengthy, and high-intensity relationships had strong PO levels. Yet, younger and newer relationships with lower intensity could quickly develop high PO levels, depending on the routes and roots in place.

Also, one very long-serving CFO, who I thought would have high PO levels, only expressed moderate levels. He was nearing retirement age and consequently had reduced engagement and activity levels with CFOC. This emphasises the importance of the first-order concept, the CFO's personal context, in determining the feelings of PO and reinforces the need to work to sustain PO using the roots and routes.

POSITIVE CULTURE AND FULFILLING WORK

CFOs frequently cited the positive culture and nature of the fulfilling work at CFOC as contributing to the roots and routes of PO.

PRODUCT AND MARKET FIT

This helps to identify the appropriate clients for CFOs. The client which is too small needed to be more established to benefit from CFOC's services, and CFOC isn't delivering its core part-time product to the client who engaged it as an interim solution. These factors impacted the feelings of PO felt by the client and CFO.

Disabling dynamics

LACK OF PO BETWEEN CLIENTS AND CFOC

My research indicates that, as anticipated, most clients had little or no relationship with CFOC at the time of the study. Most, if not all, of their communications and interactions, are with the CFO after the engagement starts. These low levels of PO between clients and CFOC are a disabling dynamic and an opportunity to strengthen the whole system.

Developing relationships between the firms of C-suite providers and their clients by introducing activities promoting PO will balance the system and maximise sustainability over time. For example, business owners suggested building a client community where like-minded clients could network and receive mutual support. This would benefit the roots of PO, like having a place and self-identity, and routes such as investing self and knowing intimately through joint activities and discussions with other entrepreneurs. The clients recognised that firms of C-suite providers are uniquely positioned to gather and assimilate learnings from their whole client base and develop thought leadership and best practices which could be shared with the clients both by function and sector.

The overall opportunity for interaction between clients and their C-suite provider is less than the naturally more intense relationships between clients and their C-suite professional and between the C-suite firm and their professionals. Nevertheless, establishing moderate PO levels between clients and the C-suite firm would balance the system and enable clients to receive total value from the firm's resources. It could also provide a pathway for clients to experience C-suite services from several team members gaining the most appropriate C-level professional for their growth stage and challenges or opportunities as they arise.

LESS SUPPORT FOR LONG-TERM CFOS AND CLIENTS

Several longer term CFOs with stable portfolios and established clients state that support from CFOC focuses very much on helping them build their portfolios in the first place. They consider this critical to getting started, for which they are very grateful. However, they note there is an opportunity to receive further support from CFOC to add value to their long-term clients now that they are up and running. Their lower PO levels back this up.

If we pursue this thought process, very high levels of PO between C-suite professionals and clients and lower levels of PO between the C-level professional and their firm could indicate that the professional is at risk of permanently joining the client.

For CFOC, its focus historically has been on finding and winning clients. In the past, it has generally been left to the CFO to keep the client happy. This could be driving the reduced feelings of PO of these longer term CFOs towards CFOC and is an area requiring attention. These CFOs felt less connected to and supported by CFOC, so they gravitated towards their clients to fill this void.

One CFO shared how he is devoted to his clients and has a customer-focused identity:

> [M]y loyalties are my four clients ... if there's a conflict, my clients come first.

This same CFO explained he needed a stream of ideas and activities to take to his clients as support from CFOC.

This finding again emphasises that PO needs to be balanced across the whole system between the different relationships. C-suite firms must build support and connection for their established team members, which will go a long way to balancing PO levels and ensuring these professionals continue to thrive with the firm and their clients for the long-term.

Unclear role of RD

Several CFOs requested clarification about their RD's role, believing it is mainly a finding and winning position with less support once the CFO started work. Some CFOs questioned the capability of the RDs to help them with their client delivery; others felt they needed to take on more of a pastoral role to ensure the newer CFOs successfully transitioned to building an entire portfolio.

The activities covered by the RD role in CFOC are key to supporting the C-suite professionals and their clients. C-suite firms focusing on learning and development and training and coaching for those fulfilling these functions will benefit enormously.

Organisational beliefs and Key Performance Indicators (KPIs)

CFOC has a belief system that measures successful relationships based on length. Several CFOs mentioned that this KPI might reflect a partial picture as some clients wish for a shorter and more impactful intervention, e.g., scaling a business quickly to sell. C-suite firms should consider including other KPIs to measure the quality of the relationship.

Heavy reliance on the RD for finding and winning clients

The CFOs rely on their RDs to help find and win clients, which places heavy dependence on having a good relationship with their RD and one with competency in this skillset. This can impact the region's growth and the ability of the CFOs to gain work.

Covid-19

Throughout this study, the UK experienced the first wave of Covid-19, with many relationships between CFOs, RDs, and clients maintained virtually. While everyone coped with this situation, some felt that conducting relationships purely virtually impacted them negatively. Several CFOs felt they prioritised their clients during this time which affected their ability and inclination to commit to virtual regional team gatherings. They felt out of touch with their RDs and fellow team members, and the lower scores for knowing intimately between CFOs and CFOC support this.

Psychological ownership pathways

I found many different pathways to creating PO as shown in Figures 9.3, 9.4, and 9.5.

Table 9.1 shows the relative strengths of the roots and routes of PO between CFOs, clients, and CFOC. While overall PO levels could be

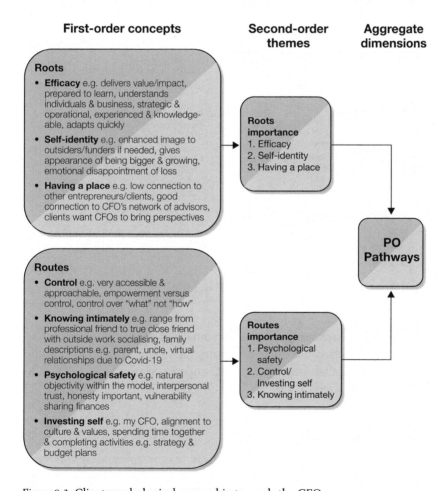

Figure 9.3 Client psychological ownership towards the CFO

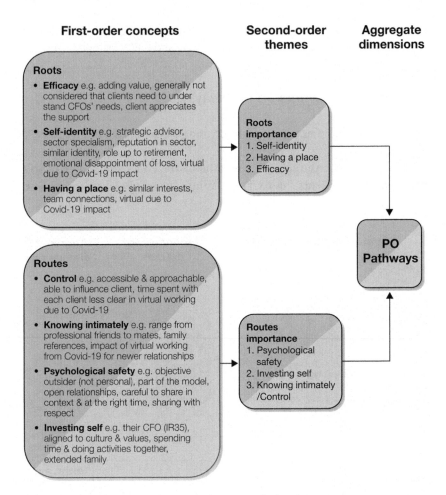

Figure 9.4 CFO psychological ownership towards the client

similar within each category, the combinations of roots and routes to reach these levels could differ depending on other factors, such as the matching of the client and CFO, CFOC organisational norms, CFO skills, and the CFO's personal context.

Roots of PO
Efficacy is important for clients and CFOs
Clients experience PO where the pathway is most affected by the roots of efficacy, then self-identity, and then having a place. Most important for clients is that the services delivered by their CFO provide the desired

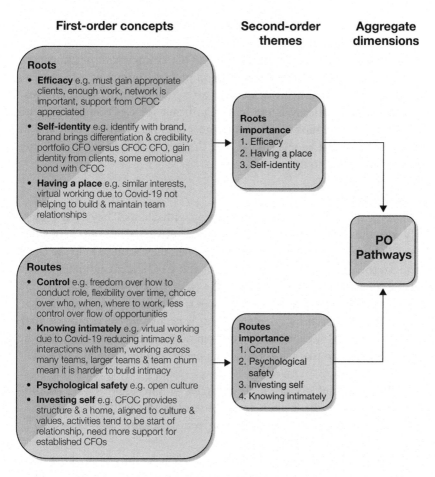

Figure 9.5 CFO psychological ownership towards The CFO Centre

Table 9.1 Relative strengths of roots and routes of psychological ownership

	Client PO towards CFO	CFO PO towards Client	CFO PO towards CFOC
Roots	1. Efficacy	1. Self-identity	1. Efficacy
	2. Self-identity	2. Having a place	2. Having a place
	3. Having a place	3. Efficacy	3. Self-identity
Routes	1. Psychological safety	1. Psychological safety	1. Control
	2. Control/Investing self	2. Investing self	2. Psychological safety
	3. Knowing intimately	3. Knowing intimately/	3. Investing self
		Control	4. Knowing intimately

outcome for them. After that, they look for a common identity and then working with like-minded individuals.

Likewise, for CFOs engaging with CFOC, efficacy is most important. The model needs to work for them and provide them a way to earn an income while experiencing flexibility, variety, and control over their lives.

Interestingly, efficacy is the least significant for CFOs engaging with clients. CFOs may rank this lowest because they have confidence that they will deliver value if clients engage, i.e., they are confident in their abilities and find it less of an unknown.

SELF-IDENTITY

This is most important for CFOs engaging with clients. They need to identify with the client. Identity is best matched between CFO and client when the CFO has a customer-focused identity, i.e., they want to help the client achieve their identity, whatever it is, or the CFO's identity matches that of the client exactly. When this isn't the case, there is a lack of alignment.

Sector focus also plays a part here. CFOs who are keen to build an identity as sector specialists gravitate towards clients who can provide that. This also works for clients, with those in niche sectors understanding the value a CFO with that background can bring, as illustrated by one CFO:

> [I]f you think about the three circles of The CFO Centre, technology, and ... client, then what I'm looking for is that to coalesce ... somewhere in the middle of that Venn diagram.

Clients state that having a CFO enhances their identity by making them appear bigger and more professional, especially in front of potential investors and funders, illustrated as follows:

> When I speak to the bank or a client, I can say I need to pass [this] by my CFO. I sound like a bigger business than I am ... which helps my brand and positioning.

> _____

> The bank is the main identity benefit of having [CFO].

> _____

> [D]ealing with a VC ... having an identity as a structured, well thought out, well-managed firm ... is critical.

There is an interesting paradox here. Clients are using an access model, which is still considered by some to be inferior to employment, to prove they have these skills in their business, therefore demonstrating the efficacy of the model.

Self-identity towards CFOC is of the least importance to CFOs. Generally, CFOs describe themselves as the CFO of their client or as a portfolio CFO rather than a CFOC CFO, as this quote illustrates:

> I consider myself a portfolio CFO ... I don't think anything at the Centre gives me identity ... it gives me support and confidence.

> I don't think I feel like ... I'm a portfolio CFO through The CFO Centre ... it gives me a sense of belonging ... and creates a brand identity in my mind.

HAVING A PLACE

Clients rank having a place lowest in strength. There are two factors to note here:

- Many clients express that they are not part of a group of like-minded people, e.g., other entrepreneurs, by being part of CFOC. At the time of the study, CFOC provided occasional opportunities for clients to get to know each other through regional ad hoc events, yet no widespread programme existed. It was also mid-pandemic, and business owners were heavily focused on their businesses; and
- Some clients feel that their CFO enables them to be with someone like-minded, yet others feel that they prefer their CFO to think differently, to bring challenge, variance, and balance to their business.

CFOs who integrate well within their clients' teams feel the benefit of these relationships, as demonstrated by one CFO:

> I gain the ability to ask more intelligent questions and for them to be more open in their responses. They don't ... put their guard up ... you get more information from people ... possibly get the chance to get referred even more often if you're seen as an insider.

Routes of PO

PSYCHOLOGICAL SAFETY MATTERS

The most favoured routes to PO for clients towards their CFO are primarily through psychological safety, followed by control, investing self, and finally, knowing intimately.

Clients want to feel safe in group settings with their CFO and be able to share confidential and personal information. Entrepreneurs and their businesses often have a single identity. The business finances are often their personal finances. The ability to share deeply personal information and to be able to be open about all their previous ways of dealing with their finances, without fear of judgement from their CFO, is vitally important. The following clients articulated this well:

> [H]e never loses his temper, and it never feels like he's patronising the people he's working with. He lands in a very considered way.
>
> ———————
>
> [W]e don't feel judged or exposed, or he belittles in any way.
>
> ———————
>
> We would feel totally comfortable telling him like, something ... is going on with the finances, and we don't know what we're doing. And it's awful and help.

The CFOs' views of their clients also show that psychological safety in the client groups is important to them, as the following quotes demonstrate:

> I don't have any sort of fear of raising issues with them.
>
> ———————
>
> [T]hey would rather hear about something than not ... they are not the sort of people that you wouldn't want to ... put your head above the parapet with. ... I think we should do that with everyone really. I think it's our job, isn't it?

Psychological safety fits well with Strategy and Leadership as Service and working in the access economy. Clients and C-suite professionals can choose to work together. For professionals, it is important to them that they enjoy working with their clients. There is no employment or long-term contract between them, so they can disengage anytime. Paradoxically, this sense of perceived freedom encourages commitment. Since each executive has a portfolio of clients and can replace a client if they wish, it reduces their dependency on any individual client for income. Both clients and executives explain that their relationship is one where challenge, objectivity, and different views are actively encouraged as part of the service. The relationships are often based on a collaboration of equals, where the expert outsider carries more weight than a subordinate insider, making challenge far easier. It is also possible that the clients have recognised a need they can't satisfy internally and want the external solution to succeed.

CONTROL

Control is a strong route for feelings of PO of CFOs towards CFOC. This could be because it is a natural part of portfolio work. CFOs are attracted to gaining control over who they work with, when, where, and how they work.

CFOs want to influence their clients yet not control them and thus avoid shadow directorship. To some extent, this is related to the UK IR35 (Inland Revenue (now HMRC) 35) regulation of portfolio working, which states that to demonstrate self-employment, the C-suite professionals must undertake their work as they determine with client control limited to practical administrative matters (meeting times, health and safety, and confidentiality etc.). The clients reinforce this view. They aren't looking to control their CFOs. They want to empower them to make decisions on how best to get the job done, and they leave it to the CFO to decide how to do the work; the clients seem more interested in the outcomes and in their CFO's expertise, advice, and views on the best ways to proceed, for the clients to then take the decisions.

Overall, the CFOs show high levels of availability, accessibility, and approachability for their clients, enabling them to feel in control. This points to strong organisational and communication skills and allows the client to feel as if they are the CFO's only client and not sharing their services with other clients. One client is particularly impressed with this way of working:

> [H]e will tell you what's going on in his diary moving forwards ... when he's not going to be available ... so you can work around that, which, is actually a very good skill.

INVESTING SELF

Conducting activities together enhances clients' and CFOs' feelings of investing in each other. These activities tend to be work-related, e.g., forecasting, strategic planning, budgeting, board meetings, and socials, e.g., such as attending Christmas parties and team building.

The more the CFO integrates into the client's team, the more they consider themselves to be part of the organisation:

> He gives me a reference point and a sounding board to what we're doing. And he approaches it slightly differently to me ... it's a good team.

> I definitely feel I belong there ... it's kind of like being part of an extended family.

KNOWING INTIMATELY

This is the least important route to PO for clients and CFOs. While some relationships between clients and CFOs are very personal, in general, the connections are at the professional level, as illustrated by one CFO:

> I think we're pretty close ... there is that thin line, isn't there that you don't want to just regress into being mates, or good, really good

friends? ... I wouldn't, for example, want to invite him down for the weekend, just because I think that that's probably a bit too involved ... I just feel that that might impede our ability to deal with the things we have to do.

For CFOs working with CFOC, there is a theme that Covid-19 has impacted the ability of the team to get together physically and detracted from building deeper relationships, as illustrated:

It's more difficult now because ... we don't have face-to-face team meetings.

CFOs who work across multiple teams felt this most.

Other considerations

AGE, GENDER, INTROVERSION, AND EXTROVERSION

I didn't find age, gender, introversion, and extroversion to significantly impact the roots, routes, and strength of PO of the relationships studied.

RETENTION SKILLS

Retention of clients by CFOs is measured within CFOC and generally represents the length of relationships. The retention levels of CFOs within this study reveal that their retention appears to be client-specific. A CFO with a high level of overall retention across their portfolio could also have higher PO levels with their client in this study. However, there are also CFOs with a lower level of overall retention yet high PO levels with their client in this research. This implies that retention is client specific and likely depends on the match between the CFO and client, the roots and routes of PO, and other contextual factors noted in the first-order concepts.

EMOTIONAL INTELLIGENCE

I did not specifically investigate this, yet other studies and CFO profiling conducted by CFOC have found that increased emotional intelligence can lead to deeper and more extended relationships between clients and CFOs.

References

Pierce, J. L., Kostova, T., & Dirks, K. T. (2003). The state of psychological ownership: Integrating and extending a century of research. *Review of General Psychology*, 7(1), 84–107. https://doi.org/10.1037/1089-2680.7.1.84

Part V

Strategy and Leadership as Service Framework: The Four Rs

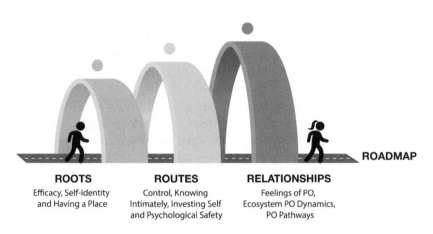

ROADMAP

ROOTS
Efficacy, Self-Identity and Having a Place

ROUTES
Control, Knowing Intimately, Investing Self and Psychological Safety

RELATIONSHIPS
Feelings of PO, Ecosystem PO Dynamics, PO Pathways

Figure V.1 The Strategy and Leadership as Service framework – The Four Rs

The strong feelings of PO found across the ecosystem in this study illustrate that PO can exist in the access economy for sharing professional services and substitute for legal employment.

PO could be the enabler of more solid and enduring relationships without the need for traditional employment and be the bridge between transactions and relationships for professional services. It could lead to a whole

DOI: 10.4324/9781003368090-15

new way of working for C-suite professionals and provide organisations with a novel, agile, and fit-for-purpose skilled workforce of the future.

Part V takes the insights from testing the concepts and details how C-suite executives can develop the roots and routes of PO in their relationships with clients and their firms of C-suite providers to create a system with PO balanced across it, in all the connections, for long-term mutual benefit.

The Strategy and Leadership as Service framework illustrates that the roots of efficacy, self-identity, and having a place, plus the routes of control, knowing intimately, psychological safety, and investing self, must be in place to create feelings of PO across the whole system.

As found and described in Chapter 9, different PO pathways are possible through various combinations of roots and routes. However, for long-term value-adding relationships to prevail and act as a substitute for legal employment, a balanced level of PO across all the relationships in the ecosystem is required.

Chapter 10 delves deeper into the roots of PO. The C-suite executives must know the roots, how to develop and deliver them, and the conditions for them to thrive.

Chapter 11 focuses on the routes of PO. Again, as a prerequisite for successful access to C-suite services, professionals must become aware of how to cultivate and hone their skills to encourage the development of these routes.

Chapter 12 concentrates on how relationships across the combined ecosystem of C-suite executives, the firm of C-suite providers, and their clients can be enhanced and kept in balance for the long term by creating feelings of PO and acknowledging there are many different pathways to build PO.

Chapter 13 then examines alternative roadmaps for implementing Strategy and Leadership as Service. How can the access economy meet the C-suite in practice? What are the barriers and obstacles to overcome for the industry to evolve? A single C-suite executive in a functional discipline of an organisation can adopt this framework. Or, by ensuring PO is felt optimally across the whole ecosystem, this concept supports a team approach which is an alternative for delivering full-time C-suite services to larger organisations. The team approach satisfies the needs of C-suite professionals who want more flexibility, variety, and control over their lives. In addition, organisations would benefit from accessing multiple specialist skillsets when needed to address their complex and growing business agendas while mitigating risk.

The Roots

10

Developing roots

The roots of PO underpin Strategy and Leadership as Service. They are the critical foundations. Without them, the whole business model is at risk. They were present in each of the relationships in the study in the order of prevalence shown in Table 10.1. In this chapter, I analyse these preferences in the context of the system and CFOC and offer deeper insights into how the roots can be implemented and stabilised in practice to become the bedrock of this way of working.

Efficacy

Jowita fully understands the importance of knowing her clients, their services, and their products inside out. She comes from a background in FMCG (Fast-Moving Consumer Goods) and big brands like Diageo. These organisations often ensure their new graduates experience all aspects of the business before settling in an area. Believing in this approach, whenever she has a new client, she asks if she can visit the factory, the retail outlets, and the back offices, to get to know the people, the product, and the whole value chain. She also makes a point of buying the product herself if possible and taking time to talk to the customers. This immersive approach quickly gets her up to speed with clients, and she does this in her own time. Clients are impressed.

DOI: 10.4324/9781003368090-16

Table 10.1 Order of prevalence of roots of psychological ownership

	Client PO towards CFO	CFO PO towards Client	CFO PO towards CFOC
Roots	1. Efficacy	1. Self-identity	1. Efficacy
	2. Self-identity	2. Having a place	2. Having a place
	3. Having a place	3. Efficacy	3. Self-identity

Morten loves working in food and drink. It's where he grew up, so to speak, in the professional world. He cut his teeth in the big blue chips and learned the ropes. Over time, he developed a love for the sector. It's his comfort zone and where he knows he can add much value to smaller organisations wanting to make it big. There's not a lot he hasn't seen in this sector, so he feels confident in his ability to impact clients. He has deep insight and an excellent understanding of the issues smaller businesses face in this sector and how to overcome them.

Antonio has a natural affinity for the fintech sector. He has good experience working in tech businesses. Given the fast nature of this sector, he is constantly investigating new emerging areas and sub-segments of the market. It means he is always up to date with the latest thinking and can impress new clients with his industry knowledge. There's another advantage, too. By being an expert C-suite professional in this specialist area, he gets to know the movers and shakers in the industry and expands his network of contacts, "You gain knowledge of people who move around the industry, and when they do other things in new companies, it's possible to get an introduction there too, which helps build my portfolio."

Jowita, Morten, and Antonio all exhibit good knowledge of their clients and industries, which enhances the efficacy they can deliver in their relationships.

The root of efficacy is all about the services being fit-for-purpose for the C-suite professional, the firm of C-suite providers, and the clients. The services must meet the desired goals of all parties. Knowing about each other's needs and the wider services offered ultimately increases intimacy.

The findings in Chapter 9 were that there was generally good efficacy from the C-suite executive towards the client. It is expected in a service relationship that the executive will be informed about the client and their industry. It's also typical for the provider to spend time assessing the needs and desires of the services required, designing their approach, and tailoring the delivery to meet these.

Most C-suite professionals in the study knew they needed to understand their clients' products and services and repeatedly made a considerable effort. Where the C-suite professional had the sector specialism required by the client, this was particularly relevant and enhanced perceived efficacy. This inside knowledge of the sector often helped to give them an extra edge, a head start, and opened doors to new industry contacts.

Having needs met is a two-way street

However, when asked to what extent the client understood the needs of the C-suite executive, most CFOs in the study took a long pause and admitted that they had yet to communicate their needs to their clients.

Some responded by sharing that they had to mould themselves to fit with the client, and the onus was on them. They wouldn't dream of asking the client to make changes. Many C-suite professionals pride themselves on being chameleon-like. They read situations with clients quickly and thoroughly and then adapt to fit the client's culture. The professionals require emotional intelligence and self-awareness to make these adaptations. Being a chameleon is helpful to a point. However, not discussing with clients how they can adjust to get the most out of the service doesn't make sense. For many clients, this is the first time they would ever have engaged with the assistance of a high-level strategic professional. They don't know what they don't know and require ongoing education to get the best out of the service.

This seems an obvious place to improve efficacy to ensure the relationship is two-way. While a service relationship exists here, and the C-suite professional expects to meet the client's needs, some balance is required. Like in any relationship, the understanding must be mutual for longevity and fulfilment. Coaching C-suite executives on how to have these conversations with their clients, e.g., explaining how best to optimise the working relationship to get the most out of the service and what needs to be in place for the professionals, will provide strong foundations for them to deliver their best work.

Understanding the needs of the C-suite team members

C-suite professionals and their clients must invest time at the start of the engagement. If the client hasn't experienced working with professionals from the access economy before they won't know how to get the most out of the relationship. In these cases, the client must be guided by their C-suite professional. This should involve clarifying expectations about how best to work together. I recommend developing a set process early on, which involves a two-way discussion on working methods, communication styles, general working practices, and understanding "the way we do things around here."

Examples of this often include clients making themselves available for their C-suite executives. Professionals can't work in a vacuum; they need regular access to the business owner, management team, and strategic and operational initiatives and decisions. An excellent way to do this is for the C-suite executive to be invited to all the board meetings and to design a cadence of regular monthly meetings and feedback sessions. Those who initiate a discussion about their readiness and openness to receiving positive or negative feedback set the tone for the relationship and give the client guidance and permission to talk openly.

The themes of service, education, and monitoring can help these conversations:

Service

C-suite professionals and clients can discuss how the service is delivered and received. A robust way to keep track of the activity required would be for the C-suite professional to draw up a workplan based on their observations, the client's stated objectives, and their initial discovery work. They could then invite the client to add to this workplan so that both parties are clear about the nature of the work, when it gets done, and the expected output. This is a live document which should be revisited regularly. As events unfold with clients, it is often the case that the scope of work can creep or change course. The workplan therefore records the agreed objectives and is used to course-correct.

Education

Educating both sides about the relevant work issues and business initiatives will be critical. Including them in briefings and updates, plus regular communication with the board and senior management, are fundamental.

Education about other services the C-suite professional can offer also fits here.

This education, however, can go deeper and move into the development of a stronger personal relationship. If the client and C-suite executive can find ways to share more of themselves, their dreams and desires, and their preferred working methods, their partnership can become even more trusting and valuable. To share personally requires the parties to be vulnerable with each other. Sharing emotions, fears, and desires can take a relationship to another level.

Monitoring

Taking a step back occasionally to monitor the overall service is also helpful. Quarterly reviews of the working relationship, inputs, and outputs between the client, C-suite professional, and C-suite firm will help here.

Agreeing the metrics for measuring value is a great way to get started. For example, metrics at the top of the business owner's list often include increasing growth and business valuation, with more detailed metrics dependent on the function provided. Then there will be the less obvious and more human measures like, time gained back by the owner from not having to run that function anymore, extra hours of sleep enjoyed due to less worry about the business, and more uninterrupted time on holiday with their family and friends, While these less tangible measures might not have appeared on the list when the business owner initially considered taking on a C-suite executive, they are likely to be the ones that matter most to them and ones that this service can deliver.

This is also true for the C-suite professional. These individuals want to make an impact, deliver value, and help their clients develop and grow. Yet, on their list of needs will be more intangible things too. They will want to be appreciated and valued. They will want to be included and feel they belong to the client's business. They will likely encourage the client to trust them and be fully open about their business. Clients who refrain from sharing openly or giving complete information to their C-suite professional will make it harder for them to deliver. Lastly, for the C-suite professional, working this way enables them to retain their independence, which means they can choose with whom they work. This will be high up on their list. Sharing their needs with their clients early on, discussing them, and making changes when needed are all part of ensuring the relationship has the best chance of success.

Relationship between the client and firm of C-suite providers

The research highlighted, for CFOC, that there needed to be a stronger relationship between the firm and the client. The C-suite professional was the face of the business to the client. This originated from the way CFOC started. Being a bootstrap start-up, privately funded, and with an emerging idea regarding a different way of working, it had few central resources in the early days. The sales and marketing machine and a sense of community attracted the CFOs who joined. They delivered all the clients' needs, tapping into colleagues to fill gaps in knowledge when identified.

As Strategy and Leadership as Service gains ground, the study has shown that firms of C-suite providers can offer further benefit to clients by delivering a collective experience. No single C-suite executive will have all the answers, skills, network, and capacity to serve a client's needs over the long-term. By introducing a more joined-up team approach, clients could work with this model beyond the entrepreneurial growth stages.

To enable a balanced system of PO across the three-way relationships shown in Figure 10.1, developing a relationship between the clients and the firm providing C-suite services is essential.

Chapter 12 explicitly covers the dynamics of PO within the entire system for providing C-suite services. It details what the relationship between the client and the C-suite provider could include and the structural changes required to strengthen the system.

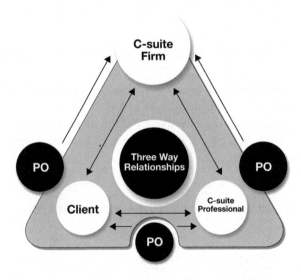

Figure 10.1 The Strategy and Leadership as Service relationships

Self-identity

> Ahmed runs a manufacturing business and acknowledges that having a CFO gives him kudos. By surrounding himself with clever people, he feels it helps his business look more grown up and capable to the outside world.

> Appearing credible to banks is an identity that Naomi wanted to portray with her business. The bank is a crucial stakeholder, and being able to introduce her CFO to her bank meant that she felt her business came across as more professional.

It was clear from the interviews that having a C-suite professional on board made a real difference to business owners and contributed to creating the identity they wanted to portray to outsiders. This was particularly apparent for businesses who wanted to secure and reassure investors and providers of finance. There was a perception that having a CFO implied the company had scale and gave the impression that it was larger than it was. In addition, it indicated the business was run professionally and had enhanced credibility. More generally, being able to refer to "My CFO" in meetings with suppliers and customers and bring these professionals to negotiate on their behalf was cited as reassuring by business leaders.

The owners of growing entrepreneurial organisations constantly strive to appear bigger than they are. There's a perception that they must look credible to attract big contracts, significant investment, high-calibre talent, and lucrative partnerships. Once they have some of these in place, it's easier to gain others. There's a herd mentality which paves the way for others to follow. A C-suite professional representing them, which is the standard in a larger business, puts these businesses into that category.

C-suite professionals focus on sector and functional experience to enhance their identity

In return, some C-suite professionals want to gain clients in their chosen functional or sector specialisms to enhance their identity as experts and help build their reputation and network in these areas. The more they can gain relevant experience through working with businesses in those sectors or with those functional issues, the more they can deepen their knowledge, build their contact base, and use this identity as an expert to differentiate themselves and attract further work.

Matching identity of client and C-suite professional

Understanding a C-suite professional's identity will help match them to clients. Those with customer-focused identities will concentrate on their client's needs, and those with other identities need to engage with similar clients to give the relationship the best chance of working for the long-term.

C-suite professionals and their C-suite firm

While all roots explored in the study exhibited a high level of PO, overall, CFOs rated self-identity with CFOC as less critical than with their clients. Many CFOs described themselves as a portfolio or fractional CFO first before mentioning their association with CFOC.

This is an interesting tension in the Strategy and Leadership as Service business model. It highlights the difference between belonging to a firm of C-suite providers and going solo.

Overall, it can be a healthy tension and has many positives. The fact the C-suite professionals are self-employed is fundamental to the model. This allows boundaries to be built within the relationships, allowing them to own their agendas and decide with which clients they want to work. They are also free to choose the type and amount of work they want. It gives the C-suite professionals agency in the relationships, which might be dwindling in employment. As discussed in Chapter 11, it helps provide some of the conditions for developing psychological safety.

Being part of a firm of C-suite professionals immediately gives the executives credibility in front of clients, i.e., they are pre-vetted, which can reassure the client and make it easier for them to engage with the concept. It also differentiates the executives from other independents in the market when talking to clients and other advisor organisations, i.e., they, too, are part of a firm. Lastly, those who want to avoid specialising in a particular sector can move quickly across industries to gain experience in new environments rather than be pigeonholed into roles where they have spent most of their career.

> An example is Vincent, a CFO with deep expertise in corporate finance. As such, when he first went out on his own as an independent, the only work he could find was in this area, doing deals. His network knew him as "the deal-maker." Yet, Vincent wanted to

change direction and further his experience working as a CFO in a business to help it grow over the long-term. He didn't want to do deal-making any more. It was too transactional. He wanted to join his clients earlier and help them develop their businesses rather than just be involved at the end when it was time to exit. Joining a firm of C-suite professionals repositioned him as a fractional CFO. It gave him access to CFO roles with business leaders at the start of their journey who accepted he had the required experience. Something he failed to achieve on his own.

Of course, the tension between being independent and part of a firm can tip the other way and have a negative impact. As shown in Chapter 12, the management of PO across the whole system to develop relationships is vital for a sustainable business model for all and for delivering the full benefit of the team to clients. Not all C-suite professionals see the benefit a team can bring. Given that these high-calibre executives are used to being seen as experts, it can be hard for them to show vulnerability in front of clients. They might feel pressured to have all the answers and find it difficult to ask for help and backup from the team or show the client they need it. C-suite professionals who are too much of a lone wolf and don't participate and contribute to the team not only run the risk that their clients miss out on the advantages of a team approach but might also lack support when they need it. They could become too reliant on their clients both commercially and for that feeling of belonging. If something out of their control goes wrong with their clients, they risk not having the relationships in the team and their C-suite firm to help them.

Being self-employed and part of a team of other like-minded professionals can bring all the benefits of independence with support and structure, thus forming interdependent relationships. It aligns well with an abundance rather than a scarcity mentality.

Tackling these issues and facilitating conversations with team members regarding the positives and negatives of being part of a team is a clear step toward increasing the self-identity between C-suite professionals and C-suite firms.

Lack of identity of clients with the C-suite firm

This study emphasises the importance of the relationship between the firm of C-suite providers and the clients. Finding ways for clients to interact with other organisations using the service fosters the formation of a common identity and is welcomed by business leaders. They want to learn from each other when operating in common sectors. Even when not, they recognise they face similar issues when navigating growth.

Having a place

> Pavin describes his entrepreneurial client as "street fighters in business." He admitted that is what he is as well, and it made them appear as "very real people" who he could identify with. He admired their tenacity and ingenuity. This communal identification made Pavin feel he fitted in and had a place in their business.

> Richard has always valued the support and backup from his regional team at CFOC. They meet regularly and are always at the end of the 'phone if he needs help with a client. However, more recently, he has taken on a buddy role to mentor new joiners to accelerate their path to building a portfolio. Through this, he has expanded his network within CFOC outside his region to a national level. He has first-hand evidence of the commonality of interests in a group of like-minded individuals, making him feel even more at home.

C-suite professionals feel at home at their C-suite firm and with their clients

This root concerns developing feelings of belonging, having a place to dwell (Ardrey, 1966), and being with like-minded individuals. The CFOs felt that by being part of CFOC, they were in a group of like-minded people, which was important to them. They felt supported, and surrounded by individuals like themselves and within a community of peers, rather than being a lonely CFO in a company. This led to enhanced feelings of PO.

It is certainly reassuring and not surprising that having a place was found to be present as a root of this research. C-suite firms are set up and designed to be a home for these individuals. To give them a community or a tribe to join. The idea is that these firms can produce so much more value to the clients they serve and each other than an individual C-suite professional on their own. The organisations encourage individual C-suite professionals to collaborate, share, and do activities together for enhanced outcomes. Together is better on so many levels. Being a team means efforts are pooled to find, win, and keep clients and strive to execute excellent client experiences. Expertise can be shared and promoted within the group for professional development and ensures clients always get access to the skills and knowledge they need at the right time. Getting together regularly in learning environments, through team meetings and conferences, enables discussion of hot topics and hard and soft skills through formal and informal learning. The design of buddy and mentoring systems for everyone means they feel supported.

Realising they had a home at CFOC was generally mirrored by the CFOs feeling like they had a home with their clients too. When a good match between a client and a CFO existed, they thought they were part of these organisations. A promising sign was when the business leader introduced their CFO to outsiders as "My CFO."

In contrast, C-suite professionals employed traditionally in companies may feel they have a home there. Still, they are on their own when it comes to being supported by peers in their functional discipline. They would have to look outside their organisation for this support, possibly undertaking external training courses and joining networking groups focused on their domain. Some C-suite professions have a regulatory body which will go some way to provide this. Still, it will be down to the individual to source this support and participate, which often gets forgotten when life and work get busy.

This is the same for C-suite professionals on their own. They need a peer community for support, guidance, and training. Notably, loneliness is a significant driver for independents to join a firm of C-suite providers. It is human nature to want to belong, and while it is possible to gain a feeling of belonging from clients, they do come and go over time. Being part of a C-suite community can be the constant that transcends client relationships.

Within Strategy and Leadership as Service, C-suite professionals can feel at home in several communities. There is the C-suite business they join directly with potentially local, national, and international teams. Additionally, if the firm is part of a wider community of providers representing other C-suite disciplines, the executives are supported by an even bigger and more diverse group. This can lead to cross-functional learning and development opportunities, direct access to a deeper knowledge base, and a broader pool of specialist knowledge within functions and sectors of the market and global geographies. As Strategy and Leadership as Service gains ground, the richness of this community provides an unrivalled opportunity for C-suite executives and their clients.

Clients' feelings of being at home with their C-suite firm

At the time of the study, clients didn't feel that working with their CFO at CFOC provided them with communal identification with like-minded people, such as other entrepreneurs and business owners.

The interviewed clients highlighted that they would welcome sharing sector insights from pooled knowledge. Business leaders identified that C-suite firms are well-positioned to gain comprehensive perspectives and learnings from their extended client base. These firms could share analysis and insights and develop thought leadership for client benefit. Most clients want to know how they compare to their peers. What could they learn from others facing similar issues? Given this study was conducted during Covid, business leaders were all facing the unknown, and there was a thirst for information about how others were coping and managing through the pandemic.

Other clients were interested in expanding their network and thought C-suite firms could help. They wanted introductions to potential customers, suppliers, and business leaders with similar issues, even if not in the same market sector.

C-suite firms and their professionals can bring together their clients with common interests, synergies, growth stages, and challenges. There is enormous potential for these business owners to feel part of a wider community. The principles of PO could inform how to develop this community, ensuring the environment fosters the roots and routes of PO to enhance its development and strengthen the whole ecosystem.

> **Top tips for C-suite professionals – how to cement the roots of psychological ownership into the relationships**
>
> *Efficacy*
> 1. Invest time at the start of relationships to learn about your client's products and services, dreams, and desires for a future state. What do they want their business to do for them? Take time to do the onboarding and induction.
> 2. Initiate a conversation early on about expectations for the relationship. What do all parties want from it in the short, medium, and long-term? How will you know when you are successful? How will you measure value and progress? What is your vision for the future?

3. Share your needs regularly, how will others get the best out of you? It must to be mutual.
4. Use the headings of Service, Educate, and Monitoring to keep the relationship on track.

Self-identity

1. Know what motivates you in your work and business e.g., Are you driven by finances and KPIs, do you put your team first, or is it all about the customer? Becoming clear about your identity will help to select the right client match for you with the same priorities.
2. Communicate your identity to your firm of C-suite executives to help them identify the best client relationships for you.

Having a place

1. Invest time to get to know and have interactions with the wider team in your clients and firm of C-suite providers. What requirements do they have that you can help with?
2. Encourage your firm of C-suite providers to develop a client community for problem solving, networking, and thought leadership.

References

Ardrey, R. (1966). *The territorial imperative: A personal inquiry into the animal origins of property and nations*. Atheneum Books.

The Routes   11

Training and coaching the routes to build psychological ownership

Learning how to develop the routes of PO will help C-suite executives to build enduring and valuable relationships in an access economy business model. Firms wanting to provide C-suite services in this way must train and coach their C-suite professionals on developing PO with their clients and creating the best environment to foster PO towards them, their service, and the firm. This will help mitigate any risk that these relationships will fail for reasons such as competition, price pressure, and lack of employment. Chiefly, all professionals in the system will experience the added benefits of future-proofing their careers for the long-term.

The first step to building these skills is knowing what the relationships need to flourish. The PO routes are control, knowing intimately, psychological safety, and investing in self. All are present in enduring relationships across the system. Table 11.1 shows the prevalence of each route in each relationship in this study.

Psychological safety

Firash explained that as their CFO, he has said things to his clients that they probably didn't want to hear. His natural style is to be honest and direct. However, he is aware that sometimes he can come across as blunt. He has had experiences where clients can take bad news personally and become emotional, which is why he takes great care and consideration when he initiates these conversations. His

DOI: 10.4324/9781003368090-17

Table 11.1 The routes of psychological ownership

	Client PO towards CFO	*CFO PO towards Client*	*CFO PO towards CFOC*
Routes	1. Psychological safety	1. Psychological safety	1. Control
	2. Control/Investing self	2. Investing self	2. Psychological safety
	3. Knowing intimately	3. Knowing intimately/	3. Investing self
		Control	4. Knowing intimately

intention is always to help improve the situation and their business and reach a better place. He explains there is a fine line between being positive and encouraging to keep the energy high while ensuring the business owner and the client team grasp the seriousness of some issues. Consequently, he seeks to create safe group working environments with his clients.

Karin owns and runs a high-tech business which experienced huge demand during Covid. She and her team worked with their CFO to build detailed growth plans and shared, "We know he has our back" and "We tell him stuff that we have never told anyone else."

A natural part of the model

Psychological safety is "Feeling able to show and employ one's self without fear of negative consequences to self-image, status, or career" (Kahn, 1990, p. 708).

Amy Edmondson of Harvard University first introduced the construct of "team psychological safety" and defined it as "A shared belief held by members of a team that the team is safe for interpersonal risk-taking" (Edmondson, 1999, p. 350).

In "Psychological safety, trust, and learning in organizations: A group-level lens," psychological safety is described as experienced at the group level within organisations as consisting of certain beliefs about how others will react when one asks a question, seeks feedback, reports a mistake, or proposes a new idea. It prescribes individuals' perceptions about the outcomes from taking interpersonal risks in their work environment (Edmondson et al., 2004).

Psychological safety is the most prevalent route to PO for clients towards their CFO and the CFOs' relationships with their clients. They shared wanting to feel safe at the group level and able to voice concerns and challenges without fear of negative repercussions. They wanted to be heard and listened to and for the environment in the business to be one which encouraged a constructive exchange of views.

Clients want to know about their CFO's issues and anxieties regarding their business and roles. Young and growing organisations don't have a full C-suite team, with the business leader often covering multiple roles personally supported by a small senior leadership team. Engaging with C-suite team members from the access economy gives them the skillsets they need to grow and scale their organisations. It also opens new perspectives and channels for leaders to gain feedback from within. Business owners and their teams crave this feedback. It is invaluable to gain insight from an experienced professional with an expanded perspective on their industry or sector. It provides a sounding board and source of knowledge to tap into, both for the business leader and the wider team. It is a different channel to tune into the organisation's pulse and heartbeat. Another leader with a different style provides an additional communication channel to the top. The C-suite executives provide support for their team and other staff members. They are another source of information and someone to confide in.

Clients also said they believed their fractional CFO gave more objective advice to them than they received from within. This is a tangible benefit of this business model. C-suite executives with a diversified portfolio do not rely on one client for their income. This takes the pressure off "saying the right things" or "what the boss wants to hear." They can be genuinely objective and testing. Knowing that their C-suite professional does not have this bias is comforting to business owners and their teams.

In turn, the CFOs felt that speaking up about sensitive issues was fundamental to their role. It helped them to do their role ethically, maintain their integrity, and deliver value to the business. They considered this to form part of the freedom they were seeking from corporate life. Many CFOs recounted that they could not have psychological safety in groups in their former corporate roles and had to "toe the party line" and cited this as a reason for leaving that environment. Plenty of C-suite professionals interviewed had come from organisations they considered political. They had to watch what they said and to whom, for fear of negative consequences. They talked about being aware of cliques and power alliances and needing to manage their career within their organisations with this in mind. For some, this weighed heavy on them and was the final straw when it came to leaving.

Working with a portfolio of clients, rather than just a single employer, helps C-suite executives feel psychologically safe in their clients' businesses.

They do not have to comply with group think or the business owners' beliefs. They have space to challenge, and freedom of choice regarding with whom they work, which is a strong anchor for respectfully sharing concerns and raising delicate topics. This sense of protection makes them braver about voicing concerns and having sensitive discussions. That does not mean it will always happen. The C-suite professionals still need an awareness of these issues and the skills to help develop the conditions to have these group conversations.

C-suite skills for creating psychological safety

When considering some of the conditions for group psychological safety to develop (Edmondson et al., 2004), it includes leader behaviour, i.e., availability and approachability, explicitly encouraging input and feedback, and modelling openness and fallibility, as well as the ability to build trusting and respectful interpersonal relationships. This aligns well with the research found in this study to support the development of PO. The other routes in the relationships, i.e., control, investing self, and knowing intimately, all support these behaviours. The ability to build interpersonal trust is a first-order concept in developing feelings of PO.

Building interpersonal trust

Mayer et al. (1995, p. 712) conceptualise trust as the

> willingness of a party to be vulnerable to the actions of another party based on the expectation that the other will perform a particular action important to the trustor, irrespective of the ability to monitor or control that other party.

While Edmondson et al. (2004) believes psychological safety and trust have much in common, and the development of interpersonal trust is a condition to create psychological safety, they are distinct. They describe three elements to distinguish the two, i.e., the object of focus, timeframe, and level of analysis as follows:

- The focus on "self" versus "other": trust equates to giving others the benefit of the doubt, whereas psychological safety indicates the need for others to give you the benefit of the doubt;

- The timeframe is interesting because decisions on whether to engage in a specific action from a psychological safety perspective are often very short-term. In contrast, trust refers to consequences across a much longer timeframe; and
- Lastly, psychological safety is experienced at the group level, whereas trust development is primarily related to dyadic relationships. whether between individuals or collectives like firms (as in supplier relationships).

An escape clause

In "Rethinking trust" (Kramer, 2009), there are seven basic rules to build trust. One of which is to write an escape clause. Kramer proposes that incorporating a straightforward way for parties to disengage allows them to trust more fully and with more commitment. The access economy business model embeds this condition without the legislative considerations surrounding employment. All parties, the client, the C-suite executive, and the firm of C-suite providers, can easily escape the relationships compared to a protracted legal battle through employment law. This can foster the building of interpersonal trust.

Time and place

The team of CFOs in the research were conscious that they had to choose the right time and place to discuss the most sensitive issues and provide plenty of context. They knew they had to raise these issues respectfully. Nevertheless, they often understood this was a valuable part of their role and found it liberating.

Mediator roles

Another role that the C-suite professionals performed was as a mediator between individuals in the leadership team or shareholder group of their clients. This is a natural progression if the relationships have psychological safety, interpersonal trust, and objectivity.

Finally, being independent and not employed by the business provides a context for the relationship that differs from employment. The balance of this objectivity with being committed and feeling as if the C-suite professionals belong to the organisation is crucial to get right for Strategy and Leadership as Service.

Control

> Yasmin knows she can always contact her CFO when he is offsite. If he doesn't pick up the 'phone immediately, he always gets back to her within a few hours and hears her out. He then lets her know when to expect any action on her issues. Yasmin believes in creating relationships with empowerment and trust. She knows her CFO is an expert, so she doesn't micro-manage. He has full control over how to do his role. She shares her needs, and they agree on the outputs, and then she lets him get on with the job.

The route of control was the most important for the C-suite professionals regarding their relationship with the firm of C-suite providers. Clients also expressed a high requirement for accessibility and communication with their C-suite executive. It is less critical for the C-suite executive regarding their clients.

Control versus influence

C-suite professionals in the access economy are not employed. To maintain their self-employed status, they must control how they do their role. They are the experts bringing their skills to their clients. The clients were very clear about this. They expected their C-suite professional to bring their knowledge and skillset to the business, to discuss with the client why and what needs to be done and then to go ahead and perform their activities in the way they thought best. Hence rather than control, influence could be a better way to describe this relationship in the context of PO between the client and the C-suite professional.

Freedom and control within portfolio work

Overwhelmingly, the CFOs believed they had control over their lives and their portfolio role as a fractional CFO and could choose how, when, where, and with whom they worked and how they managed their portfolio of clients on a day-to-day basis. This feeling of agency over their professional careers is a significant driver of Strategy and Leadership as Service. Many of them described it as having freedom.

C-suite executives attracted to portfolio work want to opt out of employment to find freedom and liberation. They get to a point when they want to design their life rather than having it created for them by their organisation. Many described being "owned, controlled, or trapped" by their previous employers, having little choice in how they spent their time, where they worked, and with whom. Most acknowledged that this was the price of being well-trained and gaining experience and skills as a professional. They wanted and welcomed this when they were younger. They were all very appreciative and grateful for the opportunities they had from their previous employers. They recognised they could design their careers to a certain extent by choosing which employers to work with. However, there is a stigma associated with jumping too quickly and too often between organisations, so there is a limit to how often they can do this.

There comes a point when the C-suite professionals believe they have enough skills and experience to offer it to others on their terms. They want to take back control from their employer and start calling the shots.

With some, there are feelings of regret:

> I have been working so hard over the years, been unavailable for my family, not been present for my kids growing up. Have I missed out on my life?

For others, there is more of a sense of excitement:

> I see this as a further opportunity to learn new skills to build a portfolio of clients and service them for the long-term, plus experience many new challenges in sector and functional development.

For those C-suite professionals who took the leap to portfolio working earlier and have been on their own, they are looking for belonging and a sense of community:

> I'm lonely and struggle to keep clients. I need support.

However, they worry that even joining up with a firm of C-suite providers, they will lose the complete independence they have created and find themselves asking:

How can I retain my freedom while being part of a group working this way?

The budding C-suite executives are all looking for their version of freedom. They want agency and space to design their life both professionally and personally. They want lifestyle balance and flexibility, to be there for their children growing up, or to pursue their hobbies, yet they also want to be wanted. They crave appreciation and value from their clients. They want to make a real impact and "see it through" with these businesses. They want variety, excitement, and challenge in their work. They desire a sense of purpose in what they are doing.

Nevertheless, on the flip side, they do not want to be entirely alone. They want some support, structure, and a community. Ultimately feeling in control of their career and how they spend their time sits high on their agenda.

The whole access economy business model of portfolio working meets these needs of the C-suite executives, striking that delicate balance between being independent and having control, i.e., being free and feeling part of something.

Freedom is a beautiful system

Freedom is one of the four existential threats described by Yalom (1980). The others are isolation, death, and meaninglessness.

Phil Jackson (2015), head coach of the Chicago Bulls from 1989 to 1998, describes freedom as a beautiful system, which sums up this existential anxiety well. Phil refers to the three-defence system, which he introduced to give some structure to the Chicago Bulls basketball team. It ultimately enabled more players to shoot baskets, thus resulting in freedom for the whole team rather than being restricted to always relying on their star player, Michael Jordan, to score.

Freedom is generally a positive concept. Indeed, in Strategy and Leadership as Service, the quest for freedom from corporate life is a fundamental philosophy. Corporate is the enemy and the antithesis of freedom. More seriously, people willingly die for freedom (May, 1999). However, in the existential sense, freedom means being free from external structures, which can lead to fear and anxiety.

We are all responsible for ourselves and our world. We make our own choices and take actions. In one sense, freedom means there are no boundaries. A feeling of being lost can result and take us to an inevitable existential conflict, the tension between our recognition of groundlessness and our desire for structure.

Freedom is not about avoiding our responsibilities, nor is it about breaking all the rules. The challenge is to balance the tension between our need for freedom and spontaneity with structure and stability.

This existential anxiety is perhaps the most interesting for Strategy and Leadership as Service to contend with and is paradoxical. The model was built to give team members freedom, yet structures, processes, and systems must be introduced for further development and scale. This should be done carefully to ensure the cultures can still accept these initiatives rather than reject them because of fear of becoming a corporate with a culture that doesn't value freedom, the very thing everyone is escaping!

The perspective that the existential anxiety of freedom brings to the relationship with structure and process provides clarity and helps communicate the need for order within portfolio work to balance freedom.

Day-to-day control

In addition to the broader concept of control that the whole Strategy and Leadership as Service business model affords the C-suite professionals, the study highlighted areas in the business model where the C-suite executives felt less in control. One of those areas was the amount of control they had over gaining opportunities to work with clients, which seemed somewhat dependent on their relationship with team members within the firm who are responsible for matching C-suite professionals with suitable clients.

C-suite professionals who take the time to educate others in their firm about their skills, experience, and working style will help them to identify clients to whom they would be best suited. It involves the C-suite professional creating a vision of their ideal portfolio of clients. This would include the sectors they would most like to work in and where they have experience, by industry, function, and business lifecycle stage. Understanding what is ideal for them and communicating this within their firm of C-suite providers will help to find these clients and identify them in business development activities. Furthermore, once the C-suite professionals are up and running with their clients, constant communication with their firm regarding the work conducted will help them understand their capacity for more work and gain valuable feedback. This three-way communication between the client, C-suite professional, and firm will undoubtedly increase the likelihood of ironing out any issues and developing long-term value-adding relationships.

Control for the client

Clients were primarily concerned with how they could access, empower, and influence their C-suite professionals. Employment brings with it the myth of control for business leaders. It is the most accepted way of working globally, and organisations believe they sit with the balance of power over how they would like their staff to behave and operate. In reality, at best, employers can influence their people, which is the same in the access economy.

While the C-suite executives can dictate how their work is done, business leaders still want to have a feeling of control that the work being carried out is in line with their expectations. The best practice is to create rolling three-month workplans with key objectives and deliverables against specific timescales. This is a vital communication tool, and regular monthly reporting meetings keep things on track and all parties appraised of developments.

One of the areas which clients are most keen to understand is how they will be able to access and communicate with their C-suite professional if they are not at their offices every day, as is usual with full-time and permanent employees. They have been used to walking over to a colleague in the office to discuss matters and value having their senior management team readily available, fostering feelings of control.

The onset of the Covid-19 pandemic has shifted attitudes regarding physical presence being the only way to work together. Before the pandemic, C-suite executives had a different working schedule at the businesses they served. Most employed staff were always present at the premises, whereas the C-suite professionals would be there one day per week or two days per month. This has its challenges. It requires thought to design robust and effective communication channels and extra skill and effort to build and maintain trusting relationships with team members remotely. At the height of the pandemic, everyone worked virtually using technology. We learnt we could collaborate this way. Many businesses have adopted a hybrid form of working post-pandemic where physical presence in the office is no longer five days per week. This has normalised the fractional model.

Accessibility and availability

Feelings of influence are enhanced for clients when their C-suite professionals are readily available and accessible, albeit not present in the office. C-suite executives need clear training in educating their clients on how this works. They need to communicate carefully with their clients upfront so that they understand when and how they can contact the C-suite professional. This is crucial to this route of PO. Given the virtual nature of work in the access economy (even before Covid-19), returning client calls quickly and promptly goes a long way to building this route. C-suite executives who respond immediately to their clients support their clients' feelings that they are not sharing their services. The clients feel the C-suite professional is "theirs". Executives with long-lasting client relationships are exceptional at communicating. They let their clients know when they can respond fully if they can't do it immediately. They must deliver on these promises as that builds trust. Most clients want to know that their C-suite professionals have heard them and that they are handling the request.

Being available also helps business leaders feel in control. It is normal to want to be in contact during business hours. However, a clear advantage of the business model is explicitly agreeing they will make themselves available when needed outside regular hours, particularly early mornings, evenings, weekends, and even holidays. This is distinct from employment, where a business leader may expect out-of-hours work that the employee feels they cannot refuse despite feeling their personal time isn't respected. Entrepreneurs tend to be "always on", constantly living their business life and often do not notice whether it is a bank holiday or late at night. The issues they encounter that they need help with from senior executives or the worries and concerns that come up do not fall neatly into a nine 'til five working week. If the C-suite professionals make themselves available and encourage their clients to contact them if they need to talk outside business hours, this feeling of control will increase resulting in enhanced levels of PO.

It is also important that the C-suite professionals communicate when they will be unavailable, as this helps to build the sharing boundary between multiple clients. Business leaders know there are other clients in their portfolios. They do not want to feel like they are sharing, even though they know they are. A good way for executives to manage this situation is to be well organised and communicate clearly in advance with clients. Asking each client in the portfolio to work similarly enables smooth diary planning. For example, letting each client know that they may take calls from other clients while on their premises works for every client and means urgent matters are dealt with even when it is not their "turn."

Approachability

How a C-suite professional responds to client needs is also critical. Clients need to feel that their C-suite executive is approachable. They need an attitude of "wanting to help and serve" at any time. If clients think their requirements are a nuisance, insignificant, or unwanted, this will detract from them wanting to ask for help.

A good example is a CFO who told me they were woken in the early morning hours when they were on holiday on the other side of the world because their business owner had forgotten they were holidaying and needed to talk about an urgent issue. The CFO recounted that their client was highly apologetic about waking them up and offered to call back at a more reasonable hour. Still, she decided to continue the conversation because, by that time, she was wide awake and wanted to help!

Always on – freedom and structure

This idea of being 100 per cent available to clients and "always on" can be considered paradoxical to portfolio working providing freedom and flexibility. Some C-suite professionals need help to adapt to this way of working. The best way to prepare and train professionals in this area is to explain the need for structure and the freedom it can create. If executives are well organised with their diaries, provide boundaries and structure to their work, and explain this clearly to their clients in advance, the clients feel they always have access when they need it. At the same time, the C-suite professional can create the freedom and flexibility they want.

As one team member at CFOC articulated:

Our intellectual property and structure set you free.

This nuance to managing a portfolio of clients is significant and salient. When busy, it is tempting to hide away to finish the most urgent work, avoiding communicating with other clients and hoping they do not need anything. Experience says this is dangerous. Inevitably other clients will also have requirements, and not responding to them creates more demands and concerns. This is where the wider C-suite team comes in. Planning for busy times, communicating availability with clients, and using colleagues to cover capacity and skill gaps are the answers to keeping clients happy and avoiding conflicts.

Knowing intimately

> I feel I know him. I feel I know his wife, his grandkids. I know what goes on in his family. He participates in our online bake-offs, comes on away days, and comes to our Christmas parties. He is fully integrated into the business. I might even say he's a friend!

> Joseph is a super, super nice guy. He's very, very friendly and easy to get on with. And we do chat and banter about stuff. And he's also supportive and compassionate about me as a person.

Knowing intimately was the least prevalent route to PO between clients and CFOs and for the CFO towards CFOC. While some relationships in the study had developed into personal friendships, most were professional friends.

It was important for both clients and CFOs to feel comfortable with each other, enjoy spending long periods together, and share information about families and hobbies without too much detail. In most cases, they did not cross a healthy line between being professional friends and mates. Some CFOs were conscious that their client could become close friends if they wanted to go that route. However, they believed it better to have some distance to keep the relationship professional and retain their ability to challenge if they wanted to.

Some clients referred to their CFO using the language of family relationships, e.g., "fatherly figure to me" or "my favourite uncle." This implied a more personal connection and closeness than strictly professional.

Relationships that had not reached the professional friend stage or where spending time together was not enjoyable had low PO, low intimacy, and ultimately were at risk of ending. CFOs with low intimacy with clients were aware that this was the case. They either persevered to enhance the relationship or were "putting up with it" for commercial reasons.

It is important for C-suite professionals with difficulties with client relationships to talk about them with colleagues at their firm of C-suite providers. This, of course, requires psychological safety. Training and coaching in relationship-building skills could unlock the issues, or another C-suite professional might better suit the client. Developing a safe culture to discuss these relationship issues is critical to resolving them successfully.

Knowing fellow team members intimately

Many CFOs wanted more intimate and friendly relationships with other CFOs, particularly in their immediate teams. Virtual working and the lack of the usual physical conferences, team meetings, and social activities during Covid-19 prevented this and resulted in low scoring of PO. This route to PO should increase as physical meet-ups have started again since the pandemic.

When C-suite executives join firms of C-suite providers, they want to belong to a community of like-minded individuals. This provides an immediate network of professional support in terms of learning from others and sharing best practices, and the opportunity to build friendships. Being on their own as an independent C-suite executive is hard work and lonely. C-suite professionals' issues with their clients are similar, regardless of the discipline. It is important to them to have a place to meet colleagues, share these challenges, and celebrate their successes.

Intimacy between clients

An area for improving levels of PO even further would be to increase the opportunities for interaction between clients. Business leaders have things in common with others with businesses in the same sector, yet there are other areas of commonality. Regardless of their specialism, growing companies will face similar obstacles and challenges to growth. Finding ways to interact and learn from others would be a further added benefit and provide a community of support for clients.

Some clients will use this more than others, and it is easy to see this as a "nice to have" rather than a priority. When Covid hit, clients wanted to talk to other business leaders about this challenge. They were searching for ideas, resources, and answers. Having a ready-made community of peers on tap would be very welcome.

Investing self

> We call him our CFO. So, you know, we do introduce him as part of the team.

> It's vital that they are aligned to our culture and values, it just wouldn't work otherwise.

Investing self with clients

Many clients felt their CFO was part of their organisation. Training CFOs to integrate themselves into the teams within their clients, e.g., the finance team, is an excellent way to do this. The more visible and helpful the CFO can be towards the other departments and units within their clients and the whole business, the higher the score in this area. In many cases, the CFOs were generally proud to say they were a member of the client, and both client and CFO described the CFO as the CFO of the client.

The CFOs who only had relationships with the entrepreneur or top team needed to be more integrated into the organisation. There is a difference between working at the senior management level and fully integrating into the business at all levels and departments.

The frequency and type of activities CFOs and clients did together influenced investing self as a route to PO. Activities included the CFO attending board or senior management team meetings alongside strategic planning, forecasting, and budgeting. These activities enabled the CFO and client to co-create and spend time together, enhancing PO.

C-suite professionals who work with the business leader and the other senior management team members rather than for them evidenced higher levels of investing self and feelings of PO.

Some C-suite professionals worked in isolation by taking instructions from the business leader and delivering the outputs. While the work might have been perfect and precisely what the business needed, levels of PO were low. The business leader didn't feel invested in the outcomes, and any competent professional could do the work.

The key to building levels of PO between a C-suite professional and the business leader and senior team is doing activities together, e.g., regular offsite away days to develop a strategy. The more a C-suite professional can integrate into the day-to-day business activity, quarterly reviews, and annual strategic planning, giving input alongside the senior management team, the more they become part of the business, and the more the business leaders feel invested.

Most clients believed their CFO must align with their culture and values, and the relationship would only work if this were the case.

Investing self within the firm of C-suite providers

Investing self between CFOs and CFOC ranked after control and psychological safety. The CFOs spend more time together and with the central team when they first start as they learn to build their portfolios. As they become more established, interaction happens at monthly meetings, sessions to share best practices, and conferences, all online during the pandemic.

Spending time and doing activities together will increase PO for C-suite professionals towards their C-suite firms. Social gatherings and learning and development programmes, which help them to build and maintain their portfolios and focus on the technical delivery of their discipline, can form part of this. Another way to increase PO is to create client communities that add value to clients and their C-suite professionals. Both clients and their C-suite will benefit from networking and further learning.

The routes to building PO dictate how a firm of C-suite providers can educate and train its professionals to create the environment and build long-term relationships across the whole system.

Top tips for C-suite professionals – how to cultivate the routes of psychological ownership within the relationships

Control

1. Ensure you are accessible, approachable, and available for your clients. Communicate your availability regularly. Be flexible.
2. Check in with clients regularly when not on-site to demonstrate your interest in their progress and to open communication channels.
3. Explain to your clients how they can communicate with you so that it fits with all your other clients and they always know how to contact you.

4. Endeavour for every client to feel like they are your only client.
5. Recognise that balancing structure with freedom brings control to your relationships.

Knowing intimately

1. Recognise the importance of sharing some personal information with clients to build intimacy in relationships.
2. Take the first steps in being vulnerable by sharing small amounts of personal information.
3. Know when you have reached the limit for a healthy professional friend relationship.

Psychological safety

1. Start building interpersonal trust from the outset by being open, reliable, and caring.
2. Prepare for difficult conversations. Consider the timing and place, but don't shy away from them – your clients want to hear your views.
3. Ask for positive and negative feedback and make time to review this.

Investing self

1. Co-create rolling three-month workplans with clients to schedule activities, desired outcomes, and discuss progress.
2. Invest in other shared activities across the organisation to foster co-creation e.g., strategy planning.
3. Find ways to immerse yourself into your clients, the best ways are those which aren't expected as a normal part of your role e.g., supporting them at an exhibition, or joining in with a charity event supported by your client, in your own time.

References

Edmondson, A. C. (1999). Psychological safety and learning behavior in work teams. *Administrative Science Quarterly, 44*(2), 350–383. https://doi.org/10.2307/2666999

Edmondson, A. C., Kramer, R. M., & Cook, K. S. (2004). Psychological safety, trust, and learning in organizations: A group-level lens. *Trust and Distrust in Organizations: Dilemmas and Approaches, 12*, 239–272.

Jackson, P. (2015). *Eleven rings*. Virgin Books Limited.

Kahn, W. A. (1990). Psychological conditions of personal engagement and disengagement at work. *Academy of Management Journal, 33*(4), 692–724.

Kramer, R. M. (2009). Rethinking trust. *Harvard Business Review, 87*(6), 68–77.

May, R. (1999). *Freedom and destiny*. W. W. Norton & Company.

Mayer, R. C., Davis, J. H., & Schoorman, F. D. (1995). An integrative model of organizational trust. *Academy of Management Review, 20*(3), 709–734. https://doi.org/10.5465/amr.1995.9508080335

Yalom, I. D. (1980). *Existential psychotherapy*. Basic Books.

The Relationships 12

The relationships needed for Strategy and Leadership as Service to work are dependent on the following:

- Fostering feelings of PO;
- Understanding that there are many pathways to creating PO within the relationships; and
- Ensuring PO is balanced in the connections across the whole system.

This chapter reviews these three themes to explore how relationships can develop effectively.

Feelings of psychological ownership

The research uncovered that the following influence the feelings of PO:

- Matching of the C-suite professional and the client;
- The C-suite firm's organisational norms;
- The C-suite professional's skills; and
- The personal context of the C-suite professional.

Matching of the C-suite professional and the client

Clients' reasons for the service
Sense-checking the clients' reasons for engaging with Strategy and Leadership as Service and being confident they can benefit is part of the

DOI: 10.4324/9781003368090-18

matching process. Again, the firm of C-suite providers will do this before introducing team members who might be the right match. Alternatively, independent C-suite executives would do this for themselves at the introductory meeting.

Fully understanding the motivations of the business leaders for their business and themselves forms a big part of this discussion. What do they want their business to do for them? What are they aiming to achieve? What are the issues, obstacles, and opportunities? What resources do they currently have? How open are they to working in this new way rather than employment? How have they performed the role up to this point? A robust fact find is required first to verify that the service would work for them and then to understand the detail of the role and gather information about the necessary culture and fit.

Right C-suite professional, right client

Finding the right match for a client will put the relationship in the best place to thrive in the long-term. Ensuring the C-suite executive has the required competencies to deliver on the functional requirements of the role is a pre-requisite, and having knowledge or experience in the sector is helpful. Most business leaders will default to wanting a professional familiar with their industry. Settling for this and thinking a match will result is naive. Challenging the business owner on why they want more sector knowledge from their C-suite executive often uncovers that they still need to think this through fully. It is just an assumption that it would be beneficial. Bringing in a team member who does not know the industry can bring another dimension of thinking to the senior team and reveal other strategies to explore. Ensuring the CEO and senior team have thoroughly specified their new C-suite team member profile is an added benefit of using a firm of C-suite professionals. These firms will work with the business leader and other senior team members to understand the role they are looking to fill. This expertise adds enormous value to specify the position correctly and the type of individual, or team, who will suit best. The C-suite provider will then select the most appropriate C-suite professional from their group or even a small team of professionals and put them forward to meet with the business leaders.

Suppose an organisation goes to market without asking a firm of C-suite providers for their involvement. In that case, the business leader must do all the vetting and run the process to find the right independent C-suite professional.

Matching a C-suite executive goes beyond functional and sector skill-sets. Getting that match right will only go so far. A C-suite executive with the requisite skills will likely deliver a good job and do what the client wants in the short term. However, it is clear from the research that long-term relationships flourish from a much deeper set of skills and foundations. There is more to the match than functional and sector experience.

Looking for C-suite professionals who have a customer focus is a great start. Those who live and breathe their clients' businesses daily and who obsess about making sure their clients are happy will take the relationship to a completely different level. These professionals will only rest at night or the weekend if they check in with their clients beforehand.

Alternatively, a C-suite executive with an identity that matches their client will deepen the relationship through their shared focus. An example of this is a business that firmly believes its success comes from caring for its people. Everything they put in place in the company is filtered through this lens before it gets actioned. A C-suite professional who shares this passion will be the most appropriate for the role compared with, for example, an executive whose focus is on financial shareholder return. The latter would constantly clash with the business leaders by wanting to make decisions to maximise profit and equity return rather than the employee experience. Another factor here arises from short versus long-term decision-making, as success originating from caring for employees is unlikely to be immediately visible in the numbers.

The identity the business portrays often aligns with the identity of the founder or CEO. It will inform the culture of the organisation, its values and beliefs, standards and norms, and ultimately the behaviours of its people. Questioning the business leaders to understand the company's culture and finally identify who would fit is crucial to finding a match.

Similar personal interests are another avenue to explore when making a match. The ability to develop the route of intimately knowing each other can come from shared experiences. Spending time together, pursuing common interests, or discussing them will bring the client and their C-suite professional closer.

Lastly, the obvious matching criteria of finding a C-suite professional who lives nearby can help to deepen the relationship. Being physically close gives the business leader a feeling of greater accessibility, approachability, and availability. The fact that the C-suite executive can "pop into the office" for an urgent meeting or at short notice adds to the perception that the C-suite professional is on hand when needed, even if this is rarely required. The adoption of technology for meetings provides an acceptable alternative for most businesses. C-suite executives reported using technology throughout the Covid-19 pandemic, which meant they did not divide up their time for clients in "days" anymore. Instead, it was minutes and hours as they hopped between Zoom rooms to service all their clients throughout the day. This efficient use of time also makes C-suite professionals more productive, which increases their capacity to work with more clients.

Organisational norms

The success of C-suite professionals in building their portfolios sits at the heart of the delivery of this service. Changing careers from being an employed full-time C-suite executive to building a portfolio, being self-employed, and working with a range of clients, often remotely, at the strategic and leadership level, requires an investment in time, skills, and energy.

Initially, many C-suite executives thinking about working this way believe it is similar to what they have done before. They could not be more wrong. Yes, the discipline in which they work is the same, and the knowledge and experience they have of their function are what the clients want from them. That is about as similar as it gets.

After that, this is a new career. It requires a learning mindset, openness, and willingness to go outside comfort zones. Deliberately naming this as a career change helps the C-suite professionals to let go of feelings that they are the expert and should know everything from the start. It helps them to adopt a beginner's mindset. They must acquire the skills to build their portfolios as a starting point. Learning to develop relationships and to find and win clients is at the core. Then once they are working with clients, they need to know how to create the routes and roots of PO to keep them for the long-term. This is the case either as an independent C-suite executive or as part of a larger organisation.

If the professional is part of a C-suite firm, the factors influencing feelings of PO are related to the set-up and effectiveness of the firm. Are they joining a mature region of the firm where there is a smooth process to finding and winning clients with a comprehensive training programme and teams of central support, or is this a brand-new geography which has only just started to introduce the concept and, therefore, resources and support might be thin on the ground?

Alternatively, starting as an independent C-suite executive will involve the individual establishing their brand, website, and marketing channels and performing extensive networking of their contacts to kick-start interest in their services.

Essentially, the level of support and appropriate training that the C-suite professional has will determine their ability to develop feelings of PO with clients. An independent C-suite professional will be on their own and will not have access to a firm's collective knowledge, accumulated best practices, and support to guide them. It will be a case of finding it out for themselves through trial and error.

C-suite skills

The two most prevalent skills for generating feelings of PO are the ability of the C-suite professional to establish appropriate boundaries between clients so that the clients do not feel as if they are sharing and, secondly, the capacity of the executive to build interpersonal trust with their client.

Sharing

In the study, most clients did not feel they were sharing their C-suite professional, even though, rationally, they knew they were. This was predominantly down to meticulous planning and communication by the C-suite executives. They educated their clients on the best way to stay in contact outside their normal working hours. They made sure they were accessible, approachable, and available when needed, communicated promptly, and gave their clients plenty of notice when unavailable.

Diary planning has become an art form for these professionals. Some meticulously divide their weeks and months with set days for each client, while others are more fluid and organise themselves week by week to fit with their clients' dynamic requirements and make sure they can attend important meetings. Both approaches work if all the clients in the portfolio play by the same rules and communications are constant.

This close attention to detail and communication makes clients feel their C-suite professional only works for them. This feeling leads to the creation of high levels of PO, and while an illusion at a rational level, it works.

When this level of care is missing, and clients do not feel they are the only client, territorial behaviour can set in. An example is a client outside of this study whose C-suite professional said they could not make an important meeting due to being on holiday. The business owner's response was:

> That is fine. I can accept that you cannot make it if you are on holiday, but I would not be happy if you were with another client.

Another potential trigger for clients becoming possessive of their C-suite professional is when their executive asks if the business leader knows of any other businesses that could benefit from the same service. Not positioning this carefully, and particularly if the C-suite is independent, means the immediate assumption by the client is that they might lose some time and focus from their C-suite professional if they introduce them to others. A further worry can creep in regarding confidentiality. Will their C-suite professional share their confidential or personal information with others? Both concerns can lead to business owners withholding introductions.

These are understandable concerns. They are easy to mitigate if the C-suite professional is part of a firm of C-suite providers, as other team members will be on hand to take on these extra engagements. Not sharing confidential information with other clients is something business leaders should expect as standard practice regardless. Professionals must be careful not to name their other clients and share learnings without compromising confidentiality. It can be beneficial to introduce clients to each other, and being clear about this communication will show up when making introductions, as it will become apparent that the clients know very little about each other's businesses despite sharing the services of the same C-suite professional.

Interpersonal trust

The ability to build trusting relationships between C-suite executives, clients, and the firm of C-suite providers fostered feelings of PO in the system.

There are many definitions of interpersonal trust, such as "Interpersonal trust refers to confidence in another person (or between two persons) and a willingness to be vulnerable to him or her (or to each other)" (Ma et al., 2019, p. 1).

The definition refers to the willingness of one party to be vulnerable with another person and have confidence that they will not harm them. Much is written about how to achieve this in relationships. For this study, I refer to The Roffey Park Institute's eight behaviours that build trust described and investigated by Dr Meysam Poorkavoos. These characteristics are important for building trust in any working relationship, employed or otherwise. However, in Strategy and Leadership as Service, the C-suite professionals have much less time with their clients to develop trust, placing even more emphasis on their ability to develop these skills. For each of the eight behavioural characteristics, I give examples of how to apply this to building trust in relationships between C-suite professionals, their clients, and the firm of C-suite providers (Park & Poorkavoos, 2016).

BEING TRANSPARENT

This refers to being open and honest with people, giving the whole story, and not hiding anything or spinning information to achieve a hidden agenda. This is one of the drivers for C-suite professionals to go self-employed in the first place and offer their services as part of the access economy. Many quoted that feeling pressurised to represent ideas or decisions in a certain way was precisely the type of environment in corporate that they came from and wanted to leave behind because they were not comfortable with it. Some said they felt pushed to present a particular view to achieve short-term results or sway decisions. While this was only happening in some corporates, they welcomed the opportunity to find an environment where they could be themselves and maintain their integrity.

The fact that they are not reliant on any one client for their income also gives C-suite professionals confidence and freedom to be completely honest and open with clients. Many shared that this was one of the first things they discussed. They specifically asked their clients to be open and honest with them, stating that they need to know all the facts and feelings of the business owner to give them the most appropriate advice.

C-suite professionals who are open can encourage their clients to be the same. Examples include carefully sharing their concerns about specific strategies and initiatives instead of holding back and inviting feedback to proposals. Facing difficult situations and encouraging discussions of sensitive topics demonstrate transparency. The C-suite executives must show care for the individuals they are dealing with in these situations to ensure the best outcomes.

STICKING TO COMMITMENTS

We must do what we say we will do; it creates a sense of reliability. Completing tasks assigned on time and delivering the results are vital for C-suite executives if they want their clients to trust them. Best practice would be to agree on the short-, medium- and long-term tasks using a workplan and regularly communicate progress. It is not just about tasks either. It can be about attending meetings and being available when they say they will be.

Of course, this works both ways. Clients need to do what they say they will do too. They must be available for their C-suite executive and deliver on the agreed actions. Some C-suite professionals report that their clients are sometimes hard to get hold of and let them down at the last minute for meetings due to having to attend to an urgent issue. Of course, this can happen occasionally, but if it is a regular occurrence, it erodes inter-personal trust and needs addressing if the relationship is to sustain in the long-term.

The same goes for the relationships between the firm of C-suite providers and their clients and C-suite professionals. Sticking to commitments with regular communication will enhance trust.

DEMONSTRATING TRUST

Trust is a generative concept, i.e., giving trust to another encourages trust to develop in return. One side, therefore, must go first here. Individuals with naturally higher levels of trust will potentially achieve trusting relationships more quickly.

An excellent example is when a C-suite executive starts working with a new business. Keen to get up and running quickly, it is common for executives to invest in the relationship and spend more time than they are charging for in the early days, essentially over-servicing. This involves giving to the relationship and trusting they will not be taken advantage of in future. Instead, they intend to gain the trust of their client more quickly. In this instance, the best practice to prevent this over-service from becoming standard and expected would be for the C-suite professional to share with the client the extent to which they are investing in the relationship above what has been agreed. Another example of giving trust first would be when a client refers their C-suite professional to a friend's business. They are extending trust, which will encourage the executive to reciprocate.

BEING PERSONAL

This is about investing in relationships at a personal level rather than a business level. It chimes with the route to PO of knowing each other intimately. Sharing personal information voluntarily to an appropriate level allows both parties to understand each other more to see what makes them tick. Sharing with others at a personal level can be difficult. Some business environments are exceptionally performance focused, with little time to invest in personal sharing. Meetings are all about KPIs and outcomes. Whatever the client's culture, it is important for C-suite professionals moving into the access economy to make time to build personal relationships, which might be taken for granted in the employed environment.

At firms of C-suite professionals, the executives seek a community of like-minded experts. They want to attend regular conferences and gatherings where they can meet up with colleagues and share more personally. The breaks and opportunities to socialise and network with colleagues are often the most popular elements of these get-togethers.

BEING CONSISTENT

Clients, C-suite executives, and providers who demonstrate consistent behaviours over time enable individuals to predict reactions in different situations. This helps us build a clear picture of each other and breeds trust. Instead of haphazard messaging, consistent communication is another way to enhance trust. It enables parties to anticipate responses and develop a dependable understanding of others.

This is important at a macro level too. Clients might require different C-suite professionals for different challenges throughout their lifecycles, and those with particularly complex or urgent needs may engage through a team approach. While the C-suite professionals are in control over how they deliver their specific skillsets, having consistency regarding the overall process of engagement, monitoring, and review of the service regardless of the C-suite professionals involved will enable clients to have confidence in what to expect and build trust in the brand. This will also give them the confidence to refer other businesses to the firm of C-suite providers and enable them to explain what they can expect from the service.

APPRECIATING OTHERS

This is about respecting others regardless of position, status, or power. Believing all relationships are equal. It is a solid route to building trust. For C-suite executives joining clients, if they show respect and appreciation for all the team members and the work they do at every level, they will create an aura of trust.

A great example is when C-suite professionals visit potential new clients. The client and their team will likely watch them when they pull up in the car park. How do they talk to the receptionist and other members of staff? Do they thank the person who brings them a cup of tea? When they leave, do they seek out and say goodbye to the team member who showed them to the boardroom? Business owners will ask for feedback from all the staff who interacted with the executive during that visit, however incidental or short. It is a job interview every time.

It goes both ways too. Many C-suite executives are fed up with being taken for granted in their employed roles. They want more appreciation and acknowledgement for their contribution. The self-employed nature of the access economy relationship encourages this behaviour, and executives report that their clients often express heartfelt gratitude for their help and guidance – something they missed in corporate.

LISTENING WELL

This is a crucial skill for building trust. Individuals who listen to the point of view of others engender trust by seeking to understand the other's position first. It also demonstrates respect by allowing the other party to feel heard. Colleagues who are listened to report feeling valued, which helps make them feel trusted.

Learning active listening skills is incredibly important for C-suite professionals. It is not easy and requires self-awareness and practice. Some find it very hard as they are used to being the expert in their field and giving advice! Active listening means without contributing. There is no joining in and telling a similar story. It is about keeping quiet, being happy to leave gaps and silence for the other to fill and following their thought process. It is about listening out for what is not said as much as what is.

Allowing others to be fully heard and listened to is a gift we can give to others. Creating situations outside of office hours with a suggestion to meet up over lunch or dinner can allow clients to have this experience and respond to thoughtful questions.

BEING VULNERABLE

In all relationships, there are misunderstandings at times, and mistakes happen. These are an opportunity to deepen the relationship. Trying to cover them up and move on quickly is the route to distrust. Instead, seeing them as an opportunity to be vulnerable and share that with others will result in a different outcome by taking responsibility for our actions and putting the situation right. It might be painful and embarrassing, but if handled well it will provide an opportunity to bring trust into the relationship.

Showing vulnerability with a client in the context of Strategy and Leadership as Service can be achieved by the C-suite executive delegating elements of their role to others as soon as possible. Clients need to expand their teams to cover extra work as they grow. At first, the C-suite executive might cover some of these tasks to understand their full scope and ensure they warrant introducing new roles into the business. Their time in the company will increase at this point. However, this can only be for a short time. They must bring appropriate skills into the team to cover these tasks and drop their time commitment back to cover the strategic elements. Hanging on to lower-level work for short-term commercial gain is a sure way for trust to break down. Instead, encouraging clients to invest in their team, transferring the knowledge to others and allowing the C-suite professional to operate at the strategic level with less time commitment will likely result in a much longer-term relationship. This self-sacrifice of the C-suite executive, making themselves vulnerable, builds trust.

C-suite personal context

Relational aspects

C-suite executives who want to build relationships and acknowledge that these are at the core of Strategy and Leadership as Service do well in creating feelings of PO. Many C-suite professionals who initially consider working this way believe the key to success is their technical skills and experience in their chosen discipline.

This is a common mistake.

Of course, these are important. However, many years of experience in their discipline, technical qualifications, big and small company experience, and non-financial board roles are hygiene factors. Most C-suite professionals adopting Strategy and Leadership as Service will have these. They do not mean the C-suite executive will be successful in this access economy business model.

This is a new career with additional relational skills needed to flourish. Developing solid relationships with clients and their teams when not working alongside them in the office can be challenging for independent C-level executives. Maintaining relationships in their network to ensure their pipeline stays topped up requires even more coordination and activity. C-suite professionals working in a firm of C-suite providers must maintain relationships across the system with their clients, network, fellow C-suite professionals, and central team members.

Personal history

The length of time C-suite executives spend working this way helps in their ability to build sustainable relationships exhibiting PO. It can take up to a year to build an entire portfolio of clients and even longer to perfect how to create lasting relationships.

Executives with outside interests, which take up more time and energy than building a portfolio, can struggle. It is not something to be done "on the side." It is a career change that requires total focus and commitment.

C-suite executives who join a firm after trying it independently do well. They have experienced what it is like to go solo and genuinely appreciate the structure and support the firm provides them. They have also realised that being a great CMO or CTO is insufficient. It is far more than that. Besides, if they are still committed to making this career change work after going solo, their determination to succeed often pulls them through.

C-suite professionals' reasons for joining

The C-suite professional's reason for joining is one of the most critical drivers for creating feelings of PO. As described in Chapter 5, some typical personas of C-suite professionals are best suited to this way of working.

Ensuring the new joiners have drivers such as making an impact on their clients' lives, creating a different lifestyle for themselves with more work-life balance, and being supported by belonging to a community of like-minded individuals will give them the most chance of success. Acknowledging their fears regarding creating an income stream and becoming used to this way of working is essential too. Pointing them to the parts of the business model which address these fears and sharing how they need to respond will mean they have complete information before embarking on their new careers.

Pathways to psychological ownership

PO develops through many different pathways and combinations of routes and roots. This gives C-suite professionals a great deal of flexibility when designing the relationships they want to have with their clients, team members, and firms of C-suite providers. They can gravitate to areas of the Strategy and Leadership as Service framework where they feel most comfortable as a starting point.

Gaining the knowledge and skills to create the environment for the roots and routes of PO to flourish and auditing their current relationships for PO are a good place to begin.

Personal development in weaker areas and learning from others with more developed skills are sensible next steps to move the dial further.

Ecosystem dynamics – the bigger picture

This theme is relevant at the system level, where the context is of a firm of C-suite providers, which delivers Strategy and Leadership as Service to their clients through a C-suite team rather than a two-way relationship between an individual C-suite professional and a client.

In the latter, there needs to be strong PO both ways to hold the relationship together for the long-term. The themes of feelings of PO and multiple PO pathways may be sufficient to do this at an individual relationship level.

However, an access economy industry consisting solely of independent C-suite professionals serving clients is not optimised. These individuals work on their own. They spend most of their time with their clients, and I encourage them to develop a sense of belonging there, but more is needed. It does not provide them with a community of peers always available and on hand where they can access support, structure, learning and development, extra capacity, and fill skill gaps.

Independent C-suite executives who are experts in a discipline may need more skills and time to find and win clients. They require training to do this and a mechanism to ensure it continues to happen when they are busy servicing clients. Most of all, they must differentiate themselves in the marketplace to stand out from all the other independents. They will need a distinct brand, vision and purpose, website, and marketing channels.

The transition to independence from employment brings many positives, such as freedom and objectivity, the ability to design balance into their lives and the opportunity to choose the clients and people with whom they want to work.

It also leaves gaps.

An overview of the market shows that independents seek out others to work with either formally or informally and search for sources of best practices and learning and development. Firms of C-suite providers help fill these gaps and offer a viable alternative to employment.

This requires moving from examining relationships between two individuals to studying an organisational system of C-suite professionals, clients, and firms of C-suite providers. Figure 12.1 considers the holistic perspective of PO development in this system.

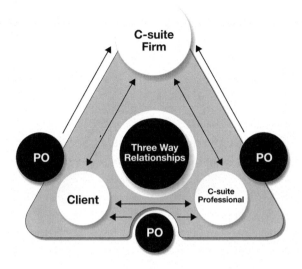

Figure 12.1 The Strategy and Leadership as Service relationships

The first-order concepts of enabling and disabling dynamics are the levers to adjust the levels of PO across the whole system.

Keeping the system in balance in the context of PO is the key to its success as a complete alternative to employment for C-suite professionals. I discuss the enabling and disabling dynamics from the insights in Chapter 9. The most critical discovery was the need to create direct relationships for C-suite firms with their clients, which sit independently from the relationship between the C-suite executive and the client.

Until the system becomes balanced with a relationship between the client and the C-suite provider, the client relationships will be wholly dependent on the skills and behaviours of their assigned C-suite professional. This puts risk in the system for all involved. The C-suite professionals might want extra support to service their clients from a time, geography, or skills perspective. Alternatively, they may need help with the relationship. Things don't always go smoothly. Despite being extremely skilled, C-suite executives can only be experts in some things. Regularly bringing in other team members to solve specialist issues will showcase the whole offering from the firm of C-suite providers, proving to clients that they can always get the answer from engaging this way. Clients, too, might sometimes like to talk to another part of the organisation about the relationship.

Furthermore, there is the opportunity to bring all the clients together and create a community where business leaders can go for networking, business development, learning, and sharing. The opportunity for C-suite firms to develop and share thought leadership within this community will be valuable to many. It could double up to enhance the experience of more established C-suite executives with stable portfolios who welcome more support.

> **Top tips for Strategy and Leadership as Service – how to optimise the relationships within the ecosystem**
>
> *Feelings of PO*
>
> 1. Matching of functional and sector skills, cultural fit, identity preferences, personal interests, and physical proximity all contribute to fostering feelings of PO between the client and C-suite professional.
> 2. Careful design of the organisational norms of the firms of C-suite providers is required.
> 3. C-suite skills most valued are developing healthy sharing boundaries between clients so that they all feel as if "they are the only one" and the ability to build interpersonal trust with clients.
> 4. C-suite professionals must carefully consider their reasons for changing career and joining the access economy at the right life stage for them, with sufficient financial support to allow time to develop their portfolios.
>
> *Pathways to PO*
>
> 1. C-suite professionals, clients, and firms of C-suite providers can choose to develop PO through many different pathways and combinations of roots and routes.
>
> *Ecosystem dynamics*
>
> 1. Enabling dynamics include optimising PO across the whole system, PO not being mutually exclusive, the work being fulfilling for C-suite professionals with a positive culture, longer relationships over extended elapsed time and good product and market fit.
> 2. Disabling dynamics can be avoided by building a community for clients and the firm of C-suite providers and delivering more support for C-suite professionals with stable portfolios.

Conclusion

Relationships are clearly at the heart of Strategy and Leadership as Service. Developing PO within each relationship and the whole ecosystem creates a sustainable marketplace.

After discussing the ingredients for this way of working, including how to apply them, it is now time to focus on the roadmaps required to build the industry.

References

Ma, J., Schaubroeck, J., & LeBlanc, C. (2019). Interpersonal trust in organizations. *Oxford Research Encyclopedia of Business and Management.* https://doi.org/10.1093/acrefore/9780190224851.013.167

Park, R., & Poorkavoos, M. (2016, October 19). *Eight behaviours that build trust.* Roffey Park Institute. Retrieved September 2, 2023, from www.roffeypark.ac.uk/knowledge-and-learning-resources-hub/eight-behaviours-that-build-trust/

The Roadmap   **13**

How the Access Economy Meets the C-Suite for All

We now know the roots, routes, and relationships required for C-suite services to thrive in an access economy business model such as Strategy and Leadership as Service. Ensuring the roots and routes of PO are in place will secure the relationships between C-suite professionals, the clients they work with, and the firm of C-suite providers.

Yet how can this way of working develop at scale? How can it become a widely accepted industry that future-proofs the careers for C-suite executives and provides a pathway to the new normal of sustainable business for all sizes of organisations across the globe?

How the access economy meets the C-suite for SMEs is thoughtfully designed and delivered to meet their needs. SMEs don't want, don't need, and can't afford a full-time, employed C-suite professional. Before learning about this business model, most entrepreneurs are at a loss when considering how to fill this gap. They know they need the skillset, yet a top C-suite professional is out of their reach and not interested in working with them full-time. The economics don't work on either side. Creating Strategy and Leadership as Service delivered by firms of C-suite providers hits the spot. Development of this industry takes time and education. Most business owners still need to hear of the concept, yet when they learn about it and understand it, they are keen to experience it and want to buy.

But what about larger organisations? How can this concept be adapted and applied to more mature, sophisticated, and advanced organisations? And why would they be interested? What value could it bring?

DOI: 10.4324/9781003368090-19

Until value to larger corporates is articulated and understood, SME business owners will see Strategy and Leadership as Service as the solution they need until they can afford a full-time employee. At that point, they will revert to the traditional employment model of recruiting a full-time individual to sit at the board table and lead the relevant function, as has been the way for decades.

Why will they do this?

It is because there is no feasible alternative. It is what larger businesses do. It is normal. It is how we do business and govern; it is how we're used to developing a career through having one job at a time and moving between them. It is what our parents did and forms part of the orthodox three-stage life of education, employment, and retirement. We think it gives us security, identity, and status. We hope it will make us financially independent.

That doesn't mean it is the best and only solution. We must ask ourselves, how else can we do this, and why would we want to? Can these full-time roles be fulfilled differently, and what could that look like? What problems would it solve and equally potentially create?

Most importantly, is there another way to better equip businesses to meet the challenges coming their way at pace and help them adapt to the megatrends the world is experiencing? What is the next iteration of the C-suite? How can organisations gear up their leadership team to make a step change to transformation, giving them the best chance for a sustainable future?

Limitations of the current C-suite model

Let's start with the status quo. As described in Chapter 1, the current traditional employment model of a board of directors with a C-suite team to deliver performance is widely adopted. A single individual represents each function or part of the business. These individuals combine to form the C-suite and work as a team to decide the strategy for the company and deliver a return to the shareholders. The directors hold the legal responsibility for running the business and governing appropriately.

Yet what is the reality facing each C-suite professional on a day-to-day basis? We know they are the face of the function to the board, who report to the shareholders. Depending on the organisation's size, they head up the role and will have teams of staff members reporting to them and for whom they are responsible.

So far, so good.

Yet the signs are that things are changing.

Disillusionment with corporate

First, as we've seen in Chapter 2, there's a growing trend of C-suite professionals becoming disillusioned with corporate life, particularly with the more traditional businesses that need help to adapt to today's fast-paced, digital world. The protocol, expectations, demands, and commitment required by larger organisations from their C-suite are becoming too much for some individuals. They ask themselves, "Why am I doing this?" The constant demands to meet shareholder return expectations at all costs are soul-destroying. Individuals are no longer willing to tolerate roles and work environments that leave them unhappy and in constant stress and fatigue.

The Covid-19 pandemic was a global experience that triggered many of us to reflect on what matters in life. It was a direct threat to our health and well-being. Some of us were forced to reassess our priorities, while others chose to. We considered questions like "Where and how do we want to live? How much time do we want to spend working? What are we doing this for, and what is our purpose?" For some of us, we were able to experience working from home for the first time. This separation from our physical office environment and colleagues gave us a new perspective on our employers and work lives. While the extroverts struggled with the lack of human interaction, the introverts generally loved it! Then came the question of returning to the office once the pandemic was in check. We had to deal with hybrid working. This experience encouraged us to re-evaluate our lives and make changes. Some left the workforce entirely, and, as described in Chapter 2, the Great Resignation ensued, closely followed by Quiet Quitting.

These phenomena are significant indicators of our dissatisfaction with our work lives. The Gallup findings report global employee engagement to be just 21 per cent in 2021, increasing to 23 per cent in 2022, but workers are still stressed with 44 per cent experiencing feelings of stress a lot during the previous day (Gallup Inc., 2023). This study is for all employees, of which the C-suite are only a tiny subset, yet it indicates that our working experience needs an overhaul.

C-suite burnout

If we focus on the C-suite in particular, a study by Deloitte, who partnered with the independent firm Workplace Intelligence to survey 2,100 employees and C-level executives across the USA, UK, Canada, and Australia, found that nearly 70 per cent of the C-suite are seriously thinking about leaving their current position in favour of one that supports their well-being, with 81 per cent choosing prioritising well-being over career progression (Hatfield et al., 2022).

The top obstacles to well-being were a heavy workload, stressful jobs, plus not having enough time off due to long working hours. Only two-thirds of the C-suite use their full holiday allocation, take short breaks throughout the day, get enough rest, and have time for their friends and family. In addition 73 per cent reported that they couldn't take time off and disconnect from work. Technology's ability to always be in touch is a double-edged sword regarding wanting downtime. Going on holiday but answering emails and taking calls throughout isn't giving our minds and bodies the rest and relaxation they need to re-energise for returning to work. The reasons for not switching off include the unmanageable work-load upon return and the fear of missing out on important emails (Hatfield et al., 2022).

This constant requirement to be "always on" and available can lead to burnout:

> Burnout is a psychological syndrome emerging as a prolonged response to chronic interpersonal stressors on the job. The three key dimensions of this response are an overwhelming exhaustion, feelings of cynicism and detachment from the job, and a sense of ineffectiveness and lack of accomplishment.
>
> (Maslach & Leiter, 2016, p. 103)

Some C-suite executives have already moved to the access economy because they have experienced burnout or have come close to it in their corporate careers. They recount many warning signs, such as waking in the middle of the night worrying about work-related issues and being unable to fall asleep, being irritable, quick to judge others, and unable to exercise or remember when they last "had fun." Sudden loss or gain of weight and not being willing to leave tasks until they are complete are all indicators that individuals could be close to a breakdown.

A move towards freedom

Of course, avoiding burnout and overwork is one reason to move towards the access economy. Moving away from a negative makes sense. Yet it's more than that. Professionals are attracted to a more positive working environment on their terms.

C-suite individuals seek more flexibility, control, and variety in their lives and want to contribute. Of course, they want to be valued and appreciated. They also want to see the results of their endeavours at the sharp end of business. They seek to have an impact and give back. They want to balance their work with living. They crave the time and space to make lifestyle choices about how much they work, when, and with whom. Most are happy to stay in corporate for a while to gain experience and some big names on their CV, knowing these will give them the credibility for a career change. But they are not prepared to stay forever. The politics and 24/7 demands of the role take their toll on a personal level, and they find themselves searching for meaning in and at work.

Of course, not all corporates are like this. Some have more progressive and supportive cultures, yet the question remains whether even these businesses can do enough to keep their C-suite talent on board.

Corporates want superhumans

Even if the C-suite professional is comfortable with their organisation's culture, the expectations and demands of the role can be extreme. A review of job descriptions of C-level positions shows the unrealistic breadth and depth of skills required in a single individual. Most high-calibre executives fall into the categories of generalists or specialists, not both. Organisations' unrelenting desire to have the best talent join their teams means they are searching for the impossible.

The uncompromising pace of change, the expectation to always be available, and to have all the information at our fingertips in real-time, stretches our human capability to the limits. Even if we could be everything to everyone, it would leave no time for anything else and is unsustainable and unenjoyable. No wonder we ask, "Why are we doing this?"

Expecting a single C-suite individual to have all the skills on an employer's shopping list is unrealistic. It is also worth asking if that is the best way to approach the role and in the organisation's interests.

If it isn't working for the individual, we also need to ask if it works for the employer. Piling the pressure onto key C-suite executives and expecting them to perform like machines is risky. Illness, absences, and staff turnover are all symptoms of burnout and unhealthy work cultures and increase the workload on those still carrying on. It's a vicious circle.

From a purely commercial perspective, depending too much on individuals, who are only human and lack sharpness and energy from overwork, increases risk in organisations. It jeopardises the completion of critical tasks or risks omitting them altogether. Too much knowledge or dependency on specialist skills sitting with a few key individuals is dangerous. A lack of collective thinking, different perspectives, and diversity of ideas will hamper innovation and creativity.

A better, lower-risk approach could be acknowledging that many C-suite roles have already expanded beyond the reach of a single individual and will continue to do so. The turbulent and changing external landscape requires a broader range of skills in a team of specialists rather than a single generalist. We need to revise our expectations and think differently about the C-suite of the future.

What's the answer?

Culture and well-being

Organisations with cultures which prioritise employee engagement and well-being will lead the way. The development of organisational cultures which are open, inclusive, and embrace diversity will promote agility and resilience for growth.

Well-being can start with health benefits, but it is much more than that. Embedding wellness activities and transparency about mental health issues and difficulties will encourage staff to be open at work. A culture which promotes psychological safety will allow employees to share and bring the discussion into the workplace without stigma. Solutions will be co-created, and new working practices will evolve.

Leaders will first require coaching and support to develop and model these behaviours. It starts with the C-suite. They will need training and support from health experts and be open to learning from Generation Z and Millennials in their teams, who will probably be the leaders in prioritising health and well-being.

One of the determinants for the long-term success and sustainability of organisations will depend on workforce well-being.

Better leaders

Leadership development is an obvious place to start progressing organisational cultures that promote well-being and enjoyable places to work.

We need better leaders.

This is a well-researched and much-written-about arena. There are many theories to learn about and adopt, plus a thriving industry of leadership consultancies and coaches to choose from for support. This isn't new. The approaches may change depending on the macro environment, but assistance has been available for decades.

Yet we still need better leaders. That issue has stayed the same.

This book isn't the place to introduce, debate, and evaluate ways to develop C-suite leadership skills to build sustainable businesses. The first point I want to make is that developing our mindset and skillset capabilities to become better leaders are a given in the future of work. The second point is that this is universal and challenging. Even with all the latest thinking about leadership and the industry of coaching and training support available, it takes time and dedication to develop these skills. The megatrends and world events that leaders must navigate are novel, complex, and relentless. It takes work to keep up, let alone get ahead!

C-suite support from the outside

We are mistaken if we think C-suite individuals are delivering on the wide range of demands in their roles. The reality is that they are already supplementing their skillsets with support from the outside.

Increasingly, a well-trodden pathway for C-suite leaders of corporates to perform their expanding and challenging roles is to bring in skills from external sources. It takes many forms and depends on the type of problem to address.

High-level, strategic thinking support will come from the big management consultancies. These organisations can bring in their teams of expert consultants and apply themselves to significant strategic issues. They have the diversity, brains, bandwidth, and deep specialist expertise to tackle these questions. Corporations can outsource this work and get on with running the company day-to-day. They provide interventions which scope and diagnose problems and propose solutions. They are not implementers, that's down to the corporate team, but they will support and guide this activity.

Another commonly used approach is to bring in much-needed specialist skills and capacity through interim executives. These individuals love working in their swimlane, either function or sector and go from assignment to assignment, solving problems and implementing solutions.

They temporarily work inside the organisation with a project focus. It's generally full-time, intensive work, and they stay to finish the job, at which point they move on. They are high-calibre professionals who require little oversight and are good at quickly assessing situations and adding value. Given that they tend to have specialisms and vast experience, there will be little they have yet to come across in these areas, so while they focus on implementation, they can also bring specialist knowledge and strategic thinking to problems.

Outsourcing businesses are also helpful for C-suite executives. They can outsource non-core and tactical activities like management accounting and compliance in the finance arena to specialists who deliver at scale, cutting down the time required for supervision and freeing up valuable headspace for the C-suite.

This external help is vital for larger organisations to keep up with their growth ambitions. It goes some way to supporting the C-suite team. However, it has limitations.

The first is that it is external. Consulting organisations deliver extraordinary expertise to solve complex problems and devise appropriate strategies. This skillset is necessary to bring in different thinking, best practice, and learnings from the wider industry. The downside is that these consultancy firms need resources to carry out their proposed strategies. Their business models do not allow them to do the implementation. Their people do not have the skillsets to execute, and the cost would likely be prohibitive. These consultants go from assignment to assignment developing world-class thinking and insight to support organisations in making breakthrough decisions. Then the organisations need to find a way to put them into practice.

Interim executives start as outsiders who temporarily join the organisation for a project. They are a halfway house solution to get things done, generally solo individuals, and seldom with the backup and support of a team. They must get up to speed with the culture and issues of the company initially before their input is optimised. Then as the project nears completion, they can become preoccupied with doing the recruitment rounds for their next assignment. Sometimes, they may even cut short their engagement to secure their next role. Most corporate initiatives do not neatly fit the time commitment of a full-time interim, as illustrated by Figure 13.1. Here I show the time commitment for full-time employment compared with interim roles. Most projects often require a gradual build-up of time initially as they gain momentum, followed by full-time focus at the height of the intensity of the engagement. Then a wind-down of time is required as the initiative integrates into business as usual. This time profile is at odds with an interim professional's requirement, which is generally entirely on or fully off and is better suited to a part-time or fractional solution, as shown in Figure 13.1.

External help is, of course, handy for corporates and serves a purpose. Let's remember, however, that the context for their involvement is to solve

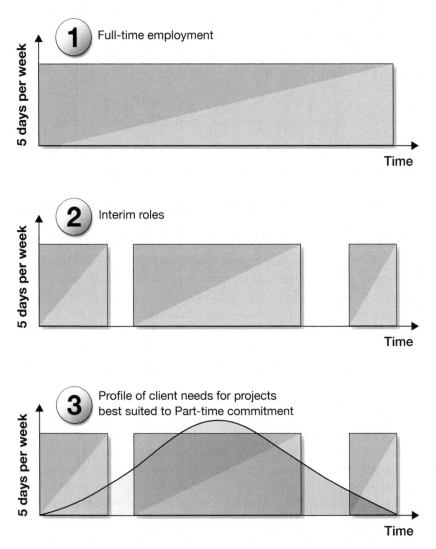

Figure 13.1 Comparison of patterns of time commitment for full-time, interim, and part-time roles

issues as they arise, which means they are generally working on a specific timeline to get the job done. The outcome is that they are interventions rather than long-term relationships.

The second limitation is that they still need to be integrated into the organisation, supervised, managed, and held accountable for their work to varying degrees. Their input is essential, has a significant contribution and will have a business case and expected return on investment. Responsibility for their work will land in the lap of the C-suite team, adding to their overflowing in-tray. Therefore C-level executives should only partially expect to devolve responsibility for this work. There will still be a level of involvement required from them, and getting that balance right is vital to their role.

In summary, C-suite professionals are questioning their roles in corporate. The demands are intense and never-ending. Their health and well-being are suffering, increasing the risk of burnout for the individual. Corporations' expectations of what these individuals can achieve are expanding due to the pressures of our complex and changing world. As the megatrends and world events develop, this pace of change and the breadth of complex problems to address will only continue and increase.

The result is that experienced C-suite professionals are leaving these roles and looking for alternatives. This is potentially a massive drain of talent and knowledge from the employed workforce. Those that stay are suffering and bringing in more and more outside help for support. The result is that things get done, but is it optimised, at what cost, and what are the associated risks?

There must be a better way!

The roadmap to the access economy C-suite for corporates

As discussed, traditional employment has limitations for organisations and C-suite professionals. Developing an access economy for these services could be an alternative and improved way to resource up to address their future challenges confidently, not only for SMEs but for mid-to-large organisations too. This requires corporates to realise the status quo will be unfit for the future, and the access economy ecosystem for C-suite professionals needs to expand.

The first obstacle to overcome for corporates is to realise that what they ask of an individual C-suite professional is becoming increasingly unrealistic and risky. A better solution using a team is worth considering.

Of course, the board will want consistency in the role and to build a long-term relationship. A Lead C-suite individual from the firm of C-suite providers can fulfil this role. This team member would not only deliver and implement specific elements of the C-suite role suited to their skillset, but also head up the relationship for the whole C-suite team of specialists required by the organisation in that particular discipline. This Lead team member would be the "face" of this C-suite function, coordinating and overseeing the team's day-to-day operations. However, they will only need to be part-time because they will have other C-suite specialists to support them. This role can form part of that C-suite professional's portfolio. Other team members will then cover further requirements of the position. These will be C-suite specialists with relevant skills for each functional project or area, e.g., treasury, systems, and capital raising in finance functions, who are called upon as and when needed. Corporates with subsidiaries or divisions in specialist areas or other market segments can be assigned other fractional C-suite professionals from the team with expertise in those areas. Global organisations spread across multiple geographies will similarly benefit as they can access C-suite executives at those locations.

This solution transforms what is possible for corporates. They move from being constrained by an individual, employed C-suite professional with limited skills, time, and energy to accessing a much-expanded set of skills, time, and specialist knowledge across different geographies through a team approach.

If the C-suite professionals move to this way of working, the corporates will still have access to the same skillsets on offer through the employed route, but now they can blend skills to ensure each part of the role has the best solution at the right time. The team will be fluid and constantly under review, with team members brought in as and when needed. Organisations can achieve an increased level of agility not available to them through the traditional employment model. Account managers from the firm of C-suite providers will liaise with the Lead C-suite professional to manage the team and meet the organisation's changing needs. Professionals replace the interim support previously used, providing a service that fits the company's time requirements by being able to ramp up and wind down to match the business issue.

Notably, the C-suite professionals will have gained freedom from corporate life. By belonging to a joined-up firm of C-suite providers, they can still have a portfolio of clients. They might be the Lead C-suite professional with some clients and provide their specialist skills to others on a fractional or interim basis. They can still choose how much they work, with whom, and when.

The power of many

The portfolio executives will belong to a community of like-minded professionals and be fully supported. The sheer scale of breadth and depth of knowledge from a global team of C-suite talent working together in this way would be unrivalled and mean they have the potential to achieve quality results and consistently get solutions to their client's problems by drawing on experiences from within the group. They will harness the power of many, as shown in Figure 13.2.

The answers they seek for their clients will always be just a few conversations away. Many C-suite professionals admit that their networks rapidly revert to silos and specialised niches once they move into a full-time employed role for an extended period. Networks are hard to maintain outside the role's demands and become dormant quickly, requiring a flurry of activity and concerted effort to revive every time an executive moves organisation. Working as a collective enables the C-suite talent to pool their

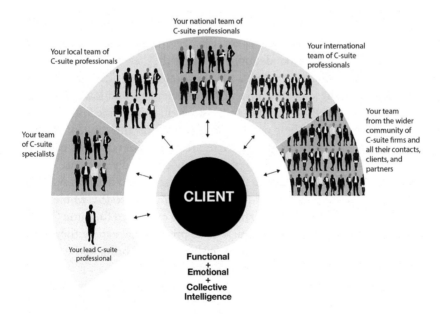

Figure 13.2 The power of many

networks and exponentially increase their contacts for business support across a range of disciplines, which further benefits them and their clients.

Further development of the access economy for C-suite professionals

The current state of development of the access economy for C-suite professionals is a growing base of independent C-suite executives moving to this way of working. These individuals are having some level of success in building their client portfolios, focusing on the SME segment of the market. There are some informal groupings of independent C-suite professionals to provide support and counter loneliness. The market is more mature in the USA, and there are regional, state, and national firms of C-suite professionals, predominantly in the CFO discipline. Again, these firms generally focus on the SME segment of the market. A small number of regional firms are going to market to work with an offering for larger corporates.

If C-suite services are to be delivered to the SME segment of the market, the ecosystem requires strong PO between C-suite professionals and their firm of C-suite providers; this provides the platform for relationships with clients.

Introducing the team approach would encourage a stronger relationship between the clients and the firm of C-suite providers. Redistribution of PO across the ecosystem will mean clients can become part of a community of businesses with a common identity and where they feel they belong.

This team approach can work for corporates. Yet it can also benefit SME clients. In these clients, given their smaller size and lower levels of complexity, an individual C-suite professional in a discipline will likely be able to fulfil most of their needs. They can call on their fellow specialist C-suite team members where there are skill, geography, or capacity gaps. Equally, having the backup of the knowledge and experience of the wider team means they can tap into this resource when needed. As these SME clients develop and grow, they can now migrate to the whole team approach instead of reverting to the traditional employed full-time C-suite model. Their incumbent part-time C-suite professional can be their Lead executive to hold the long-term relationship and then bring in the specialist skillsets from the broader team as required.

Introducing a team approach can develop a stronger relationship between the firms of C-suite providers and the clients, strengthening PO across the whole system. Clients will have "on-tap" all of the C-suite skills they need. Client communities developed by the firms of C-suite providers will enable business owners to meet with other leaders to discuss common issues, build alliances, network, and feel supported. The firms could also form sector groupings of organisations, who can learn from each other about many parts of their businesses, comparing performance while furthering their learning for how to improve.

Likewise, the C-suite professionals will have "anchor" clients where they are the Lead professionals and other clients where they support the Lead executives. They will build intimate and lasting relationships with their anchor clients, characterised by intense feelings of PO, while gaining variety and challenge through supporting their fellow team members who require assistance with their long-term clients. This builds on the current strong relationships C-suite professionals already have with their clients while enhancing PO with the firm of C-suite providers. Team members will work more closely to promote intimacy across the broader group of C-suite professionals and increase PO in that area. The C-suite executives can specialise in sectors, industries, and functions, enabling them to form deeper identities and deliver their highly developed skills to the clients who need them most.

Of course, it is still possible that even in an access economy model, the C-suite professionals can overestimate their ability to deliver for clients and take on too much work, raising their risk of burning out if this goes on for sustained periods. The firms of C-suite providers need to take this issue seriously and build checks into their working practices and utilisation levels of their team members. Using the team approach to ease the pressure on individuals must come into force in these situations.

Moving towards a team approach reframes C-suite roles. Businesses can have a deep relationship with the firm of C-suite providers, developing solid feelings of PO and gaining the right team of C-suite executives to deliver and meet all their needs as they grow. This approach would work well for all sizes of businesses, particularly those in fast-paced environments and with rapidly changing requirements.

We can imagine a new way of working by rebalancing and strengthening PO feelings across the ecosystem. This could form part of the future of work for C-suite professionals as we move towards the new normal. It gives C-suite talent more flexibility, freedom, variety, and control over their lives. They can connect with clients who need their services while developing a core identity and specialism they are known for. They work in C-suite teams, which gives them a sense of belonging to a community. In return, clients can have their diverse and varying C-suite requirements met through one service relationship performed in a joined-up way by a team of committed C-suite professionals.

This turns the traditional employment model on its head and means clients buy outcomes delivered through relationships which flex over time to meet their needs. They don't have to commit fully and completely to one individual who may or may not be the right long-term match with the best blend of skills.

Industry change for the access economy of C-suite services

Using PO as a lens for change, it is possible to innovate and map out how the access economy for C-suite professionals can develop over time through four market propositions.

Figure 13.3 shows how changes in PO between C-suite professionals and clients and between the firm of C-suite providers and clients can lead to different solutions and types of engagement.

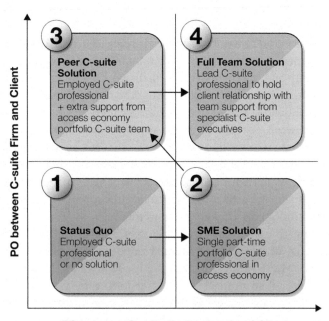

Figure 13.3 Using psychological ownership as the lens for change

1. *Status Quo – Low PO between C-suite professional and client and between the C-suite firm and client*: Corporate clients employ their own C-suite professional full-time or "make do" with no real solution if the need isn't felt strongly (e.g., smaller businesses);

2. *SME Solution: High PO between C-suite professional and client and low PO between C-suite firm and client*: The client engages with a part-time, portfolio C-suite professional from the access economy. The C-suite executive can be an independent or part of a firm of C-suite providers. This is the offering which is currently most widely delivered in the market. It is a good, working solution for SME businesses gaining traction globally;

3. *Peer C-suite solution for corporates: Low PO between C-suite professional and client and high PO between C-suite firm and client*: Corporate clients employ their own C-suite executive full-time and engage with a firm of C-suite professionals from the access economy to support this individual to fill skill and capacity gaps using the team approach. I believe this is the next step in developing the Strategy and Leadership as Service industry. Instead of using a hotchpotch of unconnected interim providers and external consultancies, the employed C-suite can form a long-term and deep relationship with a firm of C-suite providers and receive a committed, flexible, team service of specialists who are on-tap to meet changes in demand across a range of geographies and functions as needed. Knowledge of the client will build up over time within the firm of C-suite providers enabling the teams to get up to speed quickly as requirements change; and

4. *Full Team solution for all sizes of organisations: High PO between the team of C-suite professionals and client and between the C-suite firm and client*: Clients of all sizes engage with the full team approach of a C-suite firm from the access economy. They will be assigned a Lead C-suite professional to maintain the relationship as the team changes over time. The Lead team member will coordinate and manage a team of specialist C-suite executives to deliver the skills and services as and when required. The Lead team member will likely work part-time, and other team members will flex their time up and down as needed.

The research for this book found that the levels of PO between C-suite professionals and their firms of C-suite providers were the strongest, probably because this relationship is the constant in the system and outlasts those between the executives and their individual clients. I expect these PO levels to increase further in line with the progression through the four solutions due to the increased activity levels required at each stage between the C-suite professionals and their firms of providers.

Progression of Strategy and Leadership as Service

The access economy industry is in its infancy, between Status Quo and an SME Solution. Strategy and Leadership as Service is an emerging phenomenon and a niche service. As such, there are no published data on its development. Globally there are millions of mid-tier SME organisations, most surviving without C-level support, demonstrating the scale of the opportunity for industry growth.

A future development for firms already offering C-suite services for SMEs would be to promote deep relationships with clients to strengthen the whole system and create client communities.

The next logical step towards providing a solution for larger organisations would be to offer a team approach to incumbent C-suite employees through the Peer Solution. Instead of being supported by a wide range of unconnected interims and consultants, they can expand their reach and skillset through a long-term relationship with a firm of specialist C-suite providers. It is more realistic for corporates to experiment with this Peer Solution in the short term rather than move to the whole team approach. By engaging with a C-suite provider over time, for projects as they arise, they will get a joined-up approach with knowledge about their business passed from one team to the next, smoothing out transitions and speeding up impact, see Figure 13.4.

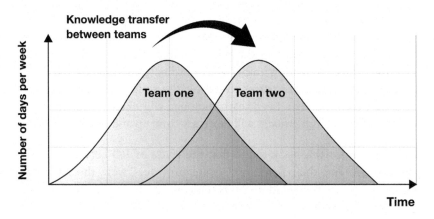

Figure 13.4 Knowledge transfer for peer and full team solutions

In time, a more considerable change for the industry would be for corporates to adopt the Full Team approach instead of employing their C-suite full-time. It comes with challenges, but making this leap in our thinking provides a solution to the issues facing these organisations.

Future generations may accelerate these changes

While this might seem a long way off now, it's worth considering how the workforce will change in the next ten years and beyond. As we progress past 2030, the Generation X leaders of corporates today will be replaced by the Millennials, and Generation Z will form the core of the available workforce. Millennial and Generation Z individuals are more likely to have started their careers in the gig economy, juggling multiple roles in a portfolio and using side hustles to experiment with entrepreneurial ventures and help them decide in which direction they want to take their lives. Not being employed will be much more accepted and usual for these individuals, and they will likely embrace portfolio working and access economy models like Strategy and Leadership as Service. However, they will lack the rigour, training, and experience currently offered by the corporates where they learn their craft. The firms of C-suite providers could step in here as they are ideally placed to fill this gap. They already fit Handy's ([1994]2002) description of the New Agents for portfolio workers, i.e., firms which support and promote individuals operating a portfolio lifestyle. They could further develop their offering to become the sustainable source of professional and personal development, training, and career experience needed to equip this upcoming talent pool with the relevant skills.

A multi-discipline solution

Finally, developing Strategy and Leadership as Service as an industry focuses on how it can substitute for employment in each C-suite function.

A further offering already being delivered to the SME market segment by the Liberti community of C-suite firms involves simultaneously fulfilling several C-suite specialisms for a client. In these situations, business leaders start engaging with one C-suite firm from the community and then see the benefit of filling out further C-suite roles in other disciplines in this way. The advantages to this are that the C-suite professionals from each C-suite firm gain support from the wider community, with all firms adopting a common philosophy and understanding how to best collaborate for the benefit of their clients.

Conclusion

The knowledge and insight provided by PO not only means that the access economy model of sharing professional services can deliver solid and enduring relationships, but it also provides the pathway for Strategy and Leadership as Service as a future way of working in the new normal for all sizes of organisations.

References

Gallup Inc. (2023). *State of the global workplace report – Gallup: The voice of the worlds' employees*. Gallup.com. Retrieved August 13, 2023, from www.gallup.com/workplace/349484/state-of-the-global-workplace.aspx

Handy, C. ([1994]2002). *The empty raincoat: New thinking for a new world*. Arrow.

Hatfield, S., Fisher, J., & Silverglate, P. H. (2022, June 22). *The C-suite's role in well-being: How health-savvy executives can go beyond workplace wellness to workplace well-being – for themselves and their people*. Deloitte Insights. Retrieved March 26, 2023, from www2.deloitte.com/us/en/insights/topics/leadership/employee-wellness-in-the-corporate-workplace.html

Maslach, C., & Leiter, M. P. (2016). Understanding the burnout experience: Recent research and its implications for psychiatry. *World Psychiatry, 15*(2), 103–111. https://doi.org/10.1002/wps.20311

Part VI

The Changing Face of the C-Suite

Conclusion

Advantages, Challenges, and Future Directions for the Access Economy C-Suite

I close this book by addressing its central purpose: to provide a stronger evidence base for changing the nature of the C-suite to align with the developing needs of C-level professionals and the external challenges facing organisations. The team-based approach to engaging top talent is made possible by an access economy business model using PO to ensure relationships can be solid and enduring.

This ground-breaking way of working for the C-suite, Strategy and Leadership as Service, challenges the ubiquitous employment model. It allows C-suite professionals to break ties with corporate life to enjoy freedom, control, flexibility, and belonging while delivering much-needed functional, emotional, and collective intelligence to organisations.

This final chapter highlights the advantages to both C-suite professionals and organisations of engaging with Strategy and Leadership as Service, whether as individuals or in teams using the Four Rs: the roots, routes, relationships, and the roadmap.

This business model is already proven and working effectively with SMEs. However, it isn't well known and is in its infancy regarding take-up. While a rethink of the traditional C-suite set-up is long overdue, it still needs to happen. There are some downsides and barriers to making this shift.

I then go on to distinguish this approach from consulting business models. I consider how human resource practices within organisations must

DOI: 10.4324/9781003368090-21

change to manage accountability of this new C-suite service and how the Strategy and Leadership as Service business model impacts other factors such as managing business risk and corporate governance.

Finally, I consider the study's limitations and the directions for further research, along with the significance to practice, theory, and the future of work.

Advantages to C-suite professionals and organisations

Whether individually or in teams, the C-suite executives successfully adopting this access economy business model will develop deep specialisms and be able to work across a portfolio of clients in these areas – giving them freedom, purpose, variety, and flexibility in how they work. They will be serial masters, working in their flow. They can choose who they work with and move away from traditional job security to income security, their diverse portfolio of clients protecting against redundancy, sector traumas, and business failures. Their careers will be future-proofed as they learn how to find, win, and keep clients, ensuring they can access the market and make a living. Through developing their knowledge and skillsets in the Four Rs, they will learn about the key ingredients for long-lasting relationships and how to put these into practice. They will know their clients' businesses, enjoy a shared identity and feel at home. They will be accessible, available, and approachable to their clients. The relationships will be intimate and develop through shared activities and investing in their clients' businesses. Yet they won't be wholly dependent on any one client, which provides space to create psychological safety giving them the freedom to challenge constructively.

Being off the payroll with a clear remit for strategy and leadership means they bring in other resources to do lower-level work. This ensures the client gains the appropriate level of skills for each role. When they are client-side, they deliver the value only they can achieve. The client gets them at their best, and they gain fulfilment from their roles.

They will feel a sense of belonging to their client's business and their firm of C-suite providers. These are not mutually exclusive. Their tribe of peers will provide support, protection, knowledge-sharing, problem-solving, learning and development, camaraderie, and social interaction. It will be somewhere they feel safe.

This team-based approach allows executives to learn from others and share their ideas – they are not one-person bands struggling for personal and professional development.

Organisations with the most challenging strategies will need a team approach. These companies will benefit from the knowledge and skills of a collective of C-suite professionals. This approach will likely involve a Lead C-suite executive to manage the client relationship with a team of specialists called in to work on specific projects as they arise. There will always be capacity and the most appropriate skillsets available. Skills, time, and knowledge won't restrict the organisation, reducing risk and enabling it to seize opportunities. It will always get the answer.

To sum up, this new way of working is revolutionary in meeting the needs of C-suite professionals and organisations.

Downsides and barriers to adoption

Ownership versus access

It is legitimate to ask why Strategy and Leadership as Service is still in its early stages of adoption. More and more entrepreneurial businesses globally are taking on part-time C-suite services, and a limited number of larger organisations are engaging with the approach. Yet, it is still early days in terms of market penetration. What's holding us back?

One response is that it takes time for some services to gain traction. Take the accounting profession, for example. This originates from 4000 BC, with the first accounting firm in the UK established in the 1850s (ICAEW, 2023). In comparison, Strategy and Leadership as Service is only just beginning.

Yet there's more to it. The traditional C-suite set-up needs to move with the times. What will it take to make that shift? Can organisations ever fully let go of the comfort blanket of the employment contract for their C-suite?

It is still customary to employ and own talent rather than access it. Something is reassuring for business owners about having their people all to themselves, focusing entirely on their priorities. The default assumption of businesses is that Strategy and Leadership as Service has a place and is helpful. It fills a gap and can deliver short, medium, and long-term value. Yet most still believe it is the stepping stone to the employed role.

For C-suite professionals and organisations, believing employment is the best way to secure future talent is misguided. Indeed, for the executives, portfolio working through a model like Strategy and Leadership as Service ticks most of their requirements. As the generational make-up of the C-suite moves from Generation X to Y and Z, it may be the preferred way for these individuals to engage. It could become the only way for businesses to keep their competitive edge and access the talent they need. We've seen it with the new business models for music streaming, viewing films, transport, and holidays. It's feasible to believe that we will access talent rather than employ it in the future.

Corporate is the enemy

The C-suite professionals working in the access economy are rejecting corporates. They view being part of a C-suite firm as enhancing their independent identity as a professional rather than taking it away. Working in this different way is a new concept to many, and sometimes it takes effort for C-suite executives to shake off their memories of corporate. Many C-suite professionals cite "becoming corporate" as a reason to fight against any structure or process introduced by their firm of C-suite providers. This is a paradox when they often advocate this way of working to their clients! Nevertheless, many have wounds from corporate life and resist structure, process, and accountability when it is applied directly to them.

Not being corporate, therefore, can become a crucial part of the culture of firms of C-suite providers and unite the team. Corporations can sometimes be seen as the enemy. C-suite executives in the access economy are happy to help their clients scale and become a larger otganisation or get acquired by a corporate, but they want something other than a corporate culture themselves. More positively, they seek a distinction from the most constraining and internal political aspects of corporate life that stifle creativity and threaten integrity.

More consistency is required as a firm of C-suite providers scales, so we have a dilemma. How can these firms scale up and bring in process, structure, and consistency without becoming the corporate beast that most of their team have rejected? If approached incorrectly, history could repeat itself, which could be an additional barrier to adoption. The firms of C-suite providers need to carefully build their cultures to address the needs of their C-suite professionals while at the same time having enough structure and process to grow.

Legislation and regulation

The emergence of the gig economy has led to some countries stepping up their regulation regarding gig workers' rights and taxation.

The lower end can be exploitative, with low pay, little protection for workers and a "take it or leave it" attitude to the work available, as there will always be someone else willing to do it. Businesses gain access to a community of flexible contractors, so they will likely have it covered no matter where or what type of work they offer. They pay workers per contract with little or no add-on costs for holidays, sick pay, or benefits required, which can work out quite lucrative for organisations. The flip side is that these workers may not be as invested in their company as their permanent employees.

This means there is no safety net for these gig economy workers. They don't have access to healthcare and retirement benefits, and they are responsible for paying their taxes which can be an added burden. Most worrying is that these contracts could be the first to go if a company wishes to reduce costs.

Some individuals have no choice but to take on gig economy roles as it is the only work available for the low-skilled. In these situations, these workers welcome increased legislation and regulation to ensure they are treated fairly with some protection, particularly when the gig work on offer is dressed up as a contract but has employment characteristics. There is also an argument that governments are subsidising the companies using gig workers because they are more likely to be entitled to state benefits that would otherwise be paid for by the contractor or employer. To get to grips with contract work and employment, some governments have created legislation for businesses and workers to determine the nature of the work, e.g., IR35 legislation in the UK.

Overall, the gig economy typically has a low commitment from both sides, the gig workers and the companies that take them on.

Yet, as Strategy and Leadership as Service has shown, it doesn't have to be like this. It is a different perspective at the privileged end of the gig economy. Professionals are actively seeking out this type of work. They want the freedom and flexibility to work this way. They realise they must price their work to allow for holidays and sick leave. They are generally more knowledgeable regarding the rules for paying their taxes; if not, they recognise they need to take advice to ensure they are compliant.

Most importantly, they recognise the risk that low commitment can lead to temporary relationships. They see the value in having a diverse portfolio of clients, which brings income security and confidence to challenge their clients. By consciously learning to implement the Four R's, they can take full advantage of this access economy business model and develop PO to ensure the commitment is high both ways with interdependent relationships. Enlightened organisations benefit from a committed and engaged, joined-up team of C-suite professionals, available on tap, with the right skillsets and mindsets for each type of role as it arises and consistently striving to deliver the best outcome for the business.

As gig work gains more traction (there are already estimated to be over 50 million people having experienced gig work in 2022 in the US) (Buffett, 2022), it's important to distinguish between the privileged and lower ends of the gig economy. The current IR35 legislation in the UK and other equivalents globally focus on the nature of the role and relationship between the client and the gig worker. Generally, several tests must be satisfied for the work to fall outside IR35 and be true self-employed work. Strategy and Leadership as Service delivered by Liberti has been carefully designed to comply fully with this legislation. Yet, blunt instruments of regulation assuming one size fits all could damage the adoption of new business models like Strategy and Leadership as Service going forwards.

Distinction from consulting models

While there are some similarities, there are critical differences between Strategy and Leadership as Service and consulting business models. Consulting firms work from the "outside in" instead of the "inside out." They advise rather than implement. They adopt highly leveraged business models where a team of individuals with different levels of skills supports senior partners with top-level skills. In comparison, Strategy and Leadership as Service is non-leveraged, with all C-suite executives operating at the same expert level.

For mid-tier firms, the types of consultants brought in tend to be those focused on these entrepreneurial businesses, e.g., mid-tier accounting firms with consulting arms or specialist boutiques. For the midmarket and larger corporates, the consultants will be the more well-known organisations like the Big Four accountants and global management consulting organisations.

Businesses frequently take on consultants at various times during their lifecycle, for specific interventions or on a more regular basis to help them grow. While companies do not employ their Strategy and Leadership as Service professionals, which is the same for external consultants, that is where the similarity ends. It is, in fact, a very different proposition from consulting.

First, consultants tend to work on specific projects to solve problems, i.e., temporary interventions. They are outsiders. They help an organisation fix a problem or exploit an opportunity. They are the experts in that issue and bring their knowledge and approach to assist the business in moving forward. They tend to focus on diagnosing the problem and putting forward solutions. At this point, while they can advise the internal team to implement the answer, they generally do not deliver the implementation themselves. This is very different to Strategy and Leadership as Service, which is heavily focused on delivery by seasoned C-suite executives working inside the organisation and for the long-term, too, not just on and off for problems as they arise. The C-suite professionals delivering the Strategy and Leadership as Service business model will likely be the ones the consultants advise.

The consultant business model is also generally very heavily leveraged. The consulting team will include a lead partner, director, manager, associates, juniors and analysts. This highly leveraged team has different skillsets at each level doing the most appropriate work. In contrast, access economy professionals operate a non-leveraged business model. All are experts in their fields with specialisms. They will mentor and train individuals with lower-level skillsets in their clients.

Other types of advisors, such as coaching organisations, peer networking groups, and portfolio workers offering consulting products, again, have similarities with Strategy and Leadership as Service. They often involve their people working with organisations on a self-employed basis. Still, like the other consulting models, they work from the "outside in" and are not implementers, working internally for the long-term.

Changes to human resource practices

If we aren't going to employ our C-suite going forwards, what will be the implications for our human resource practices? Remuneration can be more straightforward. We will move from yearly salaries with bonuses and benefits to agreed amounts for the role depending on the time commitment and outputs generated. There can still be fixed and variable elements if needed. The relationship will be something other than employment. It will be a business-to-business contract. The variable elements can relate to the delivery of agreed stretch goals.

The key focus needs to be accountability. Even if the individuals aren't employed or present in the office daily, they will still be held accountable for their roles. The C-suite professionals will agree on the activities, responsibilities, and outcomes upfront and put a workplan in place to schedule everything. This document will be a crucial communication tool for the business and executive to use to manage expectations, discuss progress and issues, share value created, and course correct if needed. A cadence of regular reviews, at least quarterly, ensures the relationship stays on track.

Until access economy business models become more mainstream for the C-suite, these relationships are monitored and scrutinised even more carefully than roles being carried out by an employed individual, as has been reported by business owners. The fact that these roles can be stopped at any time and are outside the payroll, compared with the more fixed and permanent employment roles, encourages business owners to check that they are receiving value regularly. This could be a good thing. It's easy to forget the month-in and month-out payroll cost of employment, and in many countries, it is almost impossible to make changes rapidly. Moving to an access economy model could help keep the relationship between the business and C-suite professionals healthy and consistently delivering value.

Recruitment practices will be affected by moving to an access economy business model. Human resource professionals must build relationships with firms of C-suite providers who can source the appropriate team to deliver what's needed. Even though the connections can endure, the form may change over time, with different team members joining as needed. For smaller organisations with straightforward requirements, one team member will likely deliver the service with support from the wider team as required. For larger organisations, for those with complex needs, the team's make-up is likely to be much more fluid. Team members will come and go depending on their specialisms. However, it will work well if a C-suite team leader manages the resource allocation and is the primary point of contact for the relationship with the business.

Managing risk and corporate governance

Having the ability to bring in specialists for each piece of work, as and when required, while always having a relationship with a Lead C-suite professional who heads up the service will de-risk the business considerably. Employees who go outside their area of expertise to fill a gap increase risk, and, of course, there's the opportunity cost of time not spent doing their expected role. It's crucial for organisations that individuals with the appropriate qualifications and experience deliver their roles. Businesses that employ a C-suite executive can become constrained by one set of time and skills, one network, one mindset and so on. They can only augment this by buying in external interim or consulting skillsets. These fill capacity and skill gaps but aren't joined up (usually, they are sourced separately) and will require oversight and management from the incumbent C-suite professional.

This is not the case for Strategy and Leadership as Service. In theory, there are infinite specialist options available for the business. The team of C-suite professionals are accustomed to working together, have well communicated, and tried and tested, methodologies of work and take responsibility for implementing and delivering the function. As discussed throughout this book, over-reliance on individual C-suite team members and expecting them to be superhuman increases business risks. Strategy and Leadership as Service is the antidote.

For corporate governance purposes, it is essential for C-suite professionals delivering Strategy and Leadership as Service to work strategically and operationally for the organisation and for board members to hold the fiduciary duties. This way, strong corporate governance is upheld, and the board can hold the leadership team accountable for performance. Responsibilities are segregated to ensure essential business areas receive complete and proper focus.

Limitations and further opportunities for research

The research investigating the role of PO in Strategy and Leadership as Service has focused on the Liberti business model. This field of research would benefit considerably from a thorough and more widespread quantitative study of client-supplier professional services relationships in the access economy. This would validate the findings that PO can form the basis of these relationships and be a substitute for traditional employment. In addition, validating the importance of the roots and routes of PO and establishing which are most salient through related field interventions designed to test each root and route are recommended. Further studies on how different individual and situational factors impact PO in the access economy and how target attributes develop would be beneficial.

If the access economy for professional services is to become a valid alternative to traditional employment, I advocate a more widespread study of this segment of the economy. What would be required structurally, economically, culturally, and behaviourally for access to be accepted widely as a substitute for employment in professional services as part of a society-wide change? Is it the access economy relationship that encourages more freedom and flexibility or the employed model that loses it?

The new system is already emerging: the pandemic has forced widespread behavioural change with remote working, which has generally had favourable responses. The escalating threat of climate change encourages some members of society to use the access economy to increase sustainability, and the SME economy has a growing awareness of its benefits. The innovators, networks of interacting agents, and practising communities are developing, yet we are still not at the tipping point. Further work is required to fully understand and illuminate the road to this new way of working as part of the future of work, with PO within the access economy for professional services contributing to this new world.

Significance to practice, theory, and the future of work

This research and body of work are relevant to practice. Training and coaching part-time C-suite professionals to develop PO with their clients, fellow team members, and any intermediating organisation can lead to enduring and valuable relationships in the access economy.

It extends the theory as it indicates that PO can be present in the professional services context of the sharing economy, with many pathways to its development. Through PO, we could benefit from access while having feelings of ownership.

If we design the system carefully and maintain PO across the whole ecosystem, service offerings like Strategy and Leadership as Service will develop to disrupt and challenge the traditional employment model and shape the future of work. We will finally realise that "You are what you can access" (Belk, 2014, p. 1595).

References

Belk, R. (2014). You are what you can access: Sharing and collaborative consumption online. *Journal of Business Research*, 67(8), 1595–1600. https://doi.org/10.1016/j.jbusres.2013.10.001

Buffett, J. (2022, August 16). *Workers on the gig economy: 2022 statistics*. Zety. Retrieved April 2, 2023, from https://zety.com/blog/workers-on-gig-economy

ICAEW. (2023). *Timeline*. Retrieved April 2, 2023, from www.icaew.com/library/historical-resources/timeline

Appendices

Appendix 1: Examples of Existing Research

Research	Context	Method	Findings
Atasoy & Morewedge, 2018	Digital & physical versions of the same goods	Experimental	Differences in PO for physical and digital goods mediated the difference in value, with digital versions of the same goods being ascribed less value than their physical counterparts. The marketing, psychology, and economics of physical and digital goods are all influenced by the features of an object's ability to attract PO before it is purchased.
Bardhi & Eckhardt, 2012	Car sharing	Qualitative	Access does not produce a sense of joint or perceived ownership
Carrozzi et al., 2019	Augmented reality (AR) holograms	Quantitative experimental	Study one demonstrates how customers can feel the PO of digital products by customising AR holograms. The social adaptation mechanisms of assimilation and differentiation that underlie the relationship between customisation and PO of AR holograms in social contexts are highlighted in Study two. Study three shows how these mechanisms are affected when users switch between personal or shared devices due to the affordances of AR technology.

Research	Context	Method	Findings
Danckwerts & Kenning, 2019	Music streaming	Quantitative using structural equation modelling	Music-based PO, which is positively influenced by the feeling of control over the music accessed, is positively related to service-based PO, which results from users' investment of self into the service. The findings also demonstrate a strong correlation between music-based PO and users' intention to upgrade from the free to premium service. This underscores the significance of PO for music streaming service providers, particularly those using a feature-restricted freemium business model.
Fritze et al., 2020	Car sharing & music streaming	Quantitative: Four studies using cross-sectional, longitudinal & experimental data	1. Customers increase their service consumption while decreasing material ownership when ABS customers experience feelings of PO because they see the service as a replacement for material possession (ownership). 2. By encouraging feelings of ownership and subsequent consumption, the primary antecedents of PO offer guidelines for promoting ABS. 3. Intangible services can replace material products as targets of a sense of ownership.
Karahanna et al., 2015	Social media	Quantitative longitudinal	People motivated by PO use social media because it offers opportunities to meet their fundamental PO needs. The study creates scales for measuring these needs, and empirical findings imply that they collectively influence PO motivation and social media use.

Research	Context	Method	Findings
Lawson, 2018	Digital consumption: Film streaming, i.e., Netflix	Quantitative	1. PO is possible in this context. 2. Antecedents of Investment of Self and Intimacy were found to be significant. 3. Antecedent Efficacy was found to be insignificant. 4. Duration of use was found to be insignificant.
Lee et al., 2019	Airbnb hosts	Quantitative with structural equation modelling of 224 hosts	Gaining a sense of PO, which ultimately affects how citizens behave toward the organisation and peer hosts, depends on attachment to a platform firm. The findings imply that the newly established structure should consider an attachment and PO partnership mechanism when working with specific service providers in its operational management.
Paundra et al., 2017	Car sharing	Experimental	Psychological disposition, specifically PO, of potential customers and instrumental car attributes need to be considered when developing measures to stimulate car-sharing services in society.
Peck & Barger, 2009; Peck et al., 2013	Material objects visualised	Quantitative, experimental	Two experiments show that having consumers close their eyes and imagine touching an object can increase PO and valuation. What's more, the increase is of a similar magnitude to what would be obtained by having consumers physically touch the object.
Peck & Shu, 2018; Kamleitner & Mitchell, 2018	Personal data	Review of literature	Customers are likely to feel little ownership over a good that is increasingly being taken from them and sold in markets with little to no consumer participation.

Research	Context	Method	Findings
Peck & Shu, 2018; Kirk et al., 2018	Digital technologies, e.g., websites, content, virtual worlds, gaming.	Review of literature	Consumers often come to feel PO of digital technologies. Digital technologies often facilitate the emergence of PO of non-digital technologies. Digital affordances, which are features of a digital technology object that facilitate users' abilities to appropriate or engage with the technology (e.g., interactive design elements and interfaces), appear to be important in these processes and can limit or increase users' opportunities for feeling ownership for a digital target. The degree to which consumers choose to take advantage of digital affordances and, consequently, the degree to which affordances translate into feelings of ownership are also influenced by consumers' motivational orientations and individual differences.
Sinclair & Tinson, 2017	Music streaming	Qualitative interviews and online-themed discussion groups.	Identified motivations (place, identity, control), antecedents (investing self, intimately knowing the target, pride and controlling the target) and outcomes (loyalty, empowerment, social rewards) of PO are evident in the consumers' experiences of music streaming.
Stoner et al., 2018	Material objects	Quantitative, experimental	PO drives attitudes, buying intentions, and willingness to accept products by consumers who name products.

References

Atasoy, O., & Morewedge, C. K. (2018). Digital goods are valued less than physical goods. *Journal of Consumer Research, 44*(6), 1343–1357. https://doi.org/10.1093/jcr/ucx102

Bardhi, F., & Eckhardt, G. M. (2012). Access-based consumption: The case of car sharing. *Journal of Consumer Research, 39*(4), 881–898. https://doi.org/10.1086/666376

Carrozzi, A., Chylinski, M., Heller, J., Hilken, T., Keeling, D. I., & De Ruyter, K. (2019). What's mine is a hologram? How shared augmented reality augments psychological ownership. *Journal of Interactive Marketing, 48*(1), 71–88. https://doi.org/10.1016/j.intmar.2019.05.004

Danckwerts, S., & Kenning, P. (2019). It's my service, it's my music: The role of psychological ownership in music streaming consumption. *Psychology & Marketing, 36*(9), 803–816. https://doi.org/10.1002/mar.21213

Fritze, P., Marchand, A., Eisingerich, B., & Benkenstein, M. (2020). Access-based services as substitutes for material possessions: The role of psychological ownership. *Journal of Service Research, 23*(3), 368–385. https://doi.org/10.1177/1094670520907691

Kamleitner, B., & Mitchell, V. W. (2018). Can consumers experience ownership for their personal data? From issues of scope and invisibility to agents handling our digital blueprints. In Peck, J., & Shu, S. (Eds.) *Psychological Ownership and Consumer Behavior* (pp. 91–118). Springer, Cham. https://doi.org/10.1007/978-3-319-77158-8_6

Karahanna, E., Xu, S. X., & Zhang, N. (2015). Psychological ownership motivation and use of social media. *The Journal of Marketing Theory and Practice, 23*(2), 185–207.

Kirk, C. P., Peck, J., & Swain, S. D. (2018). Property lines in the mind: Consumers' psychological ownership and their territorial responses. *Journal of Consumer Research, 45*(1), 148–168. https://doi.org/10.1093/jcr/ucx111

Lawson, D. J., & Fytraki, A. (2018). Psychological ownership implications in an access-based, digital consumption context. *Doctoral Dissertation, Master's Thesis* (Erasmus University Rotterdam).

Lee, H., Yang, S. B., & Koo, C. (2019). Exploring the effect of Airbnb hosts' attachment and psychological ownership in the sharing economy. *Tourism Management, 70*, 284–294. https://doi.org/10.1016/j.tourman.2018.08.017

Paundra, J., Rook, L., Van Dalen, J., & Ketter, W. (2017). Preferences for car sharing services: Effects of instrumental attributes and psychological ownership. *Journal of Environmental Psychology, 53*, 121–130. https://doi.org/10.1016/j.jenvp.2017.07.003

Peck, J., & Barger, V. (2009). *In search of a surrogate for touch: The effect of haptic imagery on psychological ownership and object valuation.* ACR North American Advances.

Peck, J., Barger, V. A., & Webb, A. (2013). In search of a surrogate for touch: The effect of haptic imagery on perceived ownership. *Journal of Consumer Psychology, 23*(2), 189–196. https://doi.org/10.1016/j.jcps.2012.09.001

Peck, J., & Shu, S. B. (2018). *Psychological ownership and consumer behavior.* Springer. https://doi.org/10.1007/978-3-319-77158-8

Sinclair, G. F., & Tinson, J. (2017). Psychological ownership and music streaming consumption. *Journal of Business Research*, *71*, 1–9. https://doi.org/10.1016/j.jbusres.2016.10.002

Stoner, J. L., Loken, B., & Stadler Blank, A. (2018). The name game: How naming products increases psychological ownership and subsequent consumer evaluations. *Journal of Consumer Psychology*, *28*(1), 130–137. https://doi.org/10.1002/jcpy.1005

Appendix 2: Overview of Research Steps

Research approach

Sampling

I used purposive and snowball sampling techniques (Bryman, 2016).

Purposive sampling of CFOs

I strategically sampled CFOs to select those most relevant to my research question. My sampling covered the full range of overall retention capabilities of CFOs to conduct a comparative case study with the four comparison sets covering short, medium, long, and extended retention capabilities, all measured at pre-Covid levels.

Approaching CFOs

Following the selection of CFOs, I contacted their RD first. I explained my research purpose and made them aware that I wanted to interview one of their team members, who I would ask to suggest one of their clients for an interview. None of the RDs made any changes to my selection. I then emailed the CFOs explaining my research purpose and asking for their commitment to participate.

Scheduling interviews with CFOs

On receipt of the CFO's consent, I scheduled an interview using Zoom at a mutually convenient time for approximately 90 minutes. During the Zoom session, I conducted two interviews with each CFO to cover the following:

- PO of CFO towards a nominated client; and
- PO of CFO towards CFOC.

Interviews took place over six months.

Snowball sampling of clients

I conducted a snowball sampling of clients. I asked each CFO to suggest clients with characteristics relevant to the research. We discussed each client's situation at length, focusing on their willingness to participate in the study and other aspects, such as length of engagement and depth of relationship, from the CFO's perspective.

Some CFOs thought the impact of Covid-19 on their business would influence their client's willingness to participate.

The 22 CFOs interviewed suggested 24 clients for interview (two CFOs recommended two clients each). In total, 17 clients agreed to participate. Many CFOs were keen to introduce me to clients with whom they felt they had a healthy relationship. This is a natural reaction as it is easier for a CFO to ask clients with whom they think they have their best relationships. Given my positional power in the business, the CFOs wished to showcase their strongest relationships to me.

I was happy that the CFOs chose the clients they felt would respond. Yet, I encouraged them to include clients with new and problematic relationships to gain an overall view of establishing PO in all circumstances. On reflection, the more confident and established CFOs and those with whom I already had a trusted relationship were willing to introduce me to clients with whom they considered their relationship to be sub-optimal.

Solely virtual relationships

To compare completely virtual relationships with those that started in physical settings, I chose several pairings where the client and CFO had not physically met in person.

Data collection

Overall process

To build the question set for the semi-structured interviews, I first researched other studies of PO in different contexts and reviewed their question sets. From here, I formulated some possible interview questions and tested them in early pilot interviews with clients and CFOs. I identified any issues, revised the interview questions, and finalised the guide for rollout to the complete selection set of CFOs and clients.

Interview questions

I formulated the questions regarding the roots and routes of PO by studying prior research in the field (Avey et al., 2009; Campbell Pickford et al., 2016; Chang et al., 2012; Fritze et al., 2020; Hou et al., 2009; Malhotra & Van Alstyne, 2014; Olkers, 2013).

While this was not a quantitative study, I asked participants to score the questions on a scale of one to five as follows:

1. Strongly disagree/not at all/none/unsatisfactory
2. Disagree/occasionally/a bit/below average
3. Neither agree nor disagree/sometimes/some/satisfactory
4. Agree/quite often/quite a lot/above average
5. Strongly agree/all the time/fully/excellent

This was to corroborate the qualitative responses so that I was clear on how strongly the participant felt about the question. It also enabled me to estimate how strongly CFOs and clients felt the roots and routes.

PO question

The first part of the interviews involved asking about the strength of roots and routes of PO present in the relationship.

Towards the end of the interview, I shared Figure A2.1 (adapted from Boivie et al. (2011, p. 575)) with the participants. I asked which case (A, B, C, D, E, F, G, or H) would best illustrate the degree of feelings of PO they felt towards their CFO/client/CFOC. The participant would pick the letter that most closely matched their feelings about PO. This question enabled

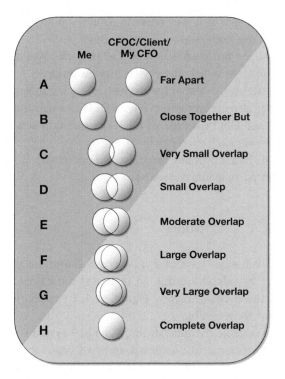

Figure A2.1 Degree of feelings of psychological ownership towards my CFO/my Client/CFOC

Source: Adapted from Boivie et al. (2011, p. 575). Used with permission of *Academy of Management Journal* from "Me or we: The effects of CEO organizational identification on agency costs" by Steven Boivie, Donald Lange, Michael L. McDonald, and James D. Westphal, in Volume 54, No. 3, 2011; permission conveyed through Copyright Clearance Center, Inc.

me to gauge the degree of presence of PO in the relationship and compare this to the stated levels of roots and routes of PO discussed earlier in the interview.

Pilot guide and final question set

After formulating the initial interview questions, I reviewed them and conducted four pilot interviews to test the question set.

The pilot interviews were well received, and the only change I made to the question set post-pilot was to introduce the questions on introversion or extroversion and identity, inspired by "The impact of technology-mediated consumption on identity: The case of Airbnb" (Festila & Müller, 2017).

I wanted to investigate if it was possible to develop any particular client archetypes from my study.

The interviewees' feedback was very positive, and I was able to include all the other questions within my final interview guide.

Appendix 3 shows the actual questions used as a guide in each of the categories of semi-structured interviews – CFO towards the client, client towards CFO, and CFO towards CFOC. The question sets were similar yet not the same for each category.

Most sections had a primary question and additional secondary questions to prompt participants if needed.

Medium and transcription

I conducted all the interviews except two over Zoom. I completed these two interviews by telephone due to technical difficulties with Zoom. When I asked the client to review Figure A2.1, I emailed it for them to review while we were talking.

Zoom was a suitable medium during Covid-19 as many CFOs and clients worked from home in lockdown and had become accustomed to video conferencing. They travelled much less and were relatively easy to contact to schedule interviews. I recorded all of the Zoom calls for future reference during data analysis.

I used AI technology, Otter.ai, linked to my Zoom account, to transcribe the interviews. It was reasonably accurate, and before coding each interview, I reviewed each transcript alongside the video recording for completeness and accuracy. All interview transcripts are stored securely and electronically.

Confidentiality

I explained to both CFOs and clients that I would not be giving them feedback from their pair due to confidentiality and that all responses would be anonymised.

Insider/outsider dilemma

As the global CEO, I will likely have influenced (consciously and unconsciously) participants' responses during these interviews. It is challenging to understand to what extent this may have happened. To counteract this, I kept to the semi-structured interview guide with each participant to give consistency and prompt my interviewees for responses without becoming deeply involved in a two-way conversation with them. Since I am Liberti's CEO and not the CEO of The CFO Centre UK, I do not have a direct relationship with the clients and CFOs, which could also have been helpful.

Other data sources

In Appendix 4, I share other data sources from the business I used in this study to contextualise the relationships.

Data analysis

Qualitative research can produce massive data sets, particularly text transcripts, if the research method comprises interviews, as does this one. Miles (1979) describes qualitative data as an "attractive nuisance" because its rich data is attractive yet tricky to synthesise into sense-making and, ultimately, theory. Unlike quantitative data analysis, there are no clear rules to follow. Instead, there are guidelines for best practices.

This research's analysis follows grounded theory (Wagner et al., 1968), including coding and thematic analysis.

Analytical approach – grounded theory

The grounded theory approach derives from the data systematically gathered and analysed through the research process. In this method, data collection, analysis, and eventual theory are closely related (Strauss & Corbin, 1998). There are two fundamental tenets to grounded theory. Firstly, the theory develops out of the data. Secondly, the approach is iterative, meaning the data collection and analysis occur in parallel, repeatedly referring back to one another.

Coding process

Coding is a critical process in grounded theory. I divided the interview data by question and then into parts (codes) within each question and gave each code a name. For example, in the question asking the CFO their reasons for joining a client initially, the first few interviews revealed emerging codes of "adding value," "the people at the client," and "the sector in which the client operated." Further interviews revealed more data for these codes and new codes. Hence, it was important to review the interviews repeatedly to capture all the codes' data.

Theoretical saturation

The coding process began as each interview was collected. The codes' development influenced the questioning in future interviews to ensure all available data on this code were collected and any other codes explored. This process is called theoretical saturation.

Constant comparison

This aspect of grounded theory is a significant phase and means that the phenomena coded under each category enabled a theoretical elaboration of that category to emerge.

Using Nvivo

I reviewed the interviews for accuracy with the Zoom video recording and imported them into specialist software called Nvivo. Each of the three categories of interviews, PO of CFO towards the client, PO of the client towards the CFO, and PO of the CFO towards CFOC, were analysed using the grounded theory approach and codes developed in the iterative process described. I could review each code's relevance by examining the number and quality of its references. I was also able to identify any outliers in the sample.

I created Nvivo Cases for each CFO and client and assigned them attributes as follows:

- Age;
- Gender;
- Strength of roots and routes as indicated by their scoring;
- Strength of PO as indicated by their scoring;
- Length of engagement with CFOC;

- Length of engagement between the CFO and the client;
- Introversion and extroversion;
- Identity; and
- Overall retention level of the CFO.

Using Excel

I recorded each question's scores and the attributes noted for each interview. I then collated the root, route, and overall PO scores for each interview within each category. I could then review which roots and routes were the strongest by category and better understand their relationship with the overall expressed PO.

I also used Excel to slice, dice, and review the data by attribute to identify trends relevant to the recorded attributes.

First-order concepts

I developed first-order concepts of the data by developing codes in Nvivo and identifying the strength of roots, routes, and PO in Excel. I grouped the codes into concepts pertinent to the research question. For example, "Sharing boundary" is a first-order concept developed from codes regarding the feelings of sharing experienced by a client, the careful organisation and communication by the CFO when they are available for each client, and how they manage their time and attention accordingly.

Thematic analysis – second-order themes and aggregate dimensions

Then from these first-order concepts, I was able to build second-order themes. Themes directly relate to the research question, build on the codes identified and provide a basis for a theoretical understanding of the data that can contribute to the literature relating to the research question (Bryman, 2016).

Second-order themes were developed using a continuous and iterative process of reviewing the first-order concepts and then stepping back to review the data from a higher perspective and within the research question's context (Heifetz & Laurie, 1997). The second-order themes emerged from this process, as did the aggregate dimensions discussed in the insights.

Outliers

Using both Nvivo and Excel allowed me to identify any outliers within the research. Outliers are incidences where an unexpected or different outcome was determined, often providing valuable insight into the data interpretation. I investigated the outliers in this study further by reviewing their context, and I discussed them in the insights section.

Limitations of comparative case study design

I acknowledge that the findings are generalisable only in this case study to the wider CFOC, Liberti community, and possibly the professional services access economy. This design aims to fully understand the role of PO, its roots and routes within a case study for sharing professional services in the access economy and use that information to theorise and inform further studies.

References

Avey, J. B., Avolio, B. J., Crossley, C. D., & Luthans, F. (2009). Psychological ownership: Theoretical extensions, measurement and relation to work outcomes. *Journal of Organizational Behavior*, 30(2), 173–191. https://doi.org/10.1002/job.583

Boivie, S., Lange, D., McDonald, M., & Westphal, J. D. (2011). Me or we: The effects of CEO organizational identification on agency costs. *Academy of Management Journal*, 54(3), 551–576. https://doi.org/10.5465/amj.2011.61968081

Bryman, A. (2016). *Social research methods* (5th edn). OUP Oxford.

Campbell Pickford, H. C., Joy, G., & Roll, K. (2016). Psychological ownership: Effects and applications. *Saïd Business School WP*, 32. https://doi.org/10.2139/ssrn.2893092

Chang, A., Chiang, H. H., & Han, T. S. (2012). A multilevel investigation of relationships among brand-centered hrm, brand psychological ownership, brand citizenship behaviors, and customer satisfaction. *European Journal of Marketing*, 46(5), 626–662. https://doi.org/10.1108/03090561211212458

Festila, M. S., & Müller, S. D. (2017). The impact of technology-mediated consumption on identity: The case of Airbnb. *Proceedings of the 50th Annual Hawaii International Conference on System Sciences*, 54–63. https://doi.org/10.24251/hicss.2017.007

Fritze, P., Marchand, A., Eisingerich, B., & Benkenstein, M. (2020). Access-based services as substitutes for material possessions: The role of psychological ownership. *Journal of Service Research*, 23(3), 368–385. https://doi.org/10.1177/1094670520907691

Heifetz, R. A., & Laurie, D. D. (1997). The work of leadership: Leaders do not need to know all the answers. They do need to ask the right questions. *Harvard Business Review*, 124–134.

Hou, S. T., Hsu, M. Y., & Wu, S. H. (2009). Psychological ownership and franchise growth. *International Journal of Entrepreneurial Behaviour & Research, 15*(5), 415–435. https://doi.org/10.1108/13552550910983004

Malhotra, A., & Van Alstyne, M. (2014). The dark side of the sharing economy … and how to lighten it. *Communications of the ACM, 57*(11), 24–27. https://doi.org/10.1145/2668893

Miles, M. B. (1979). Qualitative data as an attractive nuisance: The problem of analysis. *Administrative Science Quarterly, 24*(4), 590–601. https://doi.org/10.2307/2392365

Olkers, C. (2013). Psychological ownership: Development of an instrument. *SA Journal of Industrial Psychology, 39*(2), 1–13. https://doi.org/10.4102/sajip.v39i2.1105

Strauss, A., & Corbin, J. M. (1998). *Basics of qualitative research: Techniques and procedures for developing grounded theory.* Sage Publications, Incorporated.

Wagner, H., Glaser, B. G., & Strauss, A. L. (1968). The discovery of grounded theory: Strategies for qualitative research (book review). *Social Forces, 46*(4), 555. https://doi.org/10.2307/2575405

Appendix 3: Question Sets

1. Client interviews regarding CFO

How does PO impact client-supplier relationships in the access economy for sharing professional services?

Scale 1–5:
Explain scoring:

1. Strongly disagree / not at all / none / unsatisfactory
2. Disagree / occasionally / a bit / below average
3. Neither agree nor disagree / sometimes / some / satisfactory
4. Agree / quite often / quite a lot / above average
5. Strongly agree / all the time / fully / excellent

Context setting

1. To begin, please tell me a bit about you and your business.
2. Initially, what were your reasons for engaging your part-time CFO?

Relationship overview

3. How would you describe your relationship with your part-time CFO?
4. What are the most important things to you about the relationship?

Explore Roots of PO – characteristics of service offering

Efficacy relating to intimacy

5. To what extent does your part-time CFO really understand your needs? (Scale 1–5)
   - Do you feel comfortable describing the service of part-time CFOs to someone who is not familiar with it?
   - Are you familiar with the range of services your part-time CFO can provide?
   - To what level are you knowledgeable about the services that your part-time CFO offers? (Scale 1–5)

Self-identity relating to identity

6. To what extent does having a part-time CFO help you to achieve the identity you want to have? (Scale 1–5)
   - Does having a part-time CFO help you narrow the gap between who you are and who you want to be?
   - Is having a part-time CFO central to your identity? Part of who you are?
   - If you could no longer have a part-time CFO, would you feel part of your identity had been taken away?
   - Do you derive some of your identity from having a part-time CFO?
   - How does having a part-time CFO enable you to feel? What is your view of having a part-time CFO?

Having a place relating to communal identification

7. To what extent does using a part-time CFO allow you to be part of a group of like-minded people? (Scale 1–5)
   - To what extent does using a part-time CFO allow you to belong to a group of people with similar interests (Scale 1–5)
   - What interactions do you have with other part-time CFO users? Of your CFO? Of The CFO Centre or industry as a whole? How well do you know other users?

Explore Routes of PO – activities users undertake in response to the characteristics

Control

8. How much control do you feel you have over your part-time CFO? Objectives? Actions? Time? Input? (Scale 1–5)

- How do you determine their input and output? How easy is this to do?
- How accessible is your part-time CFO when not in your office? How responsive?
- How approachable is your part-time CFO? Do they ever pop in?
- What does your part-time CFO give you?

Knowing intimately

9. How intimately do you feel you know your part-time CFO? (Scale 1–5)
   - How much personal information do you share with them? What's stopping you?
   - What type of bond would you say you have with your CFO?
   - What feelings do you have towards them? Friends beyond work?
   - How comfortable do you feel spending time with your part-time CFO?

Psychological safety

10. To what extent do you feel psychologically safe? (Scale 1–5)

(Psychological safety is "feeling able to show and employ one's self without fear of negative consequences to self-image, status, or career" (Kahn 1990, p. 708)).

Investing self

11. To what extent do you feel your part-time CFO is part of/a member of/belongs to your organisation? Would you say your part-time CFO is your CFO? Scale (1–5)
    - How do you introduce your part-time CFO to outsiders? Your staff? Are you proud to say "This is my CFO" to people you meet?
    - What activities do you do together? What do you create together?
    - Are your part-time CFO's values aligned with yours and those of your organisation? Do they fit with your organisation's culture?
    - Do you feel the need to defend your part-time CFO when they are criticised by outsiders and therefore support their goals and policies?
    - Are your common interests with your part-time CFO stronger than your differences?

General questions

Typology
12. On a scale of 1–5, where 1 is introverted and 5 is extroverted, where would you say you sit on the scale?
13. On a scale of 1–5, where 1 is profit or income-focused, and 5 is purpose-focused, where would you say you sit on the scale?

Sharing
14. What level of usage do you have of other sharing services and products? E.g., Airbnb, Uber, Spotify? (Scale 1–5)
    - What is your attitude towards sharing assets and services?
    - How are these other services and products similar or different to sharing your part-time CFO?
    - How do you feel about sharing your part-time CFO with other businesses and business owners? Do you know the other clients?
    - How do you feel about introducing other business owners to your CFO or The CFO Centre to work together?
    - What could other clients in The CFO Centre community give you? What could you gain from them?

Substitutive value
15. To what extent is having a part-time CFO a good substitute for employing one? (Scale 1–5)
    - What circumstances would motivate you to employ a CFO?

Ownership
16. If the circle on the left represents you and the circle on the right represents your part-time CFO, which case (A, B, C, D, E, F, G, or H) would best illustrate the degree of feelings of PO you feel towards your CFO (See Figure A3.1 adapted from Boivie et al. (2011, p. 575)).

Mediator role
17. How would you describe your relationship with The CFO Centre? (Scale 1–5)
    - What does The CFO Centre do for you?
    - What interactions have you had?
    - What could it do for you?
    - How would you describe your relationship with your Regional Director (RD)? What could they do for you?

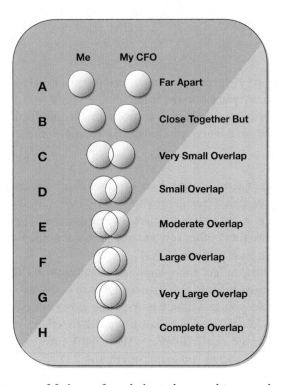

Figure A3.1 Degree of feelings of psychological ownership towards my CFO

Source: Adapted from Boivie et al. (2011, p. 575). Used with permission of *Academy of Management Journal* from "Me or we: The effects of CEO organizational identification on agency costs" by Steven Boivie, Donald Lange, Michael L. McDonald, and James D. Westphal, in Volume 54, No. 3, 2011; permission conveyed through Copyright Clearance Center, Inc.

Exit question

18. Are there any other questions you feel I should have asked but didn't?

2. CFO interviews regarding client relationships

How does PO impact client-supplier relationships in the access economy for sharing professional services?

Scale 1–5:
Explain scoring:

1. Strongly disagree/not at all/none/unsatisfactory
2. Disagree/occasionally/a bit/below average
3. Neither agree nor disagree /sometimes/ some/satisfactory

4. Agree / quite often / quite a lot / above average
5. Strongly agree / all the time / fully / excellent

Context setting

1. First, please tell me a bit about you and your portfolio of clients.
2. What were your reasons for joining [Client Name] as part-time CFO?

Relationship overview

3. How would you describe your relationship with your [Client Name]?
4. What are the most important things to you about the relationship?

Explore Roots of PO – characteristics of service offering

Efficacy relating to intimacy
5. To what extent does [Client Name] really understand your needs? (Scale 1–5)
   - Do you feel comfortable describing the product or service of your [Client Name] to someone who is not familiar with it?
   - Are you familiar with the range of services your [Client Name] can provide?
   - To what level are you knowledgeable about the services that your [Client Name] offers? (Scale 1–5)

Self-identity relating to identity
6. To what extent does being the part-time CFO of [Client Name] help you to achieve the identity you want to have? (Scale 1–5)
   - Does being the part-time CFO of [Client Name] help you narrow the gap between who you are and who you want to be?
   - Is working with [Client Name] central to your identity? Part of who you are?
   - If you could no longer work with [Client Name], would you feel part of your identity had been taken away?
   - Do you derive some of your identity from [Client Name]?
   - How does working with [Client Name] enable you to feel? What is your view of working with [Client Name]?

Having a place relating to communal identification
7. To what extent does working with [Client Name] allow you to be part of a group of like-minded people? (Scale 1–5)

- To what extent does working with [Client Name] allow you to belong to a group of people with similar interests? (Scale 1–5)
- What interactions do you have with other members and employees of [Client Name]?

Explore Routes of PO – activities users undertake in response to the characteristics

Control

8. How much control do you feel you have over your [Client Name]? Objectives? Actions? Time? Input? (Scale 1–5)
   - How accessible is [Client Name]? How responsive?
   - How approachable is [Client Name]?
   - What does [Client Name] give you?

Knowing intimately

9. How intimately do you feel you know [Client Name]? (Scale 1–5)
   - How much personal information do you share with them? What's stopping you?
   - What type of bond would you say you have with [Client Name]?
   - What feelings do you have towards them? Friends beyond work?
   - How comfortable do you feel spending time with [Client Name]?

Psychological safety

10. To what extent do you feel psychologically safe with [Client Name]? (Scale 1–5)

(Psychological safety is "feeling able to show and employ one's self without fear of negative consequences to self-image, status, or career" (Kahn 1990, p. 708)).

Investing self

11. To what extent do you feel you are part of or a member of or belong to [Client Name]? Would you say you are the CFO of [Client Name]? Scale (1–5)
    - How do you introduce yourself to outsiders? Other staff? Are you proud to say "I am the CFO of [Client Name]" to people you meet?
    - When asked to describe your profession, how do you respond?
    - What activities do you do together? What do you create together?

- Are your values aligned with those of [Client Name] and the organisation? Do they fit with the organisation's culture?
- Do you feel the need to defend your [Client Name] when they are criticised by outsiders and therefore support their goals and policies?
- Are your common interests with your [Client Name] stronger than your differences?

General questions

Typology
12. On a scale of 1–5, where 1 is introverted, and 5 is extroverted, where would you say [Client Name] sits on the scale?
13. On a scale of 1–5, where 1 is profit-focused and 5 is purpose-focused, where would you say [Client Name] sits on the scale?

Sharing
14. What level of usage do you have of other sharing services and products? E.g., Airbnb, Uber, Spotify? (Scale 1–5)
    - How are these other services and products similar or different to sharing part-time CFO services?
    - What is your attitude towards sharing assets and services?
15. How do you feel about sharing your services with other businesses and business owners?
    - How do you feel about asking for client referrals?
16. How much information do you share about this aspect of the service with each of your clients?
    - To what extent do you encourage your clients to get to know each other?

Substitutive value
17. To what extent is having a part-time CFO a good substitute for employing one? (Scale 1–5)
    - What circumstances would motivate you to be employed by [Client Name]?

Ownership
18. If the circle on the left represents you and the circle on the right represents [Client Name], which case (A, B, C, D, E, F, G, or H) would best illustrate the degree of feelings of PO you feel towards your Client (see Figure A3.2 adapted from Boivie et al. (2011, p. 575)).

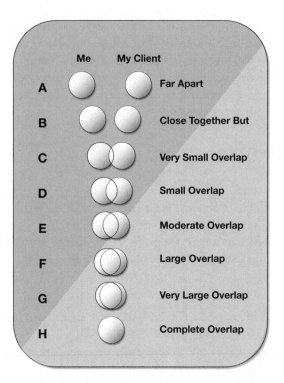

Figure A3.2 Degree of feelings of psychological ownership towards my Client

Source: Adapted from Boivie et al. (2011, p. 575). Used with permission of *Academy of Management Journal* from "Me or we: The effects of CEO organizational identification on agency costs" by Steven Boivie, Donald Lange, Michael L. McDonald, and James D. Westphal, in Volume 54, No. 3, 2011; permission conveyed through Copyright Clearance Center, Inc.

Exit question

19. Are there any other questions you feel I should have asked but didn't?

3. CFO interviews regarding The CFO Centre

How does PO impact client-supplier relationships in the access economy for sharing professional services?

1. Scale 1–5:

Explain scoring:

1. Strongly disagree/not at all/none/unsatisfactory
2. Disagree/occasionally/a bit/below average

3. Neither agree nor disagree / sometimes / some / satisfactory
4. Agree / quite often / quite a lot / above average
5. Strongly agree / all the time / fully / excellent

Context setting

1. First, could you tell me about you and your reasons for joining The CFO Centre as a part-time CFO?

Relationship overview

2. How would you describe your relationship with The CFO Centre?
3. What are the most important things to you about the relationship?

Explore Roots of PO – characteristics of service offering

Efficacy relating to intimacy
4. To what extent does The CFO Centre really understand your needs? (Scale 1–5)
    - Do you feel comfortable describing the product or service of The CFO Centre to someone who is not familiar with it?
    - Are you familiar with the range of services The CFO Centre can provide?
    - To what level are you knowledgeable about the services that The CFO Centre offers? (Scale 1–5)

Self-identity relating to identity
5. To what extent does being a part-time CFO of The CFO Centre help you to achieve the identity you want to have? (Scale 1–5)
    - Does being a Principal of The CFO Centre help you narrow the gap between who you are and who you want to be?
    - Is working with The CFO Centre central to your identity? Part of who you are?
    - If you could no longer work with The CFO Centre, would you feel part of your identity had been taken away?
    - Do you derive some of your identity from The CFO Centre?
    - How does working with The CFO Centre enable you to feel? What is your view of working with The CFO Centre?

Having a place relating to communal identification

6. To what extent does working with The CFO Centre allow you to be part of a group of like-minded people? (Scale 1–5)
   - To what extent does working with The CFO Centre allow you to belong to a group of people with similar interests? (Scale 1–5)
   - What interactions do you have with other members of The CFO Centre?

Explore Routes of PO – activities users undertake in response to the characteristics

Control

7. How much control do you feel you have over your role at The CFO Centre? Objectives? Actions? Time? Input? (Scale 1–5)
   - How accessible are other members of The CFO Centre team? How responsive?
   - How approachable are members of The CFO Centre?
   - What does The CFO Centre give you?

Knowing intimately

8. How intimately do you feel you know your immediate team at The CFO Centre (Scale 1–5)?
   - How much personal information do you share with them? What's stopping you?
   - What type of bond would you say you have with them?
   - What feelings do you have towards them? Friends beyond work?
   - How comfortable do you feel spending time with them?

Psychological safety

9. To what extent do you feel psychologically safe with your team at The CFO Centre? (Scale 1–5)

(Psychological safety is "feeling able to show and employ one's self without fear of negative consequences to self-image, status, or career" (Kahn 1990, p. 708)).

Investing self

10. To what extent do you feel you are part of or a member of or belong to The CFO Centre? (Scale 1–5)

- How do you introduce yourself to outsiders? Are you proud to day "I am a member of The CFO Centre" to people you meet?
- When asked to describe your profession, how do you respond?
- What activities do you do together with your team? What do you create together?
- When asked to describe your profession, how do you respond?
- Are your values aligned with those of The CFO Centre? Do they fit with the organisation's culture?
- Do you feel the need to defend The CFO Centre when it is criticised by outsiders and therefore support its goals and policies?
- Are your common interests with The CFO Centre stronger than your differences?

General questions

Typology

11. On a scale of 1–5, where 1 is introverted and 5 is extroverted, where would you say you sit on the scale?
12. On a scale of 1–5, where 1 is profit or income-focused, and 5 is purpose-focused, where would you say you sit on the scale?

Ownership

13. If the circle on the left represents you and the circle on the right represents The CFO Centre, which case (A, B, C, D, E, F, G, or H) would best illustrate the degree of feelings of PO you feel towards The CFO Centre (see Figure A3.3 adapted from Boivie et al. (2011, p. 575)).

Role of RD

14. How would you describe your relationship with your Regional Director (RD)? (Scale 1–5)
    - What does your RD do for you?
    - What interactions have you had?
    - What more could your RD do for you?

Exit question

15. Are there any other questions you feel I should have asked but didn't?

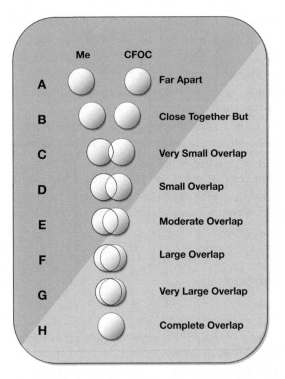

Figure A3.3 Degree of feelings of psychological ownership towards CFOC

Source: Adapted from Boivie et al. (2011, p. 575). Used with permission of *Academy of Management Journal* from "Me or we: The effects of CEO organizational identification on agency costs" by Steven Boivie, Donald Lange, Michael L. McDonald, and James D. Westphal, in Volume 54, No. 3, 2011; permission conveyed through Copyright Clearance Center, Inc.

References

Boivie, S., Lange, D., McDonald, M., & Westphal, J. D. (2011). Me or we: The effects of CEO organizational identification on agency costs. *Academy of Management Journal*, *54*(3), 551–576. https://doi.org/10.5465/amj.2011.61968081

Kahn, W. A. (1990). Psychological conditions of personal engagement and disengagement at work. *Academy of Management Journal*, *33*(4), 692–724.

Appendix 4: Other Data Sources

Other data sources used from within CFOC to give context to the relationships:

- Billing pattern through Covid-19;
- Age of Client and CFO;
- Gender of CFO and client;
- Lifecycle stage of CFO portfolio;
- Stability of CFO portfolio;
- Length of client relationship;
- Frequency of visits or interactions with client each month;
- Retention history of CFO; and
- Length of time as CFOC CFO.

Appendix 5: Scorings of Psychological Ownership from Interviews by Root and Route

Table A5.1 Scorings of psychological ownership from interviews by root and route

Mean Averages		CFO to CFOC	Client to CFO	CFO to Client
Roots	Efficacy	4.32	4.59	3.42
	Self-identify	4.14	3.41	4.25
	Having a place	4.23	2.47	3.63
	Total	**12.69**	**10.47**	**11.30**
Routes	Control	4.59	4.29	3.58
	Knowing intimately	3.32	3.94	3.58
	Psychological safety	4.50	4.59	4.38
	Investing self	4.32	4.29	3.79
	Total	**16.73**	**17.11**	**15.33**
	Overall total	**29.42**	**27.58**	**26.63**

Index

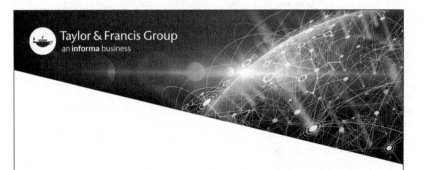